Rainier
& Grace

RAINIER
& GRACE

Jeffrey Robinson

SIMON & SCHUSTER

LONDON • SYDNEY • NEW YORK • TOKYO • TORONTO

First published in Great Britain by
Simon & Schuster Ltd in 1989

Copyright © Jeffrey Robinson, 1989

Simon & Schuster Ltd
West Garden Place
Kendal Street
London W2 2AQ

Simon & Schuster of Australia Pty Ltd
Sydney

British Library Cataloguing-in-Publication Data available
ISBN 0-671-65503-5

Typeset by Selectmove in 11/13pt Trump Mediaeval
Printed and bound in Great Britain by
Richard Clay Ltd, Bungay, Suffolk

Contents

Acknowledgements   *page*   vi

Avant Propos   vii

Chapter 1: Dawn   1
Chapter 2: Rainier at Home   4
Chapter 3: The Birth of Modern Monaco   21
Chapter 4: A Public Romance   45
Chapter 5: The Private Story   68
Chapter 6: The Taming of SBM   92
Chapter 7: Teamwork   112
Chapter 8: Midday   138
Chapter 9: Grimaldi Inc.   141
Chapter 10: Monte Carlo Chic   163
Chapter 11: Grace   186
Chapter 12: Caroline, Albert and Stephanie   207
Chapter 13: Living in a Fishbowl   232
Chapter 14: The Accident   258
Chapter 15: Dusk   275
Chapter 16: Rainier Reminisces   277

A Personal Note   297

Index   302

Acknowledgements

For help and assistance with this project I wish to thank Rupert Allan, Daniel Aubry, Pierre Berenguier, Michel Boeri, John Carroll, Dario Dell'Antonia, Julian and Phyllis Earl, Ken and Bonny Feld, Gant Gaither, Virginia Gallico, Wilfred Groote, Robert Hausman, Khalil el Khoury, Mary Wells Lawrence, Regis L'Ecuyer, John Lehman, André Levasseur, Luisette Levy-Soussan, George Lukonski, Judith Mann, Francis and Josiane Merino, Jean Marie Moll, Stirling Moss, Ricardo Orizio, Richard Pasco, Lix Paton, Prince Louis de Polignac, Francis Rosset, Marquis Livio Ruffo, André Saint Mleux, Francine Siri, Robert Sobra, Jackie Stewart, Clare Sychrava, David Thieme, Robert and Maureen Wood, and John Westbrook.

To this list I add Leslie Gardner, Robert Ducas, Nick Brealey and, as usual, La Benayoun.

I am especially indebted to Nadia Lacoste for her kindness, affection, guidance and assistance.

However, this book could never have been written – at least not by me – without the cooperation of four very special people.

I will be forever grateful to Prince Albert, Princess Caroline and Princess Stephanie for their time, their recollections, their secrets, their trust and their friendship.

But I am most appreciative of all to His Serene Highness Prince Rainier III.

He not only gave me his blessings to write this book, he also opened his heart to me.

And I am deeply touched.

Avant Propos

ONCE UPON A TIME there were a sunny few acres that jutted into the greenish-blue sea, nestled between white pebbled beaches and dark arid hills.

It was a fairy-tale land, ruled by a handsome prince and his beautiful princess.

It is still the diamond in the pearl necklace the French call *La Côte d'Azur.*

In one respect, it is a kind of Garden of Eden, despite the fact that nowhere nearby do they grow apples. Instead they grow marinas.

In another, it is a sort of Disneyland, an amusement park for grown-ups less interested in Mickey Mouse and Donald Duck than in expensive food, expensive wine, expensive flats, expensive yachts, expensive jewellery, expensive cars, expensive women, expensive sacrifices to the sybarite Gods.

It is a dinosaur from another age.

But then, maybe, life was simpler once upon a time. Or perhaps, like the song says, time's rewritten every line. At least it seemed simpler.

It was an era of tea dances and buttered scones, when gentlemen dressed for their late morning walk and women in bone corsets carried parasols. A less hurried age. A gentler age. A time for a hundred visions and revisions before the taking of a toast and tea.

Monaco is both a place and an image.

It is indeed a fairy-tale.

Except this time the handsome prince and his beautiful princess did not live happily ever after.

And Monaco can never be the same without her.

She was the person who, perhaps more than anyone else, was able to capture the romance of the French Riviera.

She sprinkled it around wherever she went.

She had a tremendous gift for that.

It's not only that she had good taste, she also gave a lustre of real glamour.

She cast the spell of a princess wherever she went.

She was superior in the same way that Peter Pan was superior.

You never had the impression with her of greed, of taking, of stretching too far, of going too far. Anything she had she worked for. She gave much more than she got. She was an idea. She was all about refinement, something gossamer and lovely. She was blonde. She was beautiful. She dressed beautifully and she spoke beautifully. She had a lovely, light laugh. She really was the fairy-tale princess with a magic wand.

She lived almost exact 26 years and six months in the United States as Grace Kelly, movie star. And almost exactly 26 years and six months as Princess Grace of Monaco.

As Grace Kelly she won an Academy Award.

But as Princess Grace, she reached a height of stardom that no mere actress could ever have attained. She was the first woman to have her funeral broadcast by satellite around the world on Euro-vision. Nearly 100 million people watched and mourned with her family.

Prince Rainier turned out to be an even greater star-maker than Alfred Hitchcock.

Her death affected people in much the same way that John Kennedy's death did. First there was disbelief. Then there was shock. Then there was anger. Then a lingering sadness set in.

And that lingering sadness remains.

A sense of personal loss flowed over people who never shook her hand, never wrote her a letter, never knew anything more about her than what they'd seen in the movies or read in a magazine.

Like John Kennedy, for one brief, shining moment there was Camelot.

People who knew her well still can't believe she's gone.

They never thought she could die.

They never even saw her ageing.

They always thought perhaps one day she might just vanish through a wall, might one day just disappear.

There is still something so special about her that in Monaco today, right now, this very minute, if you look for her, if you listen for her, if you think about her, then she is still here, somewhere, everywhere.

It's just that one grows up to believe that fairy-tales are supposed to have happier endings.

*   *   *   *

Of course, this book is for Grace

1

Dawn

*T*HERE'S a slight chill in the air as the sun starts to climb its way over the edge of the horizon, far out to sea.

The water goes from pale grey, a mirror of the sky, to a stunning blueish green as the morning steadily sneaks into the corners of the port and lights a building there that is strawberry pink.

It lights 'Le Rocher', the rock overlooking the harbour that juts into the sea where the Prince's Palace sits guarded by its ancient ramparts. It lights the high-rise apartment houses that line the Avenue Princess Grace, along the fabulously expensive stretch of sea-front called Monte Carlo Beach. It lights the old villas, piled almost one on top of the other along the face of the hill that stares down at the casino and the Hôtel de Paris and the Cafe de Paris and the Mediterranean behind them.

At first everything seems flat.

All of the colours seem washed out.

But the early morning sun casts a special light that you only find in the south of France, especially after the night-time Mistral has swept away the clouds. It's an intense, dustless, crystal clear light which brings colours alive in such a way that you think to yourself – nowhere else on earth have colours ever been quite like this.

The sun catches the buildings almost unawares.

For a second it turns them all into a pale pinkish orange. But almost before you notice it, that's gone. Now you see red and yellow and some of the buildings are a soft, rich, Assam tea golden shade – gold in this case being an appropriate colour considering the price of real estate here.

Now you also see awnings opening across thousands of balconies – blue awnings and pink awnings, and faded red awnings that have lived through too many summers, and bright yellow awnings that have just been bought.

The night train from Barcelona pulls into the station on its way to the Italian border town of Ventimiglia. A voice with a marked accent announces over a loud-speaker, 'Monte Carlo, Monte Carlo, deux minutes d'arrêt.'

The morning train from Ventimiglia pulls into the station on its way to Nice and Antibes and Cannes and the man with the marked accent makes the same announcement again. Monte Carlo, Monte Carlo, a two-minute stop.

The first room-service shift has already begun at the Hermitage and the Hôtel de Paris where the smallest croissants on earth arrive promptly, in a basket with coffee and orange juice at a cost of 113 francs or £11 or $19.50.

A lone helicopter flies the length of the beach.

At La Vigie restaurant on the cliff behind the pink stucco 1930's style Old Beach Hotel they're already setting up the buffet lunch tables. While an old man in a boat with an outboard engine sails by. And two women take an early morning swim together, dog-paddling and talking all the way out to the far buoy.

Gardeners are trimming rose bushes on the road up to Le Rocher.

A very big yacht leaves the port ever so slowly.

A police officer in his well-starched red and white uniform directs traffic at the Place d'Armes.

A sometimes-famous tennis player poses next to a swimming pool for a fashion spread before going up to the Tennis Club to spend the next three hours working on his sometimes devastating back hand.

Two rather pretty German girls walk back to their tiny studio flat after a night at Jimmy'z disco.

A teenage Italian boy stands behind the service bar at the Moana, washing glasses and listening to music on a portable radio while a teenage French boy piles chairs on top of tables so that the dance floor can be buffed.

A middle-aged man in a blue work smock runs a vacuum cleaner over the carpets in the casino.

An old woman dressed in black makes her way through the narrow streets of Le Rocher toward the Cathedral. The quarter is empty, except for a single policeman walking slowly past the Oceanographic Museum and a black robed priest taking some fresh air on the church steps before the dawn mass. The old woman dressed in black gives the priest a simple nod and moves into the darkened church, crossing herself and mumbling under her breath, hurrying past the altar to a series of crypts. She stops in front of a single marble slab where it is written, 'Gracia Patricia,' and still mumbling, she crosses herself again. She pauses for only a second, then leaves the church and hurries towards the large open place in front of the Palace. Two Carabiniers are guarding the entrance, another is standing near the smaller side door and a fourth is walking casually through the street where a thick black chain keeps cars from parking just there. The old woman dressed in black stops at the end of the street and looks at the Palace, to see the Prince's ensign flying there. She nods and crosses herself again.

*   *   *   *

2

Rainier at Home

THERE was never any mistaking them.

Not those two.

No matter how hard they tried to remain anonymous, there was always someone who'd spot them, who'd know their names.

One night in London, after dining at a Japanese restaurant with friends, Rainier and Grace asked the waiter to get them a taxi. When it arrived the two couples piled in.

But as soon as they did, the driver started laughing.

He chuckled all the way to Connaught Hotel where Rainier and Grace got out.

And he kept on chuckling all the way to the other couple's flat in Chelsea.

Finally the other couple simply had to know, 'What's so funny?'

'It was the little Japanese fellow who hailed me,' the driver said. 'I couldn't figure out what he wanted. I couldn't figure out what he was talking about because he kept saying over and over again, "Glazed cherries, glazed cherries." So who gets into my cab? Grace Kelly.'

* * * *

The Principality of Monaco fits snugly between the French

Maritime Alps and the sea, a crab-shaped pocket that stretches no more than two miles along the beach and never more than a few hundred yards inland.

A city state of 30,000 people, roughly only 5000 are Monégasque, making the principality unique as the natives are outnumbered by foreigners five to one. The majority are French, with Italians, British and Americans well accounted for. Although Monaco can boast residents from nearly 90 other countries.

Less than half the size of New York's Central Park or just about the same as London's Hyde Park, it was once described by Somerset Maugham as 'a sunny spot for shady people' because its 480 acres were made famous by bright sunshine, mild winters, the most glamourous casino in the world, millionaires, movie stars, courtesans, yachts, expensive restaurants, expensive hotels, expensive apartments, jewellery stores, banks, Formula One race cars, stamps, high-priced black tie suppers straight out of a Scott Fitzgerald novel and no income taxes.

Not that everyone who lives there is a millionaire.

Yet Monaco's residents do have the highest per capita net worth of any state in the world. Monaco is also where you find the world's highest ratio of population to automobiles, with 30,000 people owning more than 15,000 cars. There is no poverty to speak of. The state is extremely benevolent when any of its citizens suffer social problems. The standard of living is, even by French Riviera criteria, impressive.

Then too, so are the prices.

Two-thirds of the way from Nice to Ventimiglia, the principality is completely surrounded by France. The border is made of flowers and French money is interchangeable with Monaco's. French is the official spoken language, although English and Italian are close runners-up. There's a local tongue called Monégasque – it sounds more like Italian than French – but the only time you ever really hear it these days except in a high school class is at weddings, when the bride's father gets mellow and leads his old school pals in a chorus of traditional songs.

The Monégasques are not French and they staunchly defend their right never to become French. They have no standing army and have never seen their federal budget slip into deficit.

For nearly 2,000 years the Rock and the old fortress where the Palace sits was ruled by a succession of peoples: Phoenicians, Ligurians, Romans, Barbarians, Saracens, the Counts of Provence, the Church, the Genoese and the Ghibellines.

Towards the end of the thirteenth century the Grimaldis were just another clan of wealthy ship owners and merchants from Genoa. When the Guelphs went to war with the Ghibellines – in a kind of medieval version of the Ewing–Barnes feud – the Grimaldis weighed in on the side of the Guelphs. But they were backing the wrong Godfather. When the Ghibellines took the upper hand, the Grimaldis decided they would stay healthier if they were living somewhere else.

And they might well have been destined for historical obscurity as a family in exile except for the Grimaldi known as François 'Le Malizia' – Frank the Spiteful.

He wanted revenge.

The Phoenicians and the Greeks had both constructed temples on a slice of rock jutting out to sea some 100 miles east of Genoa that came to be called Monoecus, after the local name for the god Heracles. But neither of them could hold onto it and by the year 1162 it had been claimed by the Ghibellines. They valued it so highly that they built an almost impenetrable, four-turreted, 37-sided, high-walled fortress there. Overlooking a tiny, natural harbour, the rock protected the eastern approach by land and sea to the Bay of Genoa.

The garrison would be a big prize for anyone who could claim it and François was convinced he knew a way. On the night of 8 January 1297 he donned the heavy brown robes of a wandering Franciscan monk. Banging on the wooden gate he begged refuge. The unsuspecting guards allowed him to enter. Before they could shut the gates, Le Malizia pulled a sword from under his robes, his henchmen rushed in, the massacre began and the Genoese were taken by complete surprise. Within a few hours the Grimaldis had declared the rock to be their own.

Today, Monaco's coat of arms boasts a pair of friars wielding swords.

Over the next 100 years the Grimaldis lost Monaco twice and regained it twice, although by the first quarter of the 15th century they'd pretty well established their feudal rights over Monaco and the two neighbouring towns of Roquebrune and Menton. They were officially allied with France until 1524 when the ruling prince made a deal with Spain for 'rights to the sea'. That meant he could levy a tax of two per cent on the value of merchandise in the hold of any ships passing within sight of the rock. It was a decent family business until the middle of the 17th century when a later ruling prince realigned Monaco with France. Then the French Revolution got in the way. The Grimaldis were removed from their throne and Monaco was annexed to France.

In 1814, the family's claim was restored by the Treaty of Paris. Although the following year the Treaty of Vienna placed Monaco under the protection of the Kings of Sardinia and it wasn't until 1861 that Monaco was once and for all recognised to be an independent state.

As the 33rd ruler of Monaco, Prince Rainier III not only represents the oldest ruling family in Europe but, since the death of Japan's Hirohito, he's become the longest-serving monarch in the world.

For the most part the years have been good to him.

The 26-year-old, dark-haired, dark-moustached, slightly awkward Prince who ascended to the throne in May 1949 is today a handsome, self-assured man in his late 60s. His hair and his moustache are snow-white but his natural shyness is still evident, only barely hidden by a well-practised reserve.

Right after his marriage to Grace Kelly in 1956, he bought a farm called Roc Agel in the hills behind Monaco, some 3,000 feet above the sea, on the mountain called Mont Agel, near the Monte Carlo Golf Club – which, despite its name, happens to be in France.

Now, just after dawn, in slacks, a golf shirt and a comfortable pair of old loafers, he points out with great pride how he's personally worked so much of the land.

'I put in about 400 trees here. I also made all the paths around the property. I drove the bulldozer myself. You know, it's very satisfying to do that, to work with your hands. I have a workshop here where I can weld iron and metal or make things with bits of iron and bolts. It gets me away from reading official papers. That's one of the reasons I don't read a lot of books any more. After three or four hours a day of reading papers I just want to get away and do something manual.'

The property is not huge, but behind the always guarded gates and surrounded by his trees there's a medium-sized, modern stone house at the end of a long asphalt driveway. There's a swimming pool and three tiny cottages on the property, which have been turned into playrooms for his grandchildren. There are swings and a merry-go-round and a lot of dogs. There's a fair-sized vegetable patch for lettuce and tomatoes and a large group of apricot, apple, cherry and plum trees. He keeps poultry for eggs and a couple of Jersey cows for fresh milk. In addition there are four llamas, a hippopotamus named Pollux and a rhinoceros he bought in England which was already called Margaret.

'They both weigh about two tons. But you can go up to the rhino and walk around and she'll follow you like a dog. The hippo is also quite domestic.' He pauses for a moment, then adds, 'I love animals,' as if there could be any doubt about someone who keeps a rhino and a hippo at home. 'I believe I understand them. When you show them you're the boss, that you're not afraid, that you mean them no harm, you can have a real communication with them.'

It seems he collects animals the way some people collect stamps.

It all began in 1953.

His six-year love affair with the French actress Gisèle Pascal had just ended. He needed time to be by himself, to get away from Monaco for a while, so he took his boat and headed for Conakry, in what was then French Guinea, on the west coast of Africa.

'I had a little Citroën 2CV that I tied down to the deck so that when we docked I could take a long drive inside the country. My manservant in those days, Coki, was from a village called Kankan, about 350 or 400 miles due east of the coast. One of our objectives was to get him home to buy a wife. He didn't have enough money so I staked him. I bought half his wife. Well, we got there and he chose the woman he wanted. He gave her parents enough goats, sheep and beads and made arrangements for her to arrive in Monaco around Christmas. When she didn't show up we both got anxious about it. A few months later we learned that her mother had sold her to somebody else. Someone made a better offer and we got cut out of the deal. He and I were both very sad.'

Once he was ready to come home, Rainier played Noah and filled his ark.

'I bought a couple of ostriches and three chimps, a few baboons and some crocodiles which we packed in crates but had to water every day in order to keep their skin from cracking. I had my chaps build a shack on the aft of the boat and we kept the animals there. I was happy to feed them every day but none of the crew would clean out, so for the whole trip back a friend and I did that every day, too.'

He says he was just starting to get to know the animals when they stopped to refuel at Dakar.

'Two of the baboons got loose. You can imagine what we must have looked like chasing them all over the port. We attracted quite a crowd with this weird boat full of animals.'

Back home, he installed them in the gardens below the Palace. When word got out about his collection, friends started giving him gifts to help it along. The King of Morocco sent a couple of lions and the King of Siam offered a small baby elephant, although the elephant quickly outgrew the place and Rainier gave it to a safari park where they could keep it better.

'Today my collection is the Monaco Zoo. I run it myself. It's very popular because visitors can get as close as is safely possible to the animals. But these days there are so many safari parks, both good ones and bad ones, that people have gotten a little tired of zoos.'

Even if the public has tired of zoos, he hasn't.

A few years ago he heard about a circus going bust, knew they had some good animals all born in captivity, and couldn't resist.

'I bought an entire herd of big Manchurian camels, some dromedaries, an African buffalo, two guanacos and a couple of ponies. I had them delivered to Marchais, my family estate between Paris and Brussels, and put them out in the pasture with the cows.'

That family estate, the Château de Marchais, is a country property at the foot of the Ardennes, no less than six times the size of Monaco. It includes a pair of working farms and some very fine shooting.

And since the camels have moved in, it's also become something of an unexpected tourist attraction.

'It's very funny to see people drive by in a car. I can almost hear the wife say, "Look at the camels over there," and the husband says, "What do you mean, camels?" Then you hear the brakes jammed on and you see the car back up. Come to think of it, I guess it is a little strange to see camels grazing with cows in the French countryside.'

In addition to animals he says that, every now and then, he also caters to a fancy for automobiles. At the last count he owned 45.

'I have cars but I can't say that I am a serious collector. If a car comes up in a sale and appeals to me because it's a special model, I may buy it. I enjoy cars but I'm not terribly passionate about them.

I've got cars ranging from a 1903 Dion up to a 1938 Packard eight cylinder.'

As the garage at the Palace is these days so crowded with the collection, Rainier has asked the state for space to create a museum.

'The cars are all in driving order but I'm not sure driving them is always a good idea. The Packard, for instance, is a very heavy car with no power steering. People must have been terribly strong in 1938. I drove the car for an afternoon and had to stay in bed for three days afterwards.'

If the 225-room Palace in Monaco, with its small private apartments and large, formal halls is where the Prince and his family have their official residence, Roc Agel is where Mr and Mrs Grimaldi were often happiest to spend their time.

The main house is a mixture of chintz and rustic. The large living-room is comfortable, with every sign of being lived in. There are bedrooms enough for all the children and now Caroline's children too. The kitchen is modern, much of it having been shipped from America because Princess Grace didn't see anything at all romantic in trying to prepare meals in what was originally a typically cramped, badly equipped European kitchen.

'Grace was pretty good at doing barbeques. She also used to like to cook breakfast for the family.'

While he's got a full household staff here, at the Palace and at Marchais, he says that every now and then he does some cooking too. 'But only for fun. I'm not a great cook by any means although I can do a terrific crêpe Suzette. I used to do pancakes with maple syrup in the morning for the children and was very good with Aunt Jemima mix.'

Roc Agel is also a special place for music, a place where he can take the time away from phone calls and official appointments to listen uninterrupted to tapes and records.

'My father was very knowledgeable about music and knew all the composers of his day. I once tried to learn to play the saxophone but didn't get very far because it's a difficult instrument and especially painful for people around you while you're learning. So I stopped that and took up the drums. I still sometimes play them for fun. I like music immensely although I'm by no means a great musician. I happen to love Tchaikovsky. I guess I'm a great fan of romantic music. On the other hand I'm not that fond of Mozart because I find it repetitious and I don't like Wagner because it's too clashy, too Teutonic. I don't like any of the Wagnerian operas because I don't like the sound of the voices. But I like Italian opera, which I think is the best. Grace loved classical music, especially Bach, enjoyed opera and of course loved ballet. But she wasn't very fond of Wagner either. She liked jazz and so do I. Music has always played a role in our family life and there was always music playing. Grace would play music when she painted or pressed flowers. She even did gymnastics to music. And this, I'll have you know, was long before Jane Fonda and aerobics.'

Perhaps not surprisingly, the man you find at Roc Agel is not necessarily the same man you see in Monaco.

Monaco is where he must be prince.

This is a place to be a grandfather.

His friends are quick to point out that he changes when he's here, that at Roc Agel he's less formal, more relaxed. He's always been reserved, a man very aware of his position and the image that goes along with that. But when he's at Roc Agel he shows himself to be a simple man. And, they add, it's only when you see the difference that you start to understand his role is not an easy one.

At the end of the last century a play was written about one of Rainier's ancestors, Prince Florestan. It was called *Rabagas* and was advertised as a political comedy. The most touching part of the piece is Florestan's monologue on the weight of his responsibilities.

'If I go for a walk, it is found that I have too much idle time. If I don't go for a walk then I am afraid of showing myself. If I give a ball I am accused of wild extravagance. If I do not give a ball then I am mean and avaricious. If I hold a review I am attempting military intimidation. If I do not hold a review I am afraid I cannot trust the troops. When fireworks are let off on my birthday, I am wasting the people's money. When I suppress the fireworks, then I do nothing for the people's amusement. If I am in good health it is because I am idle and take no trouble over public matters. If I am in bad health, that is the result of debauchery. If I build, I am wasteful. If I do not build, then what about the working classes? Everything I do is proclaimed detestable and what I do not do gives even greater offence.'

More than a century later, Rainier claims, that speech still touches close to home.

'It's as true today as it was then. It's a very thin line to walk. And it took me quite some time to figure out where that line is because it's not something you can just learn. You have to feel your way. My grandfather would say to me, "Don't go to too many things. You must choose where to be seen, otherwise the Prince's presence doesn't means as much." But no one ever told me if ten events were too many or if five were not enough. In the beginning I had a tendency to go whenever I was asked, to shake hands, to give away cups and prizes, to be seen. It took a while to know how much is the right amount. That's something I've tried to teach my son Albert who will one day succeed me. He's got to be seen around in the beginning and he should go to a lot of things. But then he must start choosing so that his participation, his presence, is something of value, something people will look forward to.'

In other words, the job requires a certain aloofness.

'At times I must be aloof because aloofness gains respect. Otherwise people see you everywhere and it doesn't mean anything when you give your patronage to something. I'm not saying to my son that he shouldn't walk around and be accessible, but part of my job and the job he will inherit from me is in learning where to draw the line between being accessible and being over-familiar. That might not be a difficult thing to do for say, the President of the United States or the Prime Minister of England or even the Mayor of Paris. But it's especially difficult here because the place is so very small.'

Does that mean, he's asked, there's no question of ever strolling out of the Palace in a pair of Bermudas and heading to a pizza joint at the port for a beer?

He thinks for a moment. 'I guess nowadays I could but I wouldn't be inclined to. Albert can. He's younger and that's more the trend these days. But he mustn't do it every day. He goes out with friends and plays tennis at the Country Club and goes to the stadium to work-out. That's good. However he'll have to draw the line when he succeeds because he can't then have fellows coming up to him on the street saying, "Hey Al, let's go jogging." The rules change when he becomes the sovereign. Nowadays it's even more difficult than it was when I was his age. Sure, going down to the port for a pizza with some friends might be fun. But I'm very aware of the fact that, with the press as active as they are, a picture might be taken of me there and who knows what the caption under it will say.'

Rank may have its privileges yet it is not without a price.

When Albert was five or six he was sitting with a group of children who were each in turn asked by an old lady, 'What would you like to do when you grow up?' One little boy said he wanted to be a fireman and another said he wanted to be a policeman, the way children always answer that question. Then she turned to Albert and asked him. He answered, 'I don't have any choice.'

Rainier shakes his head. 'I'm not sure he understood until now just what that really means. He's discovering, as I did, that it's not always easy knowing who to trust. Albert's had to learn the hard way that some fellows who've been seen around with him were really only interested in what he could do for them. That it was a one-way street. Now he's much wiser about that sort of thing and tries to find out who people are before he allows them to get close. He has to protect himself, especially here, again because it's so small. We live under a microscope.'

Fast to admit that Monaco is the kind of place where gossip can run wild – he snickers, 'Gossip was invented in Monaco!' – Rainier is equally frank about some of the people around him.

'I have hangers-on, yes, very definitely. Again, that's something Albert and I have talked about. I've said to him, you can always judge your friends by their attitude towards you and their willingness to help you in a disinterested way. Real friends are the main hardship in this life. I constantly have people pretending friendship one day and suddenly asking favours the next. I think the sign of true friendship is when someone has been around for a very long time and has never asked for anything. But that's so rare. At the end of the day, after 40 years as the ruling Prince of Monaco, I suspect I could actually name all the people around me who have never asked for anything. I think I could count them on the fingers of one hand.'

His efforts to prepare Albert, who is now in his 30s, for the responsibilities of the throne are a continuous process.

The two have been working closely for several years. Albert sits at his father's side at meetings, handles special chores, chairs various committees and, much like Prince Charles, is trying to carve out his own niche for the otherwise ill-defined role of ruler in waiting. Rainier has insisted that Albert take his time to learn the job, a privilege he himself did not have.

'I'd have to say that my grandfather did not adequately prepare me for the job. The fact is, I don't think he was terribly concerned with how I would get on. He was sickly at the end of his life, recently married and I guess he simply didn't feel he had a lot of time for me.'

Rainier says that although he participated in some meetings chaired by his grandfather and discussed certain things with him, such as the basics of the principality's administration, he didn't really have anyone he could count on for help when he succeeded.

'The staff who worked for him didn't seem to care much either. I was pretty much on my own. Of course, sometimes that's the best way to learn. There were so many things I suddenly had to do that I didn't have a lot of time to worry about how hard it was to learn my job. I sat down and studied all the dossiers and figured out for myself where I was going.'

Until Rainier came along, Monaco's rulers tended to regard the principality as something of a part-time job. Most of them never spent more than three or four months of the year in Monaco, and they distanced themselves from the day-to-day workings of the country. Projects were only presented at the last stages for final approval. There were no intermediate stages where the Prince could ask for revisions, or improve the text of some legislation or just put his own ideas into a project. Rainier was the first truly full-time sovereign. He was also the first Prince to approach the running of the country like the running of a business.

'I couldn't make any decisions under my grandfather's rule but I made myself aware of what was going on. I couldn't criticise my grandfather so I had to keep most of my opinions to myself, but I was in a position to form my own opinions and once I took over I moved fairly quickly to change things.'

One of the many things he did was to restructure the economic base of the country.

Monaco today no longer lives off the casino.

If it was a sunny spot for shady people in the 1930s, Rainier insists it is no longer that today.

'I'm not absolutely sure that there are more gardeners in Monaco than there are croupiers but there are probably just as many. Yes, the economy is still geared to tourism but it's a great deal more well rounded than it was 40 years ago. There's no comparison. We now have a very important convention industry.

And we now have a growing sector of light industry that has emerged as a major factor in our economy.'

Another area where he's expressed his own personality is in the influence small nations can have in the rest of the world.

'The more I travel, the more I'm convinced that the small countries of this world are very useful. To begin with, we're not interested in possessing what our neighbours have. Then, because of our size, we're vulnerable. But that very vulnerability makes small nations the best champions of peace. Our survival depends on peace. The problem is that the voices of the world's small nations are usually so feebly heard.'

Usually perhaps, but not always.

He has definitely made Monaco's voice heard to express his personal concern for the seas.

It's a passion he comes by honestly, not only because he was born and raised next to the sea but because his great-grandfather Prince Albert I was a highly respected patron of oceanographic research. In 1910 it was Albert who founded Monaco's Oceanographic Museum, which for so many years was home base for the much-celebrated marine explorer, Jacques Cousteau.

Rainier has often said that had he not been born a prince he might have liked a job that would have taken him to sea. As it is, he's become one of the world's most outspoken advocates for protection of the oceans.

'The sea is considered the ideal dump for all kinds of refuse. Fauna and flora are being destroyed and the most infuriating thing is that it's happening in the midst of mankind's general indifference. Life depends on the water cycle, so what's endangered here is life itself. And we're not talking about something that can't be avoided because no unavoidable pollution exists. It's all caused by man. Pollution can be prevented. It only takes the will and the means to fight it.'

He finds it particularly menacing that the Mediterranean has become a cesspool, with the waters between Genoa and Marseilles – Monaco is in the middle – being among the most polluted.

'Years ago I used to do some deep sea fishing. Tuna would come through the Strait of Gibraltar on their way to reproduce in the south of Sicily and pass so close we could troll with a couple of rods on a boat not far off shore. Today the Mediterranean is so filthy the tuna won't come anywhere near the coast.'

Justifiably concerned, he instructed that twice-weekly tests be made along Monaco's beaches for microbiotic pollution. A few years ago, much to his horror, it was discovered that pollution levels were far too high.

'They'd just about reached the limits where we could safely permit bathing. Genoa closed its beaches. They literally had to fence them off and put police guards on the beaches to keep people out of the water. There were huge signs everywhere saying, don't bathe in this water it's polluted. But you know what? People still tried to swim there. It's amazing.'

Compelled to act, he put together an agreement called RAMOGE, formed in conjunction with the regional governing bodies for St Raphael, Monaco and Genoa. The idea was to collectively attack pollution caused by oil tankers, seaside industry and untreated sewage.

'We got the mayors of towns along the coast interested in the fight and awakened some collective consciousness. But it never produced the results I'd hoped for. It stayed too administrative. You can always get scientists to work, you can motivate them because they understand. The problem is in motivating the bureaucrats. They won't budge because it's against their nature. They're suspicious from the start. Our biggest hurdle was the French. Instead of worrying about pollution, they were more concerned with who'd have the day-to-day authority.'

Being a man who categorically refuses to accept bureaucratic red tape when he wants something done in Monaco, and greatly aided by the fact that Monaco is small enough to be manageable, he then established a marine protection zone outside RAMOGE's authority at the far eastern end of Monaco's waters.

And that's been very successful.

Various aquaculture groups have put marine life there and the zone is now quite populated, with certain species of fish that haven't been seen in those waters for years. It's been such a good example of what can be done that there are now larger zones in France and Italy, which is exactly what Rainier always hoped would happen.

'But it's only a start,' he says. Because, as far as he's concerned, his French and Italian neighbours still have a long way to go. 'Pollution throughout the Mediterranean is nothing new. As the sea only meets the Atlantic Ocean at Gibraltar, there's very limited water circulation, a slow rate of oxygen replenishment and a lack of nutrients for marine life. According to some estimates a complete turnover of Mediterranean water takes 80 years. In other words, it's up to all of us to solve the problem because all of us, sooner or later, become the victims. Again, finding the answers simply takes the will and the means.'

Pollution of the sea can be such a problem that in Monaco they've had just about everything imaginable, from a plague of plastic balls to dead horses. It seems controls in Italy are very lax and whatever they dump into the sea washes up on Monaco's beaches. The dead horses only stopped because Rainier personally got on the phone and kicked up a hell of a row.

'When those things happen, the idea is not to go too high up the administrative scale. If you complain too high up it just gets lost. As a head of state I can deal directly with other heads of state. That works especially well with the French as long as it's not too technical. I can talk to President Mitterand about a specific question and that's fine because, in some cases, you want to get the okay right from the top. Experience shows, however if you want to discuss something of local importance, it's better to talk to someone who's directly concerned rather than send your ambassador to see the Foreign Minister.'

He claims the reason why is obvious.

'What do you expect from big governments? They get bogged down in their own bureaucracies.'

On the other hand, small governments can make things happen quickly.

'Big governments become encumbered. They become over-burdened. One of the great benefits of a small country, like Monaco, is that the contact is direct, you can get to people. Now, as the chief executive of my government, I'm not going to ask for something that's impossible because the National Council won't let me have it. But if there's something I feel should be a priority, then I can make it a priority even if the administration is holding it back. You can only do that in a small country.'

The example he loves to cite is his campaign for new-style national identity cards.

When he proposed them a few years ago, he ran head first into a National Council which simply couldn't imagine why anyone would want to replace the old one – a large, clumsy piece of cardboard that folded three times and even then was still too large for a wallet – with something the size of a credit card.

'Look at this.' He reaches into his pocket and pulls a new Monaco ID card out of a small leather *aide-mémoire*. It bears his photo, his name and his registration number – which in this case happens to be 0001. 'Great, no? It doesn't take up any space. But you'll never believe how they fought me on this. The bureaucrats kept saying no, it will never do.' He waves it about triumphantly. 'Of course, now everyone is lining up to take the credit for having thought of it.'

Suddenly an odd question comes to mind. 'What else do you keep in your pockets?'

He shrugs and searches through them to produce a packet of cigarettes, a lighter, the keys to his office safe and the keys to his desk. Out of the *aide-mémoire* he produces his driving licence and a $100 bill. 'I keep this for luck.'

'No house keys?'

'No.'

'No other money?'

'Yes, but I won't tell you how much.'

'Oh, come on.'

'Enough, so that if I'm driving to work and run out of petrol I can fill up the car.'

'Do you work every day?'

'There's always something to do,' he says. 'Even when I'm not in Monaco, there's always so much to read and there are always people to see.'

'Don't you ever think of retiring?'

'Constantly.'

'Really?'

'Of course. I'll retire someday, except I can't tell you precisely when it will happen because I don't know when. It will be when Albert and I both feel that he's ready to take over. When he feels settled and confident. It will also have to do with when Albert gets married.'

'Do you see yourself ever retiring here as a gentleman farmer?'

'No. I'm not that knowledgeable about farming.'

'What grows here?'

'Mostly rocks,' he says. 'Farming is very difficult in this region. It used to be a beet-growing area, you know, sugar beet, until the economics of the region changed and now everybody grows corn and a bit of wheat. But I'm not terribly interested in that.'

'So what will you do?'

'I have a lot of interests to keep me busy. I used to play tennis and ride horses but as I've gotten older I find I play more golf. I still ski and swim and scuba-dive every now and then. When I can find the time I also enjoy fishing. It's good for the nerves but I'm not very knowledgeable about that either. All I know is that when there's a storm they bite better.'

'Do you have any good fishing stories? You know, about the one that got away?'

He smiles, 'With me they all got away.'

'There must be more than fishing and golf.'

'There are plenty of things I'd like to do if I had the time. A mixture of travelling and seeing people I want to see, not only the ones I'm obliged to see. I'd like to spend more time in my workshop and arranging my property. I'd like to spend time at Roc Agel and Marchais and maybe even on my boat. I'd love to have the time to read all the diaries my great-grandfather left. They're handwritten accounts of his scientific expeditions.'

'That's not bad. But is that all?'

He pauses. 'Maybe not.'

'What else?'

'Oh, you know.' He grins widely. 'Get into a lot of mischief. Take my revenge on society. Be rude to people. Just do all the things I can't do now.'

*   *   *   *

The Grimaldis of Monaco

Grimaldo Grimaldi (? – c.1257)
[Uncle of Francois, 'The Spiteful']

Lanfranco (? – 1293)

Rainier I (c.1267 – 1314)

Charles I, Seigneur of Monaco (? – 1357)

Rainier II (1350 – 1407)

Jean I (1382 – 1454)

Catalan (1425 – 1457)

Claudine (1451 – 1515)
[m. Lambert Grimaldi, Co-seigneur of Monaco 1420 – 1494]

Lucien (1482 – 1523)

Honore I (1522 – 1581)

Hercule I (1562 – 1604)

Honore II, Prince of Monaco (1597 – 1662)

Hercule II (1623 – 1651)

Louis I (1642 – 1701)

Antoine I (1661 – 1731)

Louise-Hippolyte
[m. Jacques de Matignon]

Honore III (1720 – 1795)

Honore IV (1758 – 1819)

Honore V (1778 – 1841)   **Florestan I** (1785 – 1856)

Charles III (1818 – 1889)

Albert I (1848 – 1922)

Louis II (1870 – 1949)

Charlotte
[m. Pierre de Polignac]

Rainier III (b.1923)
[m. Grace Kelly, 1929 – 1981]

Caroline (b.1957)   **Albert** (b.1958)   **Stephanie** (b.1965)

3

The Birth of
Modern Monaco

*V*ISITING Houston, Texas, a few years ago, Prince Rainier
was taken to a football game at the Astrodome, the nine-
acre, climate-controlled, covered stadium that seats just over
50,000.

As the Prince gazed around at this engineering feat, his host
wondered, 'How would you like to have this in Monaco?'

'It would be marvellous,' Rainier said. 'We could be the world's
only indoor country.'

* * * *

Prince Honoré V died in October 1841.

A methodical, uncompromising man, his intentions might
have been good but his grasp of economics was non-existent.

His subjects were over-taxed, olive and lemon production was
severely regulated and the state maintained unpopular monopo-
lies, such as the exclusive right to bake bread.

Worse still, Monaco was broke.

As Honoré hadn't produced an heir, rule of the principality
passed to his younger brother, 56-year-old Florestan.

But Florestan had never even been to Monaco.

Raised by his mother in Paris, he'd acquired a taste for the arts
and once pursued a career as an actor. Married to a wealthy former

dancer named Caroline Gibert, the two lived quietly for a quarter of a century, raising their family on the Left Bank. He had neither the experience nor the ambition to rule. Furthermore, he resented having to give up his cultured existence in the capital, especially this late in life, to spend part of the year in a dark, damp palace above an isolated fishing port 600 miles away.

Unfortunately for him, he had no choice.

He arrived in Monaco in November 1841 only to be welcomed by a crowd of subjects furious with Honoré's economic policies. Taking the coward's way out, he automatically abolished the state monopoly on bread.

As a matter of fact, he would have been willing to abolish all forms of taxation, regardless of the consequences, if everybody would simply leave him alone. But his wife, now Princess Caroline, understood how the real world worked and took it upon herself to try to balance the country's books. Within a year she'd pretty much assumed the day-to-day administration of the principality.

Economic discontent, nevertheless, continued and in 1847 Roquebrune and Menton finally manifested their hostility.

As 90 per cent of the principality's revenue came from an export tax on Menton's lemons, the two communes adopted the slogan, 'Roquebrune and Menton pay, Monaco profits', declared themselves free and sought protective from the King of Sardinia. Only the village of Monaco remained loyal.

Florestan's realm was instantly reduced by four-fifths.

Frustrated by his failures and lacking any enthusiasm to continue, Florestan handed over power to his 30-year-old son, Honoré-Charles, and left for Paris. Although he remained sovereign in name until he died, he never returned.

Honoré-Charles' closest adviser was his mother and she was the one who convinced him that Monaco's future lay in the development of new businesses.

She was the one who convinced him that gambling was the future.

When his father died he took the name Charles III.

The barren hill across the port from Le Rocher where the casino was built was named for him.

And the success of Monte Carlo altered the history of Monaco forever.

When Charles III died his only son succeeded to the throne.

Prince Albert I was a tall, handsome man with a well-groomed black beard whose first love was marine research.

In those days that was a difficult, painstaking and sometimes even dangerous undertaking. Consider the fact that the method he used for soundings was nothing more sophisticated than a string with a weight tied to the end, reaching at times as deep as 10,000 feet. Yet he was totally dedicated to his self-appointed, self-funded task of exploring the seas and attained an international reputation for expertise. The charts he made of waters in northern France at the beginning of the century were thorough enough to be used by the Allied forces for the Normandy landings in 1944.

When he wasn't out to sea, or establishing the Oceanographic Institute in Monaco or setting up the smaller, lesser-known Institute of Human Palaeontology in Paris, Albert was involved with European politics.

He even tried single-handedly to prevent World War I.

In 1903, sensing that Europe might be heading for war, Albert created the International Institute of Peace, a sort of forerunner of the League of Nations. Moving it from Monaco to Paris in 1912, he hoped to get the Kaiser to sit down with the other leaders of Europe to discuss their problems. Sadly, the Kaiser had other plans.

Under Albert's reign, the casino at Monte Carlo brought the principality an era of unparalleled prosperity. But certain influential Monégasque families resented the fact that prosperity had turned Monte Carlo into a company town.

The Société des Bains de Mer – the Sea Bathing Society – was the publicly quoted company that controlled Monaco's gambling franchise. As Monaco's largest employer and by far the nation's largest source of revenue, SBM wielded a grossly disproportionate amount of political power.

Not surprisingly, the burghers of Monaco were highly suspicious of SBM.

Some 16,000 people lived there at the beginning of this century but less than 10 per cent of them were Monégasque. The natives saw foreigners getting rich and convinced themselves it was at their expense. They wanted Albert to insist that SBM share the wealth by giving priority employment to Monégasques. Albert answered that he was hard-pressed to see how he could demand that a private company employ someone simply because they'd been born in Monaco.

Certain influential Monégasque families then began to feel
that Albert had sold them out by allowing SBM to wedge itself
in between the Prince and his people like that.

Hoping to direct some of the bounty towards his subjects,
Albert created a trade promotion board. When it failed to pacify
the Monégasques, he replaced it with a Chamber of Commerce.
That didn't last two months. Next he tried forming a governing
council to oversee native business interests in the principality.

That didn't work either.

In response, a plot was hatched to force Albert's abdication and
put his son on the throne.

Recognising that it was best to offer radical change before it
was forced upon him, which it surely would have been, Albert
relinquished his powers of absolute rule.

His constitution of 1911 separated the Prince's household from
the government. The Prince remained chief executive but the
government would be composed of a Minister of State plus three
counsellors. Legislative power was to be split between the Prince
and the newly formed National Council, whose members would
be elected by the people.

It is considered to be Albert's single greatest achievement.

It was the birth of modern Monaco.

For political reasons, namely World War I, Albert suspended
the constitution in 1914 and did not restore it until 1917. When
he did, the National Council was reduced from 21 members to 12
and the powers of the judiciary were separated from the powers of
the principality's administrators.

Then, immediately following the Armistice, Albert negotiated
a long-awaited, vitally important pact with France, which was
incorporated into the Treaty of Versailles.

The Prince agreed to exercise his rights in conformity with
the political, military and economic interests of France. The
French, in turn, agreed to defend the principality's independence
and sovereignty.

From this came the accord that, should there be no heir
to maintain the line, Monaco would be formed into a French
protectorate. However, the ruling prince would always have the
option of adopting an heir should he not produce one.

In this case Albert's successor was clear.

But the French worried that there was a distant German branch
of the Grimaldi family, which could possibly one day make a

claim. And there was no way the French were ever going to allow a German to rule Monaco.

Ironically, Albert's son was born and raised in Germany.

Albert was 20 when he married 18-year-old Lady Mary Victoria Douglas Hamilton in 1869, daughter of the late Duke of Hamilton, Scotland's premier peer. The alliance had been arranged by Napoleon III. But within five months she walked out on him and went to live with her mother in Baden-Baden where their son, Louis, was born.

Albert requested and received a church annulment, then dissolved the civil marriage by decree.

Despite his official status as hereditary prince, the young Louis didn't set foot in Monaco or even meet his father until he was 11.

And when they did meet, the two did not get along.

Louis was homesick for his mother and Albert longed to be at sea.

The pair lived together, mainly in Paris, for five years, until Louis escaped to the French military academy at St Cyr. Commissioned at the age of 20 and seeking adventure, he got himself posted with the French Foreign Legion in North Africa.

Today no one really remembers why Albert and Louis didn't get along.

Rainier suspects it might have stemmed from the fact that Louis was not in the least interested in anything to do with the sea or in continuing his father's marine research. That's almost certainly why Albert left the Oceanographic Institute to France. Even though the museum and the research facility are based in Monaco, they're administered by the French. Albert must have felt Louis simply wouldn't look after it.

While stationed in North Africa, Louis fell in love with a young laundress named Marie Juliette Louvet. But Albert would not grant them permission to marry, either because she'd once been married or because she came from working-class family. Their love-child, Charlotte, was born in 1898.

Now Albert refused to recognise either their alliance or his granddaughter's legal rights.

Louis and Marie Juliette separated when Charlotte was very young. While Louis always acknowledged Charlotte to be his rightful heir, it wasn't until her 21st birthday that Albert finally gave in. He conceded that her accession to the throne was the only sensible option to perpetuate the family's hold on Monaco, insisted Louis officially name her as his successor and, just in case there might be any lingering doubt, ordered Louis to legally adopt her.

A tiny, feisty woman who always spoke her mind, Charlotte was an eccentric in the wonderful way that some women from the last century were natural eccentrics.

Married at the age of 22 to a distinguished and cultured French nobleman, Count Pierre de Polignac, she was revered by her family, especially her grandchildren who called her 'Mamou'. Rainier characterises her as a woman with a kind heart who'd been a nurse during World War I and who spent her later years helping less fortunate people, among them prisoners.

'My mother lived most of her life in Paris and at Marchais. But it was sad, really, because she was unhappy almost from the start of her marriage. She never had very good memories of Monaco. I think she was always lonely here. She didn't have any friends here. She didn't have anyone around her. Being an only daughter I'm afraid there were times in her life when she was badly torn between her husband and her father.'

To keep the family name alive, Albert required her husband to change his name to Grimaldi. He became Prince Pierre Grimaldi, Count of Polignac, by sovereign order, the day before his wedding.

Rainier describes his father as a man of old-fashioned elegance with a pencil-thin moustache. Interested in music, art and literature, he was also fluent in several languages. He took up the study of Russian late in life, approached it like a hobby and, with the help of a private tutor, learned to speak and read it fluently.

'He was a very delicate, very sensitive man. Although, looking back, he might not have been very accessible where the younger generation was concerned. I regret maybe not having listened and spoken to him more. But that might be the problem with all young people. When you're young you don't listen enough.'

Pierre and Charlotte's first child, Antoinette, was born in 1920.

Two years later Albert died and Louis became ruling prince.

Then, on 31 May 1923, Charlotte's second child, her son and heir, Rainier Louis Henri Maxence Bertrand Grimaldi, was born in the Palace of Monaco, the first of the modern princes to be a native Monégasque.

*   *   *   *

As the only grandson and eventual heir of a ruling monarch, Rainier's home was wherever the sovereign held court.

'We'd only come to Monaco for about three months of the year. It was usually in the spring around Easter when the weather was good. I liked that because there was always a lot to do and the people were very welcoming. We wintered at Marchais. The Palace of Monaco was closed. My family, my grandfather's entire staff – the cooks, valets, footmen, maids, everybody – would go to Marchais for five or six months. Except the government. They stayed in Monaco. I remember my grandfather installed a telegraph at Marchais so he could keep in touch with them. It was very exciting, something brand new for us. I can still see a secretary tapping out messages all day long. There were also a couple of months every year when the family went shooting in Scotland. But I hated that. It never stopped raining. It was very boring.'

Claiming that his childhood was 'basically a contented one', Rainier acknowledges that his parents' divorce in 1929 left him feeling insecure.

'Insecure in the sense that children of divorced parents are always getting shuffled around and are never quite certain where they belong. There are times when you doubt your parents' love.'

It had been agreed that Rainier and Antoinette would spend part of the time with their mother and grandfather and part of the time with their father.

'When we were with mother we were always being told, when you see your father don't say anything to him about me or your grandfather. When we were with father we were always being told, don't say anything to your mother or your grandfather about me. That wasn't easy. Like any child who is the product of divorced parents, I felt hurt by it.'

Nor was his childhood made any easier by tension at home. Louis found himself under severe political pressure, which began just as the 'Roaring 20s' drew to a close.

The National Council tried to force a showdown.

Under the constitution they could only make recommendations to the Prince. They had no real power. And this was one of the things they wanted changed.

Next, they were still unhappy with the way SBM seemed to operate as a state unto itself in Monte Carlo, and contended that the company somehow threatened the independence of the country. They also wanted the Prince to hold SBM to its contractual responsibility of supplying Monte Carlo with basic services such as water, gas and road maintenance. They claimed SBM had neglected its obligations by investing instead in new tennis courts and a beach.

At the same time Princess Charlotte asked her father for permission to divorce Prince Pierre.

Louis agreed to his daughter's divorce and effectively banished Pierre from the principality.

But he turned a deaf ear to his subjects.

The National Council resigned in mass protest to rally support for their cause. Pressures mounted and there was talk of replacing the Prince with a republic. The general outcry grew so unfavourable that by April 1929 Louis realised he could no longer hold out. He helped seek new shareholders with fresh capital for SBM and agreed to appoint a committee of noted jurists to recommend reforms to the constitution. Elections were then held for a new National Council.

A newspaper report of the day described Monaco as, 'A box of toys in which everything is brilliant and artificial and a little fragile and must be kept carefully fitted into its place if it is not to be broken.'

It seems that Louis never truly understood just how fragile that box of toys was.

Public agitation continued to such an extent that by December 1930 he had to suspend the constitution and rule by decree. Eleven months later he established a Monégasque Assembly and personally appointed all its members. Inspite of that, they fought him bitterly and refused to rubber stamp the 1933 budget in an open display of mutiny.

Then Charlotte tried to renounce her right to the throne.

It's often written that Louis forced her to step aside, that he never intended her to be anything more than a conduit of sovereignty. Yet a letter discovered in the Palace archives dated January 1933 shows that Charlotte was a desperately unhappy woman who simply wanted to live her own life.

'Monseigneur,' she wrote to her father, 'You' – using the formal "vous" form instead of the more familiar "tu" – 'have so often proven your affection for me and, at the risk of being a disappointment to your hopes and aspirations, I am asking your double authority as chief of the government and prince to permit me to find henceforth, in all simplicity, peace in my life.'

By her own volition she wanted to abdicate in favour of her son.

'I believe I have accomplished my duty which condemned me to remain in a marriage against my wishes, in the name of political interests in which I fear I do not have the force to assume my responsibilities.'

Louis quickly established a regency counsel to carry on in his grandson's name and agreed that when Rainier reached 21, should Charlotte still feel incapable of ruling, he would grant her request.

She formally resigned her position on 30 May 1943, the day before Rainier's 21st birthday.

Three days later Louis named Rainier as heir to the throne.

'That was not an especially joyous moment for me. It was, in some ways, very sad. My mother renounced because she felt incapable. She was unhappy. I felt sorry for her. At the same time it meant a severe change of style in my life. I suddenly had to assume a lot of responsibilities.'

At around the same time Louis had to face a pretender who cast doubts on his own desires to continue his reign.

In 1934, a distant cousin laid claim to the throne and threatened to challenge Princess Charlotte's right to succeed. He was seen off without much of a fight but the incident fostered rumours that Louis was ready to quit, that he was going to sell Monaco to the French.

According to the *New York Times* of 4 February, Louis was 'seriously embarrassed financially' and no longer had the will or the means to fight a powerful local faction who did not want Princess Charlotte to rule.

The widely circulated story was vehemently denied by the Prince's spokesmen. Yet doubt lingered.

Next, his ex-son-in-law challenged his authority as far as Rainier's schooling and welfare were concerned.

It has been agreed at the time of his divorce from Charlotte that Pierre would take charge of Rainier's education.

'My father wanted me to have an absolutely superior education so he sent me to England in 1934. I started at the Summer Fields

School at St Leonard's-on-Sea. It was a horrible place. Short pants, cold showers and canings. The only good time I had there was boxing. I won the school title in my weight class. Other than that, I hated it.'

From there he went to Stowe.

'It was a beautiful setting but I remember arriving there with my father, not knowing any of the house masters or any of the students. I found the old castle atmosphere very dreary. It rained all the time so as soon as you went out to play any games you were knee-deep in mud. Then I had to learn about things like fagging, which meant doing menial chores for the older boys. Happily they were nice fellows but the whole thing always struck me as being stupid. I wasn't very happy at Stowe either.'

So unhappy, in fact, he ran away.

'On my third day I escaped. It turned out to be much easier than I thought it would be. I left the grounds and headed for the railway station. My plan was to buy myself a ticket to London and then make my way home from there. But I guess I wasn't very good at that kind of thing. I never thought there was anything unusual about going to the railway station with my school cap still on my head.'

The moment the school authorities realised he was gone, the police were notified. And as soon as the station-master noticed a lad with a school cap on his head trying to get to London, he rang the school.

'I was picked up and promptly brought back to Stowe. The head master, an ex-military man, came to fetch me in his enormous car. I thought I was in for trouble and would be severely caned. But he took me back to his study and welcomed me home with a gigantic high tea. He didn't reprimand me at all. He said, "You must be hungry so here's something to eat." It was the first meal I'd had all day. I thought to myself, finally someone understands. But then I was put in the school infirmary because they couldn't figure out why any child wanted to run away from this heaven.'

The young Prince was officially 'under observation' for two entire weeks, confined to doing absolutely nothing, until the staff gave up trying to figure him out and returned him to his dorm and his classes.

The problem should have been obvious to them.

Even though he spoke perfect English – 'We had a British nanny so I spoke English before I spoke French' – he was a chubby, timid child, the only foreigner among 500 boys, and he'd withdrawn into his shell.

He could handle himself very competently with a pair of boxing gloves strapped onto his hands but his innate shyness outside the ring was a red flag for the school bullies.

Rainier told his father how unhappy he was. And his father must have mentioned it to someone because, before long, Louis began to fear that Pierre might try to take him out of England, somehow prevent the child from returning to Monaco or otherwise come between Rainier and his grandfather.

In August 1936, Louis filed a petition in London for custody of Rainier, seeking to restrain Pierre from removing the 13-year-old from the UK.

During the March 1937 High Court hearing it came out that Louis had made similar appeals in Monaco and France and had won both times. Among the intriguing possibilities actually considered in the London action was making an heir to Monaco's throne a ward of the British courts. In the end, the judge ruled in favour of Louis but not before the affair hit the front pages and generally served to embarrass everyone concerned.

From England, Rainier went on to Le Rosey, one of the finest of the Swiss boarding-schools.

And at Le Rosey he was very happy.

'I adored it. I was there until 1939, until the first bombing of Lyons. It was a wonderful place to go to school. There were only about 100 boys at Le Rosey in those days and the girls' school was just across the way. It was the sort of place where, if you wanted to learn, everything was possible. If you wanted to work, it was great. If you didn't, they simply didn't worry about you. We even spent part of the winter in Gstaad.'

After graduation from Le Rosey he attended the University of Montpellier where he received his BA and then spent a year in Paris studying Political Science.

By the time Rainier came home to the principality in 1944 his grandfather was ailing and the Nazis were in charge.

*   *   *   *

World War II was not one of Monaco's more glorious moments.

The Monégasques did not capitulate the way the French did. They were officially neutral. However, because the French had come into Monaco at the start of the war to build defence installations along the coast, the moment France fell the Italians took the principality on the pretext that it had been previously occupied by France. The Italians then considered annexing it, and a plot was devised with a former government minister to depose Louis. When word reached the Palace, the Prince ordered the arrest of the conspirators and only released them after Mussolini personally gave Louis all the proper assurances.

The next wave of soldiers came from Germany.

In 1943 Berlin sent a Consul General and a military commandant to Monaco.

Shortly thereafter a Gestapo unit took up residence at the Hôtel de Paris.

In the greatest tradition of any occupied lot, the management at the Hôtel de Paris now feared the worst for their prize wines and Cognacs. They promptly hid their best vintages in a vault at the far end of the cellar, then sealed the vault behind a wall made to look exactly like part of the surrounding rock. The Germans took advantage of the otherwise well-stocked cellar but never discovered the deception. It wasn't until well after the war that the treasures were safely brought out of hiding, all of them intact.

The Gestapo unit was followed into Monte Carlo by a Panzer division.

But when the Panzer general tried to check into the Hôtel de Paris he discovered the Gestapo had already claimed all the best rooms. His second choice was the Hermitage. However, the staff there refused to play host to the Nazis and littered every room, making it absolutely impossible for anyone to move in. The general was forced to settle for digs at the less desirable Hôtel Métropole. However, the friction created by his instant distaste for the local Gestapo never subsided. He spent the rest of the war doing his best to spoil any plans they had, including their proposed deportation of local Jews. Monaco never became a haven for Jews during the war but they were safer there than in Nice or Cannes or most of France, for that matter, where deportations did take place.

Once the Germans had firmly established their presence, they built Radio Monte Carlo (RMC).

Intended to broadcast propaganda throughout southern France and neighbouring Italy, RMC inadvertently served as a refuge for young Monégasques who would otherwise have been sent to forced labour camps in Germany. Few radio stations before or since have ever had so many staff librarians.

As the war progressed, someone in Berlin decided that Monaco should become a furlough base for Nazi officers. And with that decision SBM's profits soared.

Also during this phase of the war, several hundred Monégasque holding companies were created. Goering and Himmler, together with other leading Nazis and many collaborating French and Italian businessmen, used these companies to launder their looted spoils.

But the Germans weren't in Monaco long before the tide started to turn in the Allies' favour.

Increasingly short supplied, Berlin ordered that the copper roof of Monte Carlo's casino be removed so that the metal could be used in the war effort. The Panzer general from the Métropole, himself a frequent visitor to the casino, refused to comply. He even used his influence to have the casino listed by the Nazis as 'a cultural and historic monument', thereby saving it from the war.

When the Americans landed at St Raphael in August 1944, Allied planes raided Nazi encampments along the cost, bombed Monaco's harbour and destroyed some German minesweepers. But instead of sending troops down the coast towards Italy, the Americans first headed north along the Rhône towards Lyons. It was only a few weeks later that they made their way back to the Riviera.

By that time the Germans were gone.

It's said that the first Americans to reach the principality were a pair of soldiers in a jeep who, on 3 September 1944, had to ask where they were. The American writer, Irwin Shaw, always bragged about being with those first soldiers to enter Monaco. Like Hemingway in Paris who liberated the Ritz, Shaw's claim to fame was that he liberated Monte Carlo's Tip Top Bar.

Once the Americans had secured the region, Nazi barbed wire was taken down, work began to de-mine the port, gun emplacements were dismantled and collaborators were arrested.

Hearing that the Nazis had used Monte Carlo as a furlough base, the US Army officer in charge of the region, Major General Robert Tryon Frederick, decided it would be the ideal R&R spot for his troops too.

Obviously, American soldiers with money to spend would have been a greenback-godsend for the principality.

But Louis said no.

The Prince claimed there wasn't enough room in the country for so many soldiers plus the regular visitors who, now that the war was over, would soon be coming back.

Insulted by Louis' attitude towards the liberators, Frederick placed Monaco off-limits to all US service personnel. Even General Eisenhower, who toured the region in the summer of 1945, refused to set foot in Monaco, staying instead on Cap d'Antibes.

Louis was a particularly stubborn man.

Nor was this the only error of judgement he made during the war.

His general posture throughout was to play an intermediate role, doing what he could to maintain calm on all sides. It's true that he never dignified the Nazi presence by attending any of their galas but he did permit an opera written by a contemporary German composer to have its world preview in Monte Carlo. It was the only time during the war that the Salle Garnier was totally filled with German uniforms.

Louis always rationalised that there was little he could do.

He believed that, as long as the Germans left the Monégasques alone and as long as the few Jews in the principality were relatively safe, it was best for everyone to accept the status quo and not make waves.

Rainier did not agree.

His sense of honour was offended by Louis's conciliations.

He felt that his grandfather, under the influence of several people in his entourage – including a loudly pro-Vichy Minister of State whom Rainier all-too-politely describes as, 'Not a very nice man' – had failed in not taking a forceful position against the Nazis.

Rainier argued with Louis about it and as soon as he finished school he insisted on his grandfather's permission to enlist in the French army as a foreign volunteer – a necessity, as any Monégasque wishing to do military service must first receive the ruling Prince's approval.

Three months after his 21st birthday, at about the same time that the Americans arrived at St Raphael, Rainier was commissioned as a second lieutenant and assigned to the headquarter's intelligence staff of the 2nd Corps, 1st French Army.

'I suffered through the winter campaign in Alsace and saw some action. But not as much as I wanted to. I had a pretty useless job posting notices on factories. It would have been more fun if we could have blown the damn things up. Because I spoke English I was sectored off to the 36th Infantry Division in Strasbourg, the Texas Rangers, and acted as a liaison on the general staff.'

Decorated for gallantry in areas under fire, he was promoted to first lieutenant and transferred to the economics section of the French Military Mission in Berlin.

He served just over 17 months before returning to Monaco to see first-hand how the war had taken its toll.

Monte Carlo's Sporting Club, built in the early 1930s, had never been intended to last more than a few years. Now it was very much out of date.

The casino was depressingly bleak.

The Hôtel de Paris, the Hermitage and in fact all the other hotels in Monte Carlo would have to be refurbished. They all needed to have the Nazi occupation washed and painted and wallpapered away.

The entire principality was in desperate need of renovation.

So too were the ties between the Prince and SBM. While he represented the political power in Monaco, SBM continued to wield the heaviest stick of all, the nation's economic power.

Rainier tried to explain to his grandfather that changes would have to come.

But Louis had other things on his mind.

In 1946, and in failing health, he married his longtime companion, a Parisian actress named Ghislaine Marie Dommanget, and altered his will accordingly to provide for her. His only interest now seemed to be in spending his remaining years with her.

Even though, as late as 1948, they were occasionally finding German mines along the beach, Monte Carlo was still all about galas and gambling.

But Rainier knew that galas and gambling were no longer enough.

The crises of the 1930s proved that the constitution also needed to be revised. He knew the time would soon come when the sovereign would have to make severe changes, or risk the sovereignty in a clash with his people.

Louis didn't care to know what Rainier thought. He was a man from another era. He would go to his grave staunch in his belief that the Prince of Monaco should always rule by divine right.

In great frustration, Rainier walked out.

He left Monaco.

He bought a small villa at St Jean-Cap-Ferrat and lived there.

As long as his grandfather was alive, there was nothing else he could do.

*　　*　　*　　*

Rainier spent those years between the end of the war and his accession to the throne racing cars in the Tour de France Rally, skin-diving, fishing, sailing, occasionally writing poetry or going to exhibitions and otherwise quietly meeting his obligations to the principality.

Then, on 9 May 1949, Louis II passed away.

Rainier was three weeks short of his 26th birthday.

Alone, he set about trying to put his own stamp of authority on the ruling Prince's office.

One of the first things he did was to bring his father back from exile.

To honour him, Rainier established an important annual literary award – today it's called the Prince Pierre Prize – and asked his father to chair the committee. The first recipient, in 1951, was the single American member of the French Academy, Julian Green.

At the same time there were distant mutterings from his cousin who'd once tried to claim the throne. Now 79, the pretender reasserted his protest that Charlotte's adoption and later admission to full hereditary rights contravened the constitution. The best Rainier could do was ignore him, secure in the knowledge that this particular annoyance couldn't go on forever.

Next he had to deal with Princess Ghislaine, Louis's widow.

In his will, the late sovereign left 50 per cent of his estate to Rainier, 25 per cent to his granddaughter Antoinette and 25 per cent to Ghislaine. But included in the estate was property that Rainier claimed belonged to the crown, property that was not Louis's to give away. The case was heard by the specially convened Court of Revision, a secretive tribunal created specifically to settle Monaco's dynastic disputes. Consisting of ten attorneys chosen by the French Foreign Office and whose names are never disclosed, they were flown clandestinely to Monaco where they ruled in Rainier's favour. Ghislaine appealed but in the end there was nothing she could do except refuse to leave her one room at the Palace.

However the real challenges were yet to come.

Rainier's accession to the throne had been welcomed by the Monégasques as a breath of fresh air. But the honeymoon with the otherwise cantankerous National Council was short lived. They very quickly picked up with him where they'd left off with his grandfather and made demands that Rainier found unacceptable.

Led in part by a local lawyer named Jean Charles Rey, the Council regularly tried to compete with Rainier's authority. Rey later married Princess Antoinette and together they claimed that because the law did not limit succession to males, Princess Charlotte's first born was therefore Monaco's rightful heir. These days Rainier insists they never posed a serious threat, that it was just vague talk, that everything was 'up in the air'. Be that as it may, the two were quickly rebuked and, if nothing else, the much-publicised affair did little more than embarrass everyone involved. Antoinette and Rey eventually divorced, although Rey stayed on the National Council, was both public and forceful in his opposition to his former brother-in-law and often bragged that he was still 'the power behind the throne'.

In the summer of 1955, when the heavily government subsidised Monaco Banking and Precious Metals Society went bankrupt, the Council pointed a finger at four close aides of the Prince and demanded their resignations. Questions of mismanagement and conflicts of interest were raised. At first Rainier stayed loyal to his aides. Then, faced with a mass walk-out by the Council, he accepted the resignations. A few months later he reappointed the four to other posts and almost immediately eleven members of the Council quit in protest.

Rainier made little effort to appease the Council.

Legally he held the power and they did not. All they could do,
all they were supposed to do, was advise. But they were undeterred
in their opposition. They sought confrontation wherever possible,
like their bizarre stance against Rainier's plan for covering the
railroad.

Running straight through the centre of Monte Carlo, with
tracks sunk into an open ditch, trains from Nice to Ventimiglia
literally sliced the country in half. Rainier proposed to cover the
tracks and build on top of them. The council said no and tried to
withhold the money that was required. It was idiotic because the
plans were not only sound, they were paramount to the further
development of Monte Carlo.

But then the Council also fought him on making funds available to the Oceanographic Institute to afford its newly appointed
director, Jacques Cousteau. There's no doubt that Cousteau's
appointment was a world-class coup for Monaco. Yet the Council
wouldn't accept that.

In the end, of course, the Prince got the money to cover the
railroad and to afford Cousteau. But at times it appeared almost as
if Rey and a few others were using the Council in a sort of personal
vendetta against Rainier.

By 1959 the Prince decided he had no option but to suspend the
constitution and take rule by decree.

'There was no doubt that changes were needed. We couldn't
go on much longer the way we were. It hadn't yet reached the
stage where anyone was making serious threats but there was
discontent with the old constitution. I decided I wanted to create a
genuine constitutional monarchy. Not because I was being press-
ured into it but because I felt it was better to do it voluntarily
than to wait until the National Council or various political figures in the community started making specific demands. So I
approached the National Council and we worked it out together.
I gave up some power but it wasn't necessarily a difficult thing to
do because responsibilities were split too.'

Under the 1962 Constitution, which is still in force today,
executive power remains in the hands of the Prince, who appoints
a Minister of State to run the government. The Minister also represents him in matters of foreign affairs and with the Monégasque
parliament. Because everything is done in the name of the Prince,
it is only done with his approval. But legislative power was split
between the Prince and the National Council, now made up of 18

native Monégasques elected by universal suffrage to a five-year term.

Rainier explains, 'They vote the budget. They debate the laws. They vote the laws. Or they can veto the laws. They're not supposed to interfere with the executive and his duties but in reality we have clashes, especially when they make judgements about how I'm doing my job or say things like, building permission should never have been granted for such and such a project. It's difficult for elected men to look after that kind of stuff because you never really know where their own interests are. The National Council discusses each chapter of the budget and each department of the government must defend its own requirements. If the National Council isn't satisfied, it can reject what it doesn't want. So because it votes the budget it can, if it wants, block the whole system.'

*　*　*　*

Moves towards independence in Morocco, Algeria and Tunisia in the late 1950s and early 1960s meant that the *pieds noirs* – those French colonials whose families had settled in North Africa – were suddenly uprooted and forced to return to France.

A large number of them relocated along the Riviera to maintain their Mediterranean origins. And this sudden influx of families created a mini real-estate boom.

Not all of them had money but many of the wealthiest *pieds noirs* were shrewd enough to understand that the principality's tax laws could keep their funds out of the reach of the French fiscal system.

Untaxed French money in Monaco became an obsession with Charles de Gaulle.

He couldn't just go after it without some sort of provocation, so he used the entrée afforded by a long-standing dispute over broadcasting rights.

Although the studios and administration offices of Radio Monte Carlo are in Monaco, their German-built transmitter and antennae are on French territory. Once the war was over, France claimed the transmitter and antennae as spoils. When Rainier complained he was told that RMC could continue broadcasting but France would name five of the station's six administrators.

Following the crash of the Monaco Banking and Precious Metals Society, de Gaulle tried to extend French influence in both RMC and Tele-Monte Carlo (TMC) by purchasing their shares. Similarly, he wanted to limit Monaco's control of Europe Number One, an independent radio station in the Saar that, along with RMC and TMC, threatened the French state monopoly on broadcasting.

Rainier categorically refused to stand for it and used his authority to ban the sale of the stations' shares to France.

De Gaulle demanded the ban be lifted.

Rainier said no.

So de Gaulle got nasty.

The Monégasque government lined up wholeheartedly behind Rainier, with the exception of the Minister of State, a loutish French bureaucrat named Emile Pelletier. The Minister came to see the Prince in his office very late one night, the two discussed the problem and Pelletier backed de Gaulle.

Infuriated, the Prince accused him of being disloyal.

Pelletier threatened to disclose to de Gaulle information that, as Minister of State, he'd been party to in confidence. He also threatened to inform de Gaulle just how anti-French Rainier really was.

The Prince fired Pelletier on the spot.

Pelletier stormed out of the office, swearing at Rainier, and made his way to Paris where he told the Prime Minister, Michel Debré, everything he'd threatened to say.

De Gaulle, who now had the pretext he needed to get at the untaxed funds, announced that Pelletier's firing was an insult to France, demanded a revision of the Franco-Monégasque accords and warned that, if the situation wasn't normalised immediately, France would shut Monaco's border 'and asphyxiate the state'.

All these years later, Rainier is willing to concede, 'Maybe, just maybe, I was a little too harsh with Pelletier. But frankly, I was extremely annoyed with what the French were trying to do. So I slammed the door and refused to give in. Pelletier got scared. He tried to discredit me in Paris. The French were so afraid of de Gaulle anyway. The word came that de Gaulle was going to change the treaties with Monaco even though they'd been in effect since 1861 and 1918. I don't know how the general thought he could get away with it because he couldn't have done it legally. We were even prepared to go to The Hague. The treaty we've got with France stems from the Treaty of Versailles. You can't just erase that.'

With the press often making light of the dispute – they covered the story with frequent references to David versus Goliath and the plight of the Lilliputians – Monaco did not, at first, get much support from the rest of the world.

Hardly anyone considered the problem as serious as did Rainier and de Gaulle.

Only the President of the Italian Senate, Cesare Merzagora, took it upon himself to remind de Gaulle that the sovereignty of Monaco was protected by law.

Whether Monaco could have rallied support from any other countries in the world had they actively sought it, or by having gone to the World Court, is something Rainier occasionally wonders about.

'I don't honestly know, except that de Gaulle had enough enemies around the world that I'd like to think we would have gotten some countries on our side. It's just that he was such a strange man. Whenever we met, when he came to visit in Monaco or when Grace and I went to Paris on what amounted to a state visit, he was very amiable. When he came here he brought gifts for Caroline. She was just a little girl and when she was introduced to him it was as if he was her grandfather. She kept asking him questions, like if he had any ponies. He must have spoken to her for 10 minutes. Still, he was adamant about his position *vis-à-vis* Monaco.'

Despite their differences, Rainier says, he couldn't help but be impressed by de Gaulle because he was such a fascinating man and such a formidable politician.

'I always compared him to the Eiffel Tower, not because of his height but because he was something you could admire but couldn't possibly love. He was very cold. You must understand that as soon as they set foot in the Elysée, every President of the French Republic becomes a monarch. Giscard got in there and decided right away he wanted to slow down the tempo of the Marseillaise. Then he wanted to march up the Champs-Elysées because he felt the people would enjoy that. Frankly, the Parisians were furious because they'd come to see the Republican Guard on horseback. Mr Giscard d'Estaing became so regal that at official dinners he insisted on being served first, just like the King of France. It's a funny attitude.'

Not that he's saying de Gaulle went as far.

'No, he wasn't that pompous. But he was very rigorous. After all, he was a military man. He had the attitudes of a general but he behaved as a chief of state. You know how wives count very little for military leaders? Well, that was true of de Gaulle the president too. Madame de Gaulle was always three paces behind him. And yet there was surely a lot of affection between them. It's just that de Gaulle used people. If they weren't useful they were of no interest.'

When de Gaulle discovered, much to his displeasure, that Rainier would not give in without a fight, the dispute got very bitter.

'He wanted us to align ourselves on the French fiscal system. After someone somewhere in the Finance Ministry, which was then run by Giscard, got it into de Gaulle's head that a lot of the North African French money was hidden here and that it had to come to France, he took the approach that there was no need for negotiations. That his word was going to be the law. To prove his point, he ordered customs barriers set up around Monaco.'

Two companies of gendarmes stationed in Nice were put on alert.

Rumours flew around Monaco that French paratroopers were getting ready to take the Place du Casino.

On 12 October 1962, police and customs officers sealed off the border. They worked strictly by the book and harped on all sorts of petty nonsense. For example, if you had a radio in your car, they'd ask you where you bought it and demand to see the receipt. If your papers weren't in order you were turned away.

Next, de Gaulle threatened to cut off Monaco's electricity and water.

'I don't know what would have happened to us had he done that but I've always believed it could have been fatal for him. It would have been a really stupid thing to do because there was never any aggression on our part. I was giving interviews at the time trying to show that we weren't being anti-French by standing up to de Gaulle. I was only making a stand against measures that affected us, that were taken in the name of France when we were not given any chance to discuss them.'

De Gaulle's objective was, as Rainier saw it, a direct threat to the sovereignty of the principality. At one point there was actually talk around the French Foreign Ministry of dethroning Rainier, of sending him into exile.

It wasn't until the press began describing Monaco as a country under siege that things started to happen.

Many people were utterly convinced that because de Gaulle had lost the French colonies in North Africa he needed to restore his tarnished reputation by conquering Monaco. That was reflected in the heavy press criticism which followed the barricading of Monaco's borders. One otherwise right-wing newspaper even asked, 'Why does the General take an atom bomb to kill a fly?'

This was an image that particularly pleased Rainier. It also prompted a lot of mail in the principality's support, not only from people in France but from around the world. Nevertheless, it took 15 months to negotiate a settlement with Paris because de Gaulle was so stubborn.

'Once we got down to serious negotiations with the technicians at the various ministries we knew everything would be all right. We could see that they were even a little embarrassed about all this because de Gaulle had gone too far. After all the hassles, our main concession was that French people living in Monaco would have to pay French taxes as if they were living in France. We worked out a compromise that from 1963 onwards no Frenchman would be allowed to evade French taxes by living in Monaco. But then that's what de Gaulle had been after all the time.'

The customs checks disappeared, the gendarmes were stepped down and life returned to normal. Although Rainier and de Gaulle were destined to lock horns again a few years later.

When de Gaulle closed the American bases in France and withdrew French military support to NATO, Rainier announced that US ships would indeed be permitted to stop in Monaco.

'De Gaulle didn't like it when I refused to turn my back on the Americans. But this time there wasn't much he could do about it. I didn't invite them to stop here for economic reasons, even though there's always a lot of money at stake whenever a warship comes to call. The guys come ashore and they spend. I just thought de Gaulle's attitude towards the Americans was wrong. I didn't see any reason why we should have adopted that same stance.'

In the context of those times, claims former US Secretary of the Navy, John Lehman – a cousin by marriage on Princess Grace's side – standing up to de Gaulle's deliberate campaign against American interests in Europe was a brave thing to do.

'Despite the difficulties he was having with de Gaulle, Rainier continued to play host to American ships and really hung out the "Welcome" mat. De Gaulle hated that. But Rainier would not be intimidated. He was willing to take the heat. When the French were being beastly to the Americans, Rainier went out of his way to be keenly supportive. He's always been very pro-American. And this attitude preceded Grace. She merely reinforced it.'

Yet Rainier's willingness 'to take the heat' was not without its price on his nerves.

At one point during his battle with de Gaulle, the Prince wrote to a friend, 'It's terrible to feel one's smallness and fragility in front of crushing power and determination. I hope and pray that it will all come out well but in the meantime it is going to be hard, bitter and difficult.'

Maintaining that 'hard, bitter and difficult' are still the words he'd use to describe that period, Rainier believes that one of the ways he got through those times was by learning to count on Grace.

'In the beginning she said maybe I should have toned myself down a bit with Pelletier. But she could see that he hadn't fulfilled his responsibilities to me. This was the first serious diplomatic crisis in her career. It was unknown territory for her. She had to learn about it, had to find out for herself what was going on. Once she realised what was happening she backed me up all the way.'

He says they discussed what was happening at great length, he confided in her and he turned to her for support.

'She always offered suggestions but she never interfered with my decisions. I wouldn't say she was my closest adviser because she never took the position of an adviser. Instead, she was always cautioning me not to be in a hurry. She took the human side, wanting me to keep a dialogue going with the French, telling me not to push too quickly or too hard.'

He pauses for just a second.

'She and I were a pretty good team.'

*   *   *   *

4

A Public Romance

W*HEN COMEDIAN* Bill Cosby was first introduced to Princess Grace, a mutual friend suggested, 'You probably already know each other because you both come from Philadelphia.'

Cosby responded immediately, 'Yes of course we know each other. Her family owned my family.'

*   *   *   *

John Brendon Kelly, the ninth in a family of ten children, was a tough, two-fisted, hard-drinking man with an eye for the ladies who, like so many sons of immigrants to the United States, battled his way from poverty to riches to live the American dream.

His parents, hailing from County Mayo, came to the New World with nothing more in their pockets than a thick brogue and a lot of hope. John B., who was always called Jack, was born in 1890 in East Falls, one of Philadelphia's Irish working-class neighbourhoods. He was brought up there at a time when Irishmen were 'Micks' and 'bogtrotters' and the best that any 'Mick' or 'bogtrotter' could expect, if he wasn't a heavyweight boxer or perhaps some sort of celebrated drunken poet, was a job as a day labourer.

To help support his family, Jack worked after school from the age of nine in the local carpet mills, quitting school three years later to work full-time as a hod carrier and apprentice brick-layer with one of his older brothers who'd by then started his own construction firm.

But Jack was destined for better things.

He had the drive to succeed and a talent for rowing. With his back and arms strengthened by construction work, he took to sculling on the nearby Schuykil River and quickly developed into a champion oarsman. Returning from the Army after World War I in 1918, he and his Vesper Boat Club team-mates spent the next two years preparing to race at England's world-famous Henley Regatta and then at the Olympics in Antwerp. But two days before he planned to leave Philadelphia for Europe, a telegram arrived from Henley saying, 'Entry rejected'.

The official Henley explanation is now, as it was then, that Kelly could not be permitted to race because the Vesper club and all its members had been officially banned for violating the 'amateur' status of the event in 1905. It seems they'd sent oarsmen to Henley that year by soliciting donations to cover expenses. One British steward found such matters so offensive he even proposed that all Americans be outlawed, although the regatta organisation did not go that far. However, the ban on Vesper was still in effect in 1920.

Kelly, on the other hand, always offered a different reason.

He maintained throughout his life that his entry was refused because he'd once been a common labourer and that anyone who'd ever worked with his hands was therefore not eligible to compete with 'gentlemen' at class-conscious Henley.

In fact, a ban against anyone who'd ever worked with his hands did exist, not only for Henley, but for all amateur rowing in Great Britain until about 1939. The rule specifically barred anyone who'd ever been employed in, among other activities, manual labour.

So, as long as he lived, Jack Kelly accused the British of being boorish snobs who were obviously afraid that their so-called 'gentlemen' scullers could never be a match for the likes of a muscular labourer.

Whichever version is closer to the truth, the point is that Kelly took the snub personally and vowed that one day he would get even.

And his revenge has become the stuff of American sports mythology.

Not only did he go on to defeat the best of the British two months later in the Olympics – he came home with two gold medals – he then spent years training his son who, in 1947 and again in 1949, reminded the British of the earlier insult and took Henley's first prize.

Once described by his chum Franklin Roosevelt as, 'The handsomest man I've ever seen', Jack Kelly was heavy on charm, sentimentality and humour and was graced till the day he died with an athletic physique, a fearless enthusiasm to get what he wanted and a passion for politics. In 1919 he borrowed $2,500 from two of his brothers to start a company called Kelly For Brickwork which, by 1935, had become so successful that he used it as a springboard to run for mayor. Although he was defeated and never put his name on another ballot, he did flirt with the idea of running for the US Senate in 1936 and was, until 1940, head of the Philadelphia Democratic Committee. Nevertheless, throughout his life he remained a dominant backroom force in Philadelphia politics. It's often said in the City of Brotherly Love that John Kelly was so well connected that not one single building was erected in Center City between the mid-1920s and the mid-1950s without Kelly For Brickwork getting the contract.

In 1924 Jack married Margaret Majers, a woman he'd known for nearly nine years. The daughter of German immigrants, she'd been raised a Lutheran in the Strawberry Mansion area of Philadelphia. She grew up speaking German at home and stressed with her children the same strong sense of Prussian discipline that had been such an important part of her own youth. Everyone obeyed her. Not even Jack dared go up against her. Although when she insisted her children learn to speak fluent German, they hid the grammar books because they hated the language and feared that, late in the 1930s, speaking German was an unpatriotic thing for Americans to do.

A former magazine cover-girl, she studied at Temple University for two years to get herself an Associates Degree in Physical Education. That quickly led her to a job as the first woman to teach P.E. at the University of Pennsylvania. She converted to Catholicism to marry Jack and their first child, Peggy, was born within a year. Their son John – always known as Kell – followed two years later in 1927, with Grace two years after that, on 12 November 1929. Their fourth and last child, Lizanne, was born in 1933.

A stickler for routine, every part of Ma Kelly's day was pro-
grammed to a tight schedule. There was just so much time for
breakfast, just so much time for listening to the radio. There was
a specific time for piano lessons, a specific time for bed. She ran
her household with an iron hand and, when she laid down the law,
that's the way it was.

Years later, Caroline, Albert and Stephanie would get to see Ma
Kelly at her best when they spent summers with her at the Kelly
family beach house in Ocean City, New Jersey.

Rainier and Grace would bring the kids to visit their grandmother and their American cousins and at dinner time it was
Ma Kelly who sat at the head of the table. On more than one
occasion, when she spotted Rainier leaning comfortably forward,
she'd grab her fork and jab him with it, shrieking 'Elbows', until
he took them off her table.

The Kellys lived in a 15-room house built with Kelly bricks at
3901 Henry Avenue in the then upwardly mobile part of Philadelphia called Germantown. Grace was born there. Her mother
described her as a happy child, even though she was asthmatic
and suffered ear and throat infections throughout her childhood.

Interestingly enough, it might have been those bouts with
illness which inadvertently helped to turn her head towards the
theatre.

Both her parents were very keen on athletics and they more
than just encouraged their children to excel. For Jack and Ma,
athletics came a close third behind religion and schoolwork. Kell
not only won at Henley, he also took a bronze medal in sculling at
the 1956 Olympics, while both Peggy and especially Lizanne were
exceedingly good competitive swimmers. Grace played tennis,
was captain of her school field hockey team, swam and could
dive. But she never really became the athlete her brother and
sisters were. She wasn't formed in the same competitive mould.
Nor was she as besotted by sports as they were.

As those childhood illnesses often kept her in bed, she discovered the joys of reading.

Coming from a family where competition, especially in sports,
was very important, Grace was the one who found herself something of the odd one out.

Kell was his father's son. Peggy was her father's favourite. And
Lizanne was the baby of the family, so she could usually get away
with anything. Grace was neither as pretty as Peggy and Lizanne,

nor as extroverted as her sisters and brother. She was caught in the middle and, as a middle child, she tended to retreat into her protective shell.

But she was 'Fordie's' favourite and years later she'd say memories of her friendship with him were among her fondest of childhood.

Godfrey Ford worked for the Kellys as a general handyman and all-round 'Mr Fixit.' Almost a Harriet Beecher Stowe caricature, he was a kind and gentle black man from North Philadelphia who spent his life with the Kellys, who was totally dedicated to them, who watched the children grow up as they watched him grow old.

She used to love to tell stories about him, like how when the family moved to Ocean City for the summer all the other kids would have to ride with their parents except her. She got to ride in the old pick-up truck with Fordie. Ma Kelly worried they'd never arrive safely but that didn't stop Grace from piling into the front seat next to Fordie, with their luggage and even some of the family furniture pouring off the back. They'd take twice as long to get to the beach as anyone else. But they'd laugh all the way and sometimes he'd let her steer and the two of them made up stories together and sang.

Fordie might have been the first person in Grace's life to say it didn't really matter if she wasn't the athlete her brother and sisters were.

Because Ma Kelly was such a disciplinarian, Grace was enrolled at the Ravenhill Academy in East Falls, a parochial school run by nuns who rigourously stressed discipline and correct manners. But by the time she was 12 she'd convinced her mother that the less severe Stevens School would be better for her and she was allowed to transfer there.

It was at about that time she started wishing she'd been a boy.

As she later explained, her father's influence on her had been formidable. He used to lecture his children, 'Nothing is given for nothing', so Grace grew up believing that everything worth having had to be earned and the way you earned anything was through hard work. The problem with being a teenage girl in the 1940s was that the real opportunities always went to boys.

'My father was a leader of men,' she once told an interviewer. 'Whatever the cost, one had to follow him. And to follow in his footsteps it was easier to be a boy than a girl.' Still, she added, 'An enthusiastic father is a marvellous start in life.'

She'd obviously inherited his enthusiasm and that first began to manifest itself when she was taken to see a performance of the Ballet Russe. Dance enchanted her and she began to study both ballet and classical piano. Childhood illnesses now behind her, dance and gymnastics took the place of athletics. There was even a time when she thought she might like to become a professional dancer.

Then she discovered the dramatic stage.

She was 12 when she made her debut with the East Falls' Old Academy Players in a production called *Don't Feed the Animals*. She next appeared in a production of *Cry Havoc* and, much to her delight, was soon cast by the group in their version of *The Torch Bearers*, a play written by her uncle George.

She graduated from Stevens in June 1947 and applied to Bennington College in Vermont. But she'd never been too keen on maths and science and didn't have the academic qualifications they wanted.

Bennington turned her down.

And who knows how her life might have been different had they accepted her.

Instead she attended a few courses at Temple while trying to decide where her future lay. Once she made up her mind to take a serious stab at acting, she moved to New York, installed herself at the Barbizon – a residential hotel for well-bred young women – and began studying at the American Academy of Dramatic Arts.

Watching Grace, barely 18, go off to seek fame and fortune in the big city was not necessarily something that Jack Kelly found easy to accept. His own sister Grace, for whom his daughter was named, had expressed an interest in acting many years before. But her career was stopped before it ever began by her parents, because proper young ladies in those days did not do such things. As Grace herself would one day say, 'Aunt Grace made the mistake of being born just one generation too soon. I had better luck.'

Indeed she did.

She also had a pair of uncles on her father's side who made a career in the theatre appear to be a genuine possibility.

Walter Kelly, much older than her father, was an itinerant actor who had a moderate stage success in his youth playing a vaudeville character known as 'The Virginia Judge'. He went to

Hollywood in the early days of the American cinema but his career never got much further than vaudeville and he died in 1938 when Grace was nine. Yet she grew up knowing that one of her uncle's had been 'on the boards' and Uncle Walter stories were a common topic at the family dinner table.

George Kelly however, proved infinitely more successful than Walter. He was John's immediate elder brother, although the two were totally different. Where John was physical, George was a dreamer, a delicate man of moods and intellect who started in the theatre as an actor and then evolved into writing plays. He was Grace's godfather and perhaps one of her most important early influences. In 1926 he won a Pulitzer Prize for his play *Craig's Wife*, the success of which eventually took him to Hollywood where he was on the writing staff at MGM. Even though his years in Hollywood never came close to equalling his earlier Broadway promise, being George Kelly's niece did open a few doors for Grace at a time when she desperately needed an early break.

She auditioned, not hiding the fact that she was George Kelly's niece, for the American Academy with, among other pieces, a speech from *The Torch Bearers*.

Over the next two years she learned about diction and posture and how to walk on a stage. She learned how to overcome her shyness and create a character. She studied improvisation and 'The Method'.

Grace trekked down to the Bowery to watch bums stumble around so she could improvise a drunk. Then she was sent off to the zoo to study the way animals moved. Acting school was, she later said in an interview, the only place she was ever called on to play a llama.

While living at the Barbizon – which more often than not was referred to by the hoards of young men who hung out in the lobby there as 'The Amazon' because very few of the residents were anywhere near as beautiful as Grace Kelly – a friend suggested she might be able to earn some extra money by modelling. She refused at first, then let herself get talked into it and before she was 19 started working for a small agency which managed to get her work at $7.50 an hour. That was a fairly good salary in those days when you consider that most of the rest of the world was struggling to make $1 an hour. Before long her blonde, 'girl-next-door' looks – as they were then described – found their way into national advertising campaigns. She sold Ipana toothpaste, Old

Gold cigarettes, dandruff shampoo, overnight beauty creams and
several different kinds of beer. Her fee was upped to $25 an hour
and by the time she graduated from the American Academy of
Dramatic Arts in 1949 she was doing fashion spreads for newsreels
at $400 a week.

Whether or not she could have gone on to be one of the great
New York models is another matter. The problem with modelling,
as she saw it, was that modelling wasn't acting and she wanted to
be an actress.

In spite of the fact that she was George Kelly's niece and had a
rich father, Grace still paid her dues.

She made the rounds of Broadway casting calls only to be told
time and time again, 'Don't call us, we'll call you'. She was subjected to the humiliation that all actors and actresses suffer when
they're first starting out, of standing around for hours in a long line
of other hopefuls, finally being asked to read a dozen lines, then
getting stopped after just one or two by a voice at the rear of the
darkened theatre who says, 'Thank you, next please'.

She learned about rejection the hard way, by being rejected.

At nearly 5' 7" she was too tall to play the innocent little
girl which her pretty face and bright blue eyes suggested. Still,
she stuck it out and persevered until she finally landed her first
professional acting job. It was in the summer of 1949 at the Bucks
County Playhouse in New Hope, Pennsylvania, for their production of George Kelly's *The Torch Bearers*.

Uncle George had put her name forward for the part but she
didn't get it just because she was his niece. She was hired because
the director believed she'd be 'okay'. And while she might not
have been particularly remarkable in the role, she worked hard
and was good enough to be invited back for their second production of the summer, *The Heiress*.

And this time she was very good.

Flattering notices at Bucks County led to a screen test. Director
Gregory Ratoff was making a film called *Taxi* and thought she
might be right to play the young Irish immigrant. She took her
first screen test in New York but convinced herself that she'd
failed when the part went to Constance Smith.

She continued auditioning until she won the part of Raymond
Massey's daughter in a Broadway revival of August Strindberg's
The Father. He was a majestically tall actor so this time the
problem wasn't her height. It was the *New York Times*. They

gave her a passable review, but panned him. The power of the NYT being what it's always been on Broadway, the show closed in less than nine weeks.

Grace spent the rest of the winter of 1949 on the audition circuit, modelling to earn money but as an actress, otherwise out of work.

Of course, timing and luck are important in all careers. But Grace's timing, combined with her Kelly-green Irish luck, seemed to be near perfect. She was in the right place at the right time because New York in the early 1950s was where television was happening. And television in the early 1950s was fast becoming America's most important arena for aspiring actors and actresses.

Unable to land another role on Broadway, she plugged herself into the weekly television drama circuit.

She started appearing regularly and then starring in, dramas presented on the Philco/Goodyear Playhouse. That led to appearances in all the other major 'playhouse' productions of the day, such as The Kraft Television Theatre, The Nash Airflyte Theatre and The Prudential Family Playhouse.

Live television became the major training ground of the era for young actors and actresses trying to find their way into show business. And over the course of 30 months Grace worked in no less than 60 live television productions.

In 1951, just as she was starting to make a name for herself in television, she was offered her first movie, a minor part in a film called *Fourteen Hours*.

Based on a true incident, it's the story of a man standing on the ledge of a building for 14 hours, threatening to jump. It featured Richard Basehart, Barbara Bel Geddes, Paul Douglas, Debra Paget, Agnes Moorehead, Jeffrey Hunter and Howard da Silva. The film was not a success at the box office and didn't do much for Grace's career. Ironically, it does get shown on television from time to time, not only because it was her debut, but because Henry Hathaway's direction was good, Basehart was effective and Bel Geddes – Miss Ellie on TV's *Dallas* – was the best of all.

During those early years, George Kelly did whatever he could for his niece. At one point, early on, he phoned his friend, producer Gant Gaither, and suggested he see Grace work. It was the summer she was at Bucks County. Gaither agreed to drive down one weekend and meet George Kelly there. He suggested they could have dinner together before the play. But Kelly was not at all enthusiastic. Even though he wanted to help Grace, he told Gaither, 'What? Me see one of my plays performed by a summer stock company? Never.' So Gaither ended up going alone. However, he liked what he saw and knew he'd be doing George a favour if he could hire her. It took some time but he eventually gave Grace a try-out in the out-of-town previews of a play called *Alexander*. Her role was a sexy one and, even though the Albany, New York critics wrote that 'Grace Kelly was too cool to be sexy', it was that very quality which would one day make her a major movie star. Recognising her promise, Gaither told her in Albany, 'You've got the part when we come to New York.'

'She was a lovely young girl who became a magnificent woman,' Gaither recalls affectionately, almost 40 years later. 'The thing that amazed me most about her was that her judgement was always so good. She had such wonderful common sense. Long before she got married, if I was working on a show that needed help, I'd ask her to come see it. If she was critical of something she'd offer something else in its place. She had a wonderful sense of construction.'

Just before the show travelled down the Hudson to Broadway, Grace got a phone call out of the blue saying that Hollywood producer Stanley Kramer wanted her for a western called *High Noon*, to be directed by Fred Zimmermann.

She made the picture in the autumn of 1951, having spent much of that summer doing stock in Colorado playing good parts, but nevertheless still the *ingénue*.

High Noon was her first Hollywood experience.

However, her portrayal of Amy Kane opposite Gary Cooper's Oscar-winning tin-star sheriff did not make her a movie star. The film has since become a cult favourite but when she was finished, Hollywood merely said thank you and handed her a ticket back to New York.

Grace returned to the apartment she now called home at 200 East 66th Street, worked in television and pounded the pavement again looking for a part on Broadway.

Then, again seemingly out of the blue, a call came from producer Sam Zimbalist and director John Ford who wanted her for the second female lead in a picture they were going to shoot in Africa called *Mogambo*.

But it wasn't, as she originally thought, her work in *High Noon* that got her the role. It turned out to be that first screen test she'd made for Gregory Ratoff. Zimbalist and Ford had seen it quite by chance, liked what they saw and hired her. So she offed to Kenya with Clark Gable who was re-creating his white hunter role – he'd starred with Jean Harlow in the first version of the story called *Red Dust* – and Ava Gardner who was playing the female lead. And Grace's performance as the ice-cool, 'other woman', Linda Norley, earned her an Oscar nomination that year as Best Supporting Actress.

Nicely enough, she always credited Ford for her success in that picture and also with having taught her a lot about acting on screen. She used to say that he knew just how far he could push his actors without forcing them to overstep the limits of their potential. Even though she lost the Oscar to Donna Reed, who took the honours – along with Frank Sinatra as Best Supporting Actor – for *From Here to Eternity*, there was no doubt that by 1953 Grace Kelly was a star.

Alfred Hitchcock had also seen Gregory Ratoff's screen test of Grace and now he hired her to play opposite Ray Milland in *Dial M for Murder*. He followed that by putting her opposite Jimmy Stewart in *Rear Window*.

Then she made *The Country Girl* with Bing Crosby and William Holden. Ironically, a few years before, the producer who brought *The Country Girl* to Broadway had turned Grace down for the same role in which she now won the Oscar as Best Actress.

From Ipana Toothpaste to Hollywood, Grace Kelly had become a household name in America.

She was the role model for half a generation of young American girls in the mid-1950s.

They dressed like her and wore their hair like her and tried to speak like her.

If you were a young girl growing up in America in those days and you were beautiful, what you wanted to hear most was someone saying, 'You're as pretty as Grace Kelly'.

To the utter delight of MGM, with whom she'd long since signed a seven-year $750 a week contract, Grace Kelly was suddenly worth a fortune and the studio kept their books in the black by renting her out to other studios. They used her in *Green Fire* with Stewart Granger, but once that was done they hired her out to Paramount for *The Bridge at Toko-Ri* with Bill Holden and Frederick March and for the third time to Alfred Hitchcock for *To Catch a Thief* with Cary Grant.

When she returned home from the south of France – where she could see Monaco far below while they filmed the now-famous driving scene along the Grande Corniche – MGM announced that she was going to do a picture called *The Adventures of Quentin Durward* with Robert Taylor.

But when Grace read the script she hated it.

As far as she was concerned the role they had in mind for her gave her nothing more to do than walk around wearing a tall hat and watch Robert Taylor joust. She told MGM she wouldn't make the picture. They said she had to and reminded her that she was under contract. She stood her ground and refused. So MGM put her on suspension. If she wouldn't honour her contract and work for them, MGM was going to teach her a lesson and now she wouldn't work for anybody.

By early 1955, Grace Kelly's career had run headfirst into a brick wall.

*   *   *   *

For a period of about ten years, from the end of the war until the end of 1955, Prince Rainier was considered the world's most eligible bachelor.

He was handsome. Everybody knew he owned a country and reckoned he must therefore be very rich. And the woman he chose to marry would become a princess. So he was forever being invited to dinner parties only to find that an extra lady had been seated beside him.

'We thought you two would get along so well,' his host or hostess would invariably say.

Understandably, it wasn't too long before he stopped going to dinner parties.

After having fallen out with his grandfather at the end of the war, Rainier purchased a small villa in St Jean-Cap-Ferrat, on the side of the peninsula facing Villefranche. It had been going for a good price because it was on an inside cove and, although it didn't have a large garden, he could swim in the cove off a little dock. He lived there as a bachelor. Although once he ascended the throne he tended to spend the week at the Palace and go to the villa for weekends.

The villa was all the more special because he lived there for nearly six years with his friend, Gisèle Pascal.

The two met when he was a student at Montpellier. She was an actress who'd come down from Paris to do a play there. They were the same age. They also had the Mediterranean in common, as she'd been born in Cannes. They sailed together in the summer and skied together in the winter and, as time wore on, speculation mounted that they would soon marry.

But the wedding that 'informed sources' prophesied as being just around the corner, never happened.

The press, eager to keep the story alive, decided the two couldn't marry because the Monégasques would never stand for their prince wedding an actress. Yet Prince Louis had married an actress and one day Rainier would too. Next came the story that the National Council wouldn't allow the Prince to marry Mlle Pascal because she was a commoner, the daughter of a florist. That had no bearing on anything either, as one day they would also write that Miss Kelly was the daughter of a bricklayer.

Finally the story ran that they'd been forbidden to marry because she couldn't have children. Rumour had it that the National Council badgered Rainier, fearing that unless he produced an heir the principality would revert to France.

That too was nonsense.

'There was no reason for us to get married,' Rainier says, all these years later. 'We were together six years and it was fine while it lasted but I think we both felt it was long enough. It was a love affair that had come to its own end. I don't think there was any real intention on either side to get married. As long as things were good they were fine just as they were. Then it simply ended.'

Both of them were obviously affected by the break-up. After a time Gisèle Pascal went on to marry and have a child, scotching the rumour that her inability to bear children kept her from becoming Monaco's Princess. Rainier got into his boat and took that trip down the west coast of Africa.

Naturally, as soon as he returned to Monaco he was once again a prime target for the matchmakers.

Even Aristotle Onassis tried to find a bride for him.

Convinced that only someone very special would do, Onassis looked around and decided the perfect match would be Marilyn Monroe. He plotted their engagement and leaked stories to the

press hoping to force the issue. But Rainier and Marilyn weren't
to be. They never even met.

'You must understand how shy he was in those days,' says
Khalil el Khoury, a Sydney Greenstreet look-alike whose father
had been the first president of the Lebanon. El Khoury originally
came to Monaco in the spring of 1950 and, as was the custom went
up to the Palace to sign his name in the official guest book. A few
hours later the chief of protocol rang to say that the Prince would
like him to come for tea the following afternoon.

'I went to the Palace and there we sat, Prince Rainier and I, two
very young and very shy characters, neither of us terribly relaxed
with the other. We were making small talk when the Prince asked
my age. I told him. He said, "Me too." He asked me when I was
born. I told him and it turned out we were not only the exact
same age, we were born within four or five hours of each other.
That broke down the barriers.'

Their friendship has endured ever since. But it was built
gradually and, at least in the early stages, both of them found it
easier to write letters. 'We kept up a very important correspondence. He and I both like writing letters, we still do. To this day he's
an avid letter writer. I think it must be a way of communicating
meaningfully with people while still being able to hide behind
one's own timidity. It's probably easier for him to open up that
way. I'm sure that was the case when he was young because he
really was painfully shy.'

Francis Tucker was another man who knew first-hand how shy
Rainier was.

Formerly of Wilmington, Delaware, Tucker was an Irish-
American leprechaun of a priest in his 60s, complete with a
thick brogue, who served the Prince as father confessor. He'd
witnessed, perhaps more clearly than anyone else, how the Pascal
affair and the pressure to find a bride was affecting Rainier.

So he vowed to do something about it.

'Father Tucker was definitely an enthusiast,' Rainier says.
'He never hesitated to get involved with things he believed in.
I remember he once tried to group the kids from his parish into
a marching band. He bought uniforms and instruments for everybody. But most of the kids only showed up for rehearsals once or
twice and then never came again. Well, at least he tried. When he
wanted to do something he did it. He took an efficient and lively
approach to everything. That didn't always please the Bishop but

he'd been assigned to me directly by the Vatican whereas the Bishop of Monaco is assigned by the Cardinal of France. So he knew what he could get away with.'

By the mid-1950s the conniving, witty and thoroughly loyal Father Tucker had taken it upon himself to play cupid. The only problem was that he didn't know how to stage-manage a romance. He had no experience with this sort of thing at all. So he sought divine guidance.

And his prayers were answered by MGM when they suspended Grace Kelly.

*　　*　　*　　*

Rupert Allan first met Grace Kelly in the spring of 1952 in a lift at the Savoy Hotel in London.

As *Look* magazine's west coast editor, Allan had been in the UK throughout that winter – the famous last winter of the great fogs – helping to coordinate a massive lead story on Queen Elizabeth's coronation. He'd returned to the hotel one afternoon and stepped into the lift when he literally bumped into an old friend who'd just flown in from Kenya. Allan asked, 'What are you doing here?' The friend explained he'd been MGM's publicity director on *Mogambo.* Standing next to him in the lift was an unobtrusive but pretty young blonde woman wearing dark-rimmed glasses. Allan smiled politely at her as the MGM publicist announced, 'I'd like you to meet the star of our film, Grace Kelly.'

She was wearing a beige sweater, a tweed skirt, flat shoes and a string of small pearls. She had no make up on at all and struck Allan as 'a kind of Peck and Peck girl', a well scrubbed young woman straight out of *Country Life.* He thought to himself, how in the world can this be the girl who's been creating such a stir in films like *High Noon?*

They met again a few days later at a Sunday afternoon party given by Allan's great friend, Ava Gardner.

The *Mogambo* company had switched from Africa to London to shoot interiors and Gardner had rented a house near Marble Arch. But the place didn't have any chairs so everyone ended up sitting on the floor, eating and drinking, while Gardner's secretary told a story that became the hit of the party. One evening in Nairobi, Gardner and her secretary heard there was going to be a pantomime at a private club near their hotel. With nothing else to do, the two women walked over, only to be told by the maître d' that unescorted ladies were not permitted. Flushed with anger, they returned to the hotel where Gardner proceeded to ring the club and introduce herself as Clark Gable's secretary. She said that Mr Gable wished to attend the pantomime that night with six guests. The maître d' said that Mr Gable would be most welcome. Gardner said that Mr Gable was dining with his guests and would come by as soon as dinner was finished. The maître d' said he would reserve seven front-row seats for Mr Gable and added that he needn't rush, that they would hold the curtain for him. Ava Gardner and her secretary promptly went to sleep.

Gable was furious.

But Grace thought it was hysterical.

She and Allan laughed about it all afternoon.

Allan returned to California immediately after the coronation and at one point over the next few weeks mentioned to his boss at *Look* that he'd met Grace Kelly in London. *Look* assigned him to do a story on her. A far cry from the average Hollywood reporter, Allan's natural southern charm and his gentle demeanour quickly put Grace at ease. When the article ran as a cover story, she told Allan it was the best piece yet written about her. It proved to be so popular with *Look*'s readership that Allan was asked to do a second interview with Grace. The readers loved it so they told him to do a third story with her.

A sincere and long-lasting friendship took hold.

Because Grace only came to California to work, she didn't have much free time there. But what little time she did have she often spent with Allan, a reliable escort and soon her chief confidant.

In the meantime, Allan had established himself as the Cannes Film Festival's unofficial liaison with Hollywood. Not only had he been educated in France and spoke the language, but he'd once worked in Paris for the Motion Picture Association of America where one of his jobs had been to handle the American participation at Cannes.

However, by the mid-1950s American participation at Cannes wasn't what you might call overwhelming.

At the 1953 festival the paparazzi cornered Robert Mitchum and convinced him to pose with some young starlet. Not suspecting anything, Mitchum agreed. He and the starlet walked to the beach together, followed by the photographers. She took her place in front of him and, as soon as she saw that the photographers were ready, she promptly dropped her dress. Without thinking, Mitchum tried to cover her by throwing his hands across her chest. The photos were distributed worldwide. Then it was learned that the Mayor of Cannes happened to be a member of the French Communist Party and, with the McCarthy witch-hunt days still fresh in most Hollywood minds, no one in the US film world wanted to be associated with anything that could in any way be construed as un-American.

The festival organisers, desperate for American stars, turned to Rupert Allan to get them some. He said he'd try. They said the star they wanted most for the 1955 festival was Grace Kelly.

Knowing that she'd just been suspended, Allan called her in New York to ask if she'd like to go to Cannes.

But Grace said no. She'd just moved into her new apartment at 880 Fifth Avenue, near the Metropolitan Museum, had just hired a new secretary, and told Allan she needed some time away from Hollywood to put her own life in order.

Allan told her, 'You sound like an old lady.'

Anyway, she eventually confessed, there were other, more personal reasons for not wanting to go to Cannes.

She'd been there the summer before with Oleg Cassini when she filmed *To Catch A Thief*. That romance had ended but she felt that returning to Cannes now would only serve to resurrect a lot of old memories that might be best left to fade away on their own. She told Allan, 'I'd rather not go anywhere just now.'

But he wasn't going to give up.'

He said, 'Spring in Cannes will do you some good. Anyway, I'll be there so you won't have to worry about anything. I know everybody. I'll translate for you. I'll take care of everything.'

Again she said no.

He told her, 'They'll send you a round-trip, first-class ticket. The return portion can be left open so that you can have as much time as you want to spend in Europe.'

She wasn't easily swayed, but the more he persisted the more he wore her down. Finally, probably just to be polite, she told him, 'I'll think about it.'

The next thing that happened, unbeknownst to Allan, was that Paramount rang her, suggesting it would be useful if she went to Cannes because it had just been announced that *The Country Girl* was being screened at the festival.

Grace flew to Paris where she met her friend Gladys de Segonzac who'd been costume mistress on *To Catch a Thief*. A couple of days later, on the evening of 4 May, the two of them took the ultra-posh, overnight 'Blue Train' to Cannes.

Allan met them the next morning at the station.

When Grace and de Segonzac got off the train, so did Olivia de Havilland and her then husband Pierre Galante, an editor with *Paris Match* magazine.

That night over dinner Grace told Allan how she and de Segonzac bumped into de Havilland and Galante at the Gare de Lyons. She and de Havilland had never met before but, as they were in neighbouring compartments, the four of them spent some time talking, especially after breakfast early the next morning as the train swung eastward along the Mediterranean coast. They were standing in the narrow corridor looking out of the window at the sea when Galante mentioned that *Paris Match* might like to do a cover story on her. He suggested he take her to Monaco, to photograph her there in a royal setting with the young bachelor Prince Rainier.

What Grace never knew was that the photo session was not exactly Galante's spontaneous early morning idea. Having heard that Grace would be coming to Cannes, the story idea had been discussed the week before in a *Paris Match* editorial meeting.

Anyway, contrary to most reports of the incident, she never actually said yes to Galante.

She did not say she would do the photo session.

The truth is that she wasn't terribly interested in being photographed with the Prince. She'd hardly even heard of him. And anyway, Monaco was 90 minutes away. So when Galante asked, Grace gave him a polite, non-committal answer. She said it sounded like a good idea but first she'd have to see how it fit in with her schedule.

In fact, she didn't so much as give it a second thought until later that morning in Cannes when Galante told her that the Prince had agreed to meet her at the Palace the next day, Friday, 6 April, at 4 p.m.

And right away, Grace said she couldn't make it.

She explained that she had to be at an official reception for the American delegation at Cannes. As the reception began at 5.30, a 4 o'clock appointment with the Prince was absolutely out of the question. She apologised to Galante and explained that the trip to Monaco would have to be cancelled.

A few hours later, Galante informed her that the Prince had kindly agreed to advance their meeting to 3 o'clock. He kept saying to Grace how excited he was about the photo session and promised her several times that it would make a terrific cover story.

Except Grace didn't want to go.

She told Rupert Allan about it that night over dinner.

He said, 'Do you want to do it?'

She said, 'No.'

He shook his head, as if to tell her this is your own fault.

She kept saying she didn't care about the photo session, that Monaco was too far away and that she had too many things to do in Cannes.

He reminded her of his promise to handle everything for her while she was in Cannes and rubbed a little salt into the wound by saying that he could easily have got her out of the *Paris Match* commitment if she'd told him about it when she first got off the train.

She nodded, knowing that he was right.

His point made, he said, 'All right, I'll cancel Monaco for you.'

But now she said, 'I just don't know if I can. The Prince changed his schedule to accommodate mine. I'm not sure how I can get out of this politely.'

Allan said, 'I'll try to find a way.'

'I don't. . .' Grace shook her head. 'It may be too late.'

Interestingly enough, throughout her life that would be Grace's attitude towards most things. If someone asked her to make an appearance or to do an interview, she always had trouble saying no.

Rupert shrugged and, by the time Grace went to bed that night, she'd resigned herself to the trip to Monaco.

In the middle of the night one of the French labour unions called a strike. To re-enforce their position, they turned off all of the electricity in Cannes.

The next morning Grace got up, washed her hair and plugged in her portable drier. Nothing happened. She tried another socket.

It didn't work there either. Nothing worked. None of the lights came on in her room so she phoned the front desk. They gave her the bad news.

In a mild panic, she rang Allan. 'Have you noticed there's no electricity? What am I supposed to do?' She said the *Paris Match* people were waiting with a car downstairs. Also, MGM's new publicity man from Paris had just called in a fury to say that she had no right to be in Cannes because she was still under suspension by the studio and that her appearance there could cost her a lot of money.

Allan rushed to her room.

Grace's soaking hair was wrapped in a towel. She was also struggling to find something to wear that hadn't been wrinkled in her suitcase because with no electricity there was no way she could press any of her clothes. The only thing she had that didn't need pressing was a black silk dress with large pink and green print flowers. It was a beautiful dress. But it was not a good one for pictures. She didn't want to wear it. Allan convinced her she didn't have a lot of choice. Grace put it on, then parted her wet hair in the middle and put some flowers in it, hoping it would dry in the car.

As they left the room she cried, 'This is terrible.'

'If you'd told me,' Allan kept saying, 'I never would have let you agree to this. Anyway, I should have gotten you out of it last night. This is precisely the kind of thing that will happen tomorrow and the next day and the day after that unless you have them call me first.'

She nodded several times, 'Yes, you're right,' not only because she didn't have time to discuss it with him but because she knew he was right. And she was angry at herself for having gotten into this.

Allan tried to console her. He said as long as she couldn't get out of it, he'd come along too.

They went downstairs to meet the *Paris Match* people.

Winding their way through the crowded lobby of the Carlton, past movie executives and fans and a hoard of photographers, they stepped outside to the waiting car in the middle of the driveway.

Grace stopped short.

She couldn't believe how many people were planning to come with her.

There was Galante, two *Paris Match* photographers, the MGM guy from Paris and Gladys de Segonzac.

She muttered, 'How am I supposed to get into this car with all these people?'

Allan gave her a kind of 'I hate to say I told you so' shrug and begged out of trip. As there was hardly enough room left in the car for Grace herself, he waved and mumbled, 'See you when you get back.'

In the end it turned out that there were two cars.

Grace crammed into the back seat of a Studebaker with Galante, de Segonzac and the fellow from MGM. The photographers followed on their heels in a Peugeot. But they followed so closely that, just as they reached the city limits of Cannes, the Studebaker braked sharply and the Peugeot ran into them.

The damage was minimal yet it kept them from getting to Monaco on time.

By now Grace was starving. So, before heading up to Le Rocher, they made a fast detour to the Hôtel de Paris where Galante dashed into the bar and bought her a ham sandwich.

They got to the Palace just after 3 o'clock, having already rehearsed their excuses, only to be informed that the Prince wasn't yet there.

The group stood around for a while, until one of the Palace officers volunteered to give them a conducted tour. Annoyed at being made to wait, Grace and her party went from state room to state room. Everyone kept glancing at their watches. The photographers occasionally took photos of Grace against the superbly furnished background.

At 4 o'clock a valet announced that the Prince had just arrived.

Now Grace seemed nervous.

She checked herself in a mirror and asked Galante, 'What do I call the Prince? Does he speak English? How old is he?'

Rainier walked into the room wearing a dark blue, two button suit. He went straight to Grace and offered his hand.

She gave a little curtsy, as she'd been told to do.

He apologised for being late and asked if she'd like to see the Palace.

She said they'd already done the tour.

He then offered to show her the animals in his private zoo.

They walked together through the gardens, the two of them followed by the entourage from *Paris Match* and the Palace.

He introduced her to his two young lions, a bunch of monkeys and a baby tiger.

Grace kept her distance from the cages but Rainier put his arms past the bars and rubbed the back of the tiger's neck.

Grace later admitted that she was suitably impressed.

And all the time the *Paris Match* photographers kept snapping away.

On the trip back to Cannes, Galante asked her what she'd thought of Rainier. All she'd say was, 'He is charming, charming.'

At the Carlton she told Allan how the Prince had kept her waiting, how the whole thing had taken too much time and how, if she was going to do that sort of thing, she wanted to do it right. She said she was embarrassed that her dress was terrible for photographs, that her hair was wet and how the whole thing had been wrong.

Allan asked how she'd like the Prince.

And she told him too, 'He is very charming.'

Later that week Grace wrote Rainier a thank-you note.

Then she left Cannes.

Had she not been suspended from MGM she wouldn't have been free to go to Cannes. Had she taken another train down from Paris and not bumped into Galante and Olivia de Havilland, Galante might not have been able to talk to her into the photo session. Had she listened to Allan and channelled all her press requests through him, he might have easily talked her out of going to Monaco.

Fate can be an odd bedfellow.

The *Paris Match* story ran and immediately everyone started talking about a possible romance. Most people realised it was simply hype, that such stories sold newspapers. But the idea of the fairy-tale prince and the beautiful movie star was so romantic that, even if it wasn't true, people wished it was.

In the autumn, Grace was reinstated by MGM and started work on her tenth film, *The Swan*, based on a play by Ferenc Molnar, with Alec Guinness and Louis Jourdan. They did exteriors near Ashville, North Carolina, then moved to Hollywood for the studio work.

Towards the end of the year, Allan received a call from Bill Atwood, an editor at *Look* who was doing a piece on Prince Rainier. During one of the interviews, Atwood discovered that the Prince was very pro-American, although he'd never been to the States. When Atwood wondered why, Rainier told him that, as a matter of fact, he was now planning his first trip there. He said he'd be travelling in December with a priest friend, Father Tucker, and a young French doctor friend, Robert Donat, who was, by coincidence, going anyway to do some work at Johns Hopkins University in Baltimore. Rainier said he'd like to go to Florida to fish and maybe also go to California. Atwood asked if there was anybody on the west coast he'd like to meet. Rainier answered, 'Yes. That young actress I met in Monaco. Her name is Grace Kelly. I'd like to see her again.'

As far as Rupert Allan knew, Grace had never heard from the Prince after their photo session at the Palace.

'Bill Atwood phoned me and asked if I could arrange for Grace to see Prince Rainier on the set of her film and get some photos. I said I was sure I could because as far as I knew she'd liked him. When I asked her if she'd let us take some photos with Prince Rainier on the set she said, yes of course, any time. But then she made a point of saying, "Listen Rupert, this is no romance." She said, "I'm so damned tired of hearing about a romance between him and me in all the European papers. I haven't heard a thing from him since I was in Cannes."'

The photo session was arranged but shooting on *The Swan* ran overtime. Grace was annoyed because she was due back in Philadelphia for a family Christmas party. The director finally broke for the holidays just in time for her to catch her plane.

'She was living then on the west side of Los Angeles. I went home with her to help her pack. She was one suitcases short so I ran to my place to get her an extra suitcase. There were a few splits of champagne in the fridge so we wished each other Merry Christmas and drank them. She loved champagne. That's all I ever saw her drink. I never saw her drink liquor. I never saw her touch a drop of whiskey. She also loved caviar. Anyway, I took her to the airport early the next morning and put her on a flight for New York. She arrived home in Philadelphia just in time for the party. When I mentioned Prince Rainier to her in the car on the way to the airport she told me again, "Rupert, really, there is no romance."'

Except it wasn't true.

But the only people who knew that were Rainier and Grace.

* * * *

5

The Private Story

A MONÉGASQUE was travelling in South America, crossing
from Argentina into Paraguay at a small checkpoint where,
when the border guard saw his passport, he was told, *'No esta
bueno'* – It's no good.

The Monégasque demanded to know ,'What do you mean it's
no good?' He insisted, 'There's nothing wrong with my passport.'

The border guard made signs to suggest that he'd never heard
of anywhere called *La Principauté de Monaco.*

The Monégasque tried to explain where it was.

The border guard didn't seem to care. *'No esta bueno!'* He
simply wasn't going to let anyone through with such a passport.

The Monégasque did everything he could think of to convince
the border guard that such a place existed. 'Monaco. You know,
Monaco.' He said it louder each time. 'MON–A–CO!'

Then, suddenly, as if a light deep inside his head had flicked
on, the border guard's face lit up. 'Ah, yes, Monaco. Grace Kelly.'

* * * *

The official version of their love story has always gone like this:

Rainier and Grace met during the 1955 Cannes Film Festival.
They spent one afternoon together, enjoyed each other's company
– both of them used the word 'charming' to describe the other –
and didn't meet again until Christmas.

Between Cannes and Christmas, Father Tucker did his best to make a match.

He appreciated the fact that Grace Kelly was beautiful and he didn't mind that she was a movie star. Nor did it hurt that she was a fellow American. Best of all he liked the idea that she was a good Catholic girl with a good reputation.

Because Father Tucker had once served in Philadelphia, some people – Rupert Allan among them – remain convinced to this day that he used his connections there to check out Grace. It would have been very simple for him to ring the Archdiocese and ask the Cardinal's office to tell him about the Kellys. And some people – Rupert Allan among them – are equally convinced that, within a few days of the photo session at the Palace, Father Tucker had gleaned more about Grace and the Kellys from his priestly intelligence network than even Grace and the Kellys might have known.

Although he wasn't present that Friday afternoon when Rainier and Grace met, Father Tucker took it upon himself to write Grace a note saying, 'I want to thank you for showing the Prince what an American Catholic girl can be and for the very deep impression this has left on him.'

Rainier recalls the event with a large smile.

'I spoke to Father Tucker about Grace. He knew she was coming to visit that afternoon and after she left he asked how we got along. It's only natural that we would have discussed it because he and I always talked about lots of things. And yes, of course, I was impressed with her when I met her. Who wouldn't have been?'

A few months later, old friends of the Kellys arrived in the south of France. Russell and Edith Austin were 'uncle and aunt' to Grace when she was growing up. He was a dentist from Philadelphia who had a summer house near the Kellys' place in Ocean City.

The Austins were staying in Cannes, heard about the Red Cross Ball in Monaco – the social event of the Riviera season – and inquired about tickets.

When their hotel concierge reported that the evening had long since been sold out, that it was impossible to get tickets, they showed some typical American moxie. They phoned Prince Rainier's office, explained that Grace was their niece and wondered if, all things considered, they could somehow impose on

Grace's friendship with the Prince to buy a pair of tickets to the ball. The message wound up on Father Tucker's desk.

He couldn't believe his luck.

He personally delivered the tickets to the Austins with the Prince's compliments, then manoeuvered the conversation around to the Kellys and in particular to Grace. In his laughing, friendly way, he got the Austins to tell him everything they knew about Grace.

When he returned to the Palace he just happened to mention the subject to Rainier.

Later that week, at Father Tucker's suggestion, the Austins were invited to tea with the Prince. Once again Father Tucker steered the topic of conversation to Grace.

At the end of the afternoon, the Austins suggested, as Americans are wont to do, that if the Prince should ever find himself in the States he might enjoy coming to Ocean City where they would be pleased to repay his hospitality.

Rainier politely agreed to consider it.

Thanks to Father Tucker, the Austins returned to Philadelphia not merely thinking that the Prince was interested in Grace but with the clear impression that a love match might be on. And, while it's not only possible but also highly probable that they – like everyone else involved in this tale of old-fashioned match-making – have exaggerated their own role just a bit, at least Father Tucker had planted the idea in their minds.

The next thing anyone knew, Prince Rainier announced that he would go to America in December 1955.

As soon as Father Tucker got wind of this, he contacted the Austins and they persuaded the Kellys to invite the Prince to their home for dinner on Christmas day.

Late in the afternoon on 25 December, the Austins arrived at 3901 Henry Avenue with the Prince Rainier, Father Tucker and Dr Donat where, for the first time since the film festival, Rainier saw Grace.

They spent Christmas afternoon and early evening talking.

The Kellys liked Rainier from the moment they met him. Although, at least in the beginning, not everybody knew who he was or what to call him. Ma Kelly thought he was the Prince of Morocco. Grace had to explain to her mother that wasn't quite right. Jack Kelly then pulled Father Tucker aside to ask what the proper form of address was. 'Do I call him Your Majesty?'

'No,' Father Tucker said, 'he's referred to as Your Highness.'

So Jack Kelly played along and called the Prince, 'Your Highness,' even though he later explained to Rainier, 'Royalty doesn't mean anything to us.'

After dinner, Kelly drove Father Tucker to the station to catch his train back to Wilmington while Rainier and Grace, with Dr Donat in tow, went to Grace's sister's house to dance and laugh and talk until 3a.m.

Rainier and Donat spent the night in the Kelly's guest room which meant Rainier and Grace had the chance to spend part of the next day together as well.

Supposedly unbeknownst to anyone, while being driven to the station on Christmas night, Father Tucker confided in Kelly that the Prince was considering asking Grace to marry him. If Jack was surprised, he hid it well. He told the priest that he suspected something like this might be on the cards and gave Father Tucker permission to tell the Prince that as long as Grace was willing, he'd have the Kellys' blessing. Rainier waited a few days before proposing, Grace accepted and the engagement of the decade was announced to the world.

For most people, including Rupert Allan, news of the engagement came totally out of the blue.

'I was driving back to Los Angeles from a photo session for *Look* magazine at Squaw Valley when I heard on the radio that Prince Rainier of Monaco had just announced his engagement to Grace Kelly. I couldn't believe it. I kept saying, that can't be. I kept saying, they don't even know each other.'

Except they did.

The official version of their love story – that Rainier and Grace had no contact whatsoever between their first meeting in the spring of 1955 and his trip to Philadelphia that December – is not the way it really happened.

The true story of how they fell in love has never been told, until now.

This is how it happened:

Their first meeting was less than private, but the Prince says that once they got past the formalities of shaking hands and posing for pictures, once they started to walk together in the garden with the entourage far enough behind them that they could relax a bit and talk, they started to realise they had some things in common.

They'd both been lonely children.

She'd come from a family where success was based on sporting achievements, except she wasn't very interested in sports. He came from a broken home where his future responsibilities were impressed on him at an early age, where he was often reminded that he wasn't the same as other little boys and couldn't behave the same way they did.

They were both shy.

She was just learning what it was like to be a public figure, to be deprived of her privacy by the press. He'd suffered that all his life and could sympathise with her.

She didn't necessarily care for the sea in the same the way he did but she shared his love of animals and felt comfortable with him as he led her around his private zoo. She also couldn't get over the way he put his arms through the bars of the tiger's cage and played with the cat as if it was nothing more than a house pet.

She appreciated the old world charm and sophistication of European men. He liked the freshness and spontaneity of American women.

And they were both Catholic with a fundamental belief in their faith.

These days, Rainier doesn't recall exactly what he expected when he was told that Grace Kelly was coming to visit. He knew who she was but the idea of posing for publicity photos with a movie star didn't particularly excite him. When she confessed to him that she hadn't wanted to do the photo session either, they had that in common as well.

He found her gentle, naturally elegant and was captivated by her aura of purity.

She found him totally engaging, not in the least stuffy or pretentious, the way she'd expected.

He liked the way she laughed.

She discovered he was a sensitive man who, when he relaxed, had a good sense of humour. And she loved to laugh.

She wrote to him from Cannes to say thank you.

And he answered her, saying how glad he was that they'd met.

She answered his letter, saying that she too was pleased to have met him.

He wrote to her again.

And she wrote back to him.

A regular correspondence began.

Gradually, they got to know each other as pen pals.

It was easy that way. It was comfortable. They could hide behind their own letters. They could give each other time.

Slowly at first, step by step, carefully, like peeling petals from a rose, they revealed more with each letter. They wrote about the world and they wrote about life. They wrote about themselves, explained a feeling, wondered if it was shared, and confessed a secret.

By the end of that summer Rainier knew he'd found someone very special.

He'd often said how difficult it was for him to get to know a woman. The frequently quoted remark from his bachelor days was, 'My greatest difficulty is knowing a girl long enough and intimately enough to find out if we are really soul mates as well as lovers.'

Like any wealthy, handsome young man, it was easy for him to find a lover. All too often that came first and there was no time left, once word leaked out, to discover if she might be a soul mate.

This time, maybe even for the first time, he was doing it the other way around.

Long before they ever held hands, they both knew they were friends.

These days he can't recall how many letters there were.

He's not even sure they still exist.

At least, he says, he doesn't have the ones she sent to him. 'No, I didn't save them. Maybe I should have but that's not the way I am. I don't keep things like that.'

And the ones he sent to her?

He shakes his head, 'I don't know. Maybe she kept them. I suppose women do save letters. But if she did keep them I don't know where they are.'

Would you look for them, he's asked?

He takes a deep breath and after a moment's pause he says, 'No one has ever seen them. Not even my children.'

Now there's a longer silence.

'Those letters. . .' His voice gets very quiet. . . 'To be honest, I wouldn't want anyone to see them. Even if I could find them. . .' He shakes his head again. 'I know what you're thinking but even

if I could find them. . . please understand. . . I simply couldn't let
anyone trespass on that. After having lived such a public life. . .'

He stops and looks away and in an even quieter voice he says,
'Those letters may be the last secret treasure garden I have left.'

*   *   *   *

The *Paris Match* photos created such interest in the possibility of
a romance between Rainier and Grace that, on 11 October 1955,
Rainier went on Radio Monte Carlo to tell the people of Monaco
that any rumours they might hear of his impending marriage were
just that, rumours.

'The question of my marriage,' he said, 'which rightly preoccu-
pies you, interests me, believe me, just as much, and more.' He
went on to explain how certain sections of the press had been
making all sorts of speculations that were simply not true. 'My
private life has not been spared. Just give me another three years
and then we shall see.'

But before the month was out he'd decided to ask Grace Kelly
to be his wife.

'I knew what I wanted to do,' Rainier says. Then he confesses,
'But I couldn't just assume she'd marry me. I had to ask her. So I
went to the States to see her. But I couldn't ask her to marry me
if I wasn't absolutely sure she'd accept. I couldn't ask her to marry
me if there was any chance she'd say no.'

By that time they'd already secretly arranged to meet at
Christmas.

Rainier sailed for the United States on 8 December, arriving
in New York one week later. Father Tucker and Dr Donat came
along, each for their own reasons. Father Tucker was going to visit
his family in Delaware and Donat had business at Johns Hopkins
University in Baltimore. Ostensibly, the reason for Rainier's visit
was to go with Donat to Johns Hopkins for a check-up at the
university hospital. There was also talk of visiting 'friends' on
the east coast and some fishing in Florida.

While Father Tucker was let in on the secret before they sailed,
the only other people wise to Rainier's marriage plans – besides
Grace who, by this time, had good reason to believe from their
correspondence that Rainier's intentions were serious – were his

closest advisers at home. After all, the possible marriage of the Prince of Monaco was an affair of state.

According to the Franco-Monégasque treaty of 1918, the engagement announcement of anyone in line for the Monégasque throne must be preceded by a formal request for permission from the French government. Of course, French government consent is nothing more than a rubber stamp. But in 1920, when Princess Charlotte announced her engagement to Count Pierre de Polignac without first seeking such permission – even though her grandfather was sovereign Prince, her father was hereditary Prince and she was but number three in the line – a strong letter was promptly sent from the French Foreign Minister to the Minister of State that rules of protocol had to be observed.

Some time in early November, Rainier discussed his plans with the Minister of State who then spoke to the French Consul General in Monaco. On 30 November 1955, eight days before Rainier sailed from Le Havre, the French Consul General wrote to the Minister of State, 'On the eve of SAS Prince Rainier's departure for the United States where he intends to propose marriage to *une Americaine*' – the fiancée to be is not named – 'my government suggests that this is perhaps a good opportunity to bring your attention to the (1920) precedent.'

The Minister of State passed that letter on to the Prince.

Grace's name does not appear on any official correspondence at this point because Rainier had not yet revealed it to his Minister of State.

He believed no one should know her identity for a couple of reasons. It would be extremely embarrassing to both Grace and himself if word leaked out before he had the opportunity to propose. And, if she accepted, protocol again dictated that a formal announcement would have to be made in Monaco before, or at least the very same time that it was made in the US.

Right up to the point where he arrived at her front door on Christmas day, only Father Tucker knew who he had in mind.

As the week after Christmas wore on, as Rainier and Grace were seen together in Philadelphia and on 27 December in New York, the press began adding one and one and coming up with two.

The official version of the story is that he proposed to her on New Years Eve.

The truth is that he did it a few days after Christmas.

He asked her quite simply, 'Will you marry me?'

And she answered quite simply, 'Yes.'

But they couldn't tell anybody yet because this was not just an ordinary marriage, this was a Prince and head of state asking her to become his Princess. Before the world could be told there were all sorts of hurdles to cross.

First, there was her father.

A man known for usually speaking his mind, Jack Kelly pulled Rainier aside and said he hoped the Prince's intentions were serious.

Rainier answered, 'I want to marry her,' without explaining that Grace had already said yes.

Kelly gave the Prince his permission right away. But then he cautioned Rainier, 'I hope you won't run around the way some princes do because if you do you'll lose a mighty fine girl. Don't forget, she's got Irish blood in her veins and she knows what she wants.'

Next came Ma Kelly, who intended that Rainier and Grace should be married in Philadelphia. 'That's how it is in America,' she argued. 'The girl's parents arrange the wedding and Grace always promised me she wanted that.'

Rainier had to explain that this would not be just an ordinary wedding, that Grace would become the Princess of Monaco and in that regard she now had responsibilities to the Monégasques.

It took some time but Ma Kelly eventually gave in.

Then there were the negotiations for the marriage contract.

A multipaged legal document drawn up over the next few weeks by lawyers in Monaco acting for the Prince and attorneys in New York acting for Grace, it specifically outlined the rules which would govern the material side of their marriage.

In France and in Monaco, contractual agreements to establish rights to property, as defined by the Napoleonic Codes, are a traditional part of any marriage. There are three basic types: communal property, a specific division of property and a total separation of property. Most people marry under the first clause. In fact, in France, unless you specifically ask for the second or third clause, you automatically get a communal property agreement. The second arrangement is one wherein all the material things each party brings to the marriage remain their own but everything acquired after the marriage is shared. The third is simply an agreement that everything brought to the marriage plus everything acquired during the marriage will belong to one partner or the other.

It was this third clause, known in French as *Separation des biens*, under which Rainier and Grace were wed.

'It was the right thing for both of us,' Rainier explains. 'But it was absolutely a normal standard marriage contract and there was nothing out of the ordinary about it.'

If not out of the ordinary for a certain class of European – most of France's wealthiest people are married under this clause – it must have seemed quite odd to the Kellys of Philadelphia, especially because the contract stipulated that Grace would have certain responsibilities towards household costs. In other words, she would have to pay some of their bills. But again, that's a normal practice in France under such a contract.

Finally, there was the matter of a dowry.

According to the contract, it would be paid by the Kellys to the Prince for his taking Grace as his wife.

Dowries are also the norm among older European families, not just French or Monégasque, although they were hardly an everyday occurence in East Falls in 1956.

Recently, a book intending to do nothing more than sensationalise Rainier and Grace's life together made the claim that he forced an otherwise reluctant Jack Kelly to pay $2 million for the right to see Grace married to the Prince of Monaco.

That is not true.

Having seen the marriage contract, which is in Prince Rainier's private files, I can state categorically that, while certain financial arrangements were made, a $2 million dowry was not involved.

The author of that particular book acknowledged assistance from various people who now say they've either never spoken to him or that when he contacted them they refused to cooperate. Some of the most startling quotes in that book are attributed to dead people. And, if that isn't enough to cast some serious doubt on the accuracy of the author's reporting, there are also gross errors of fact.

Among them is the statement that the only reason Dr Donat went to the States with Rainier was to personally administer a fertility test to Grace before a marriage could be planned. After all, the argument went, if she could not bear children he could not marry her.

Rainier shrugs that off as utter nonsense.

'It was very much the fad in the mid-1950s for Europeans to have a thorough medical check-up in the United States. Lots of people I knew were going to places like the Mayo Clinic. My friend Robert Donat, who was a surgeon in Nice and had taken out my appendix, suggested that as long as I was going to the States anyway, why didn't I take a few days and get a check-up. He wanted me to go to Johns Hopkins. I decided, why not, as I'd never had a general health check-up before. So I went with him to Baltimore. I spent three very boring days sitting in the hospital there getting poked and prodded.'

Just as quickly, he dismisses any discussion of Grace's fertility test.

To begin with, there is no such things as a simple fertility test for women. According to a noted gynecologist, you never know for sure if the equipment works until you give it a try. A doctor can check to see that a woman ovulates and can take X-rays to see that her Fallopian tubes are clear, that there are no obstructions to fertilisation. But that's about it. So any scene that describes Grace with her ankles in the stirrups while two doctors poke and probe to make certain that she can bear the heir to Rainier's throne is not only tacky but also pure invention.

All the more so because no physical examination of any kind was required of her.

In the case of someone like Princess Diana, a physical was demanded by the crown before she could marry the heir to the British throne. A gynecologist certainly checked to see that everything was in order. Equally important, doctors also traced her family medical history to make sure that there were no genetic diseases, such as epilepsy or haemophilia, which might be passed on.

Yet, where Grace was concerned, Rainier insists, 'She didn't go through any special medical tests whatsoever. As far as I know she didn't even have a simple check-up before we got married. And there definitely was no fertility test. Had she not been able to bear children there was another option available to us. We could have adopted a child. The law is quite clear. According to the treaty with France, should there be no natural heir to the throne, the ruling sovereign may adopt a child to perpetuate the reign.'

On Tuesday night, 3 January 1956, Rainier and Grace went to the Stork Club in New York with some friends. Jack O'Brien, the theatre critic for the *Journal-American* newspaper, spotted them across the room and sent a note to their table with the waiter. It read, 'Dear Grace, I understand you're planning to announce your engagement on Thursday or Friday. Answer here please.' At the bottom he drew two boxes, one marked for each day.

After showing it to Rainier, Grace went to O'Brien's table. She told him, 'I can't answer your question tonight.'

He asked, 'When can you answer it?'

After a short pause she said, 'Friday.'

The official announcement was made on Thursday, 5 January, first in Monaco and then a few minutes later at a luncheon Jack Kelly hosted for Philadelphia dignitaries at a local country club.

On Friday morning, exactly as she'd promised O'Brien, it was front-page news.

'I've been in love before,' Grace told the press, 'but never in love like this.' Later she would confess in an interview, 'By getting married I was stepping straight into a new, unknown world and that was, I have to say, a little frightening. But I was ready for making a change in my life. And so was the Prince. I think we were lucky enough to meet at the right moment. I've always thought that a man who marries a famous woman, a woman more famous than him, can lose his own identity. I didn't want a future Mr Kelly, if you see what I mean. I didn't want to take a husband. I wanted to become someone's wife.'

So the fairy-tale Prince was going to wed the beautiful movie star.

'It absolutely was a fairy-tale romance, 'interjects Prince Louis de Polignac, Rainier's cousin and for many years Chairman of SBM. 'Everything about it was so lovely. But there's something you must understand about him. Ever since the first day he ascended to his throne, Prince Rainier always had in his mind and in his spirit the development and the love of his country. He didn't marry Princess Grace because she was right for the country. He married her because he loved her. Though I can tell you categorically that he wouldn't have married her if she had been wrong for Monaco.'

The magic of their engagement captured the public's imagination to such an extent that even today theirs is still considered one of the greatest love stories of the 20th century.

'We were both old enough to know what we wanted,' Rainier says. 'And once we saw each other again in Philadelphia I think we both realised that what we wanted to do was make our lives

together. Neither of us were children. We both understood what
marriage meant. Both of us had gone through difficult times but
both us had learned from those difficult times that what we were
each looking for was marriage. We discussed it and we thought
about it and we decided to go ahead with it. We fell in love. A
lot of people couldn't believe that. A lot of people never thought
it would last. I guess we fooled them.'

They also fooled the supposed 'Curse of the Grimaldis'.

Around the end of the 13th century, Prince Rainier I gained the
reputation among the Grimaldi clan as a great sailor and lover. He
was awarded the title, Admiral General of France for his naval
exploits. But in his amorous conquests he fared less well. After
one of his battles he's said to have kidnapped a beautiful Flemish
woman whom he took as his lover and then betrayed. Shortly
thereafter she turned herself – or was turned by someone else –
into a witch. To repay her unhappiness, she cursed him and all
those who followed with the prophesy, 'Never will a Grimaldi
find true happiness in marriage.'

Whether you believe in witches or not, it's possible that
Charles III wasn't happy in his marriage. Or that Albert I wasn't
happy in either of his. Perhaps Louis II and Charlotte were equally
unhappy in wedlock. But when you mention the 'curse' to Rainier
he grins and says, without any hesitation, 'Yes we beat the curse
too.'

*   *   *   *

The morning after his engagement to Grace was announced,
Rainier got up early and came down for breakfast, only to find
Jack Kelly already there.

His future father-in-law jumped up to give Rainier a hearty slap
on the back. 'Sleep well, sonny?'

Rainier understood what Kelly was telling him, so he smiled,
'Very well, dad.'

And their friendship was secured.

Not long afterwards Rainier returned to a joyous Monaco to
prepare for the wedding while Grace headed west to Hollywood
to make her last motion picture, the Cole Porter musical version
of *The Philadelphia Story*, called *High Society*. But within a few

months Rainier returned to the States, renting a small villa in Hollywood so that he could be with Grace.

The diamond engagement ring she wears in the film is the 'friendship' ring Rainier gave her when he asked her to be his Princess.

*   *   *   *

Over the next few months the press never let up.

They followed him wherever he went, peeked over his shoulder as he planned every stage of their wedding.

And they followed her wherever she went, as she bought what must have been the most written-about trousseau of the century.

She started at Neiman Marcus in Dallas, the Texas oil million-aires' favourite store. They made suits for her, several gowns, an assortment of street clothes, an entire wardrobe of sports clothes and even a yachting outfit, although she ordered it without the traditional pair of sailor's shorts.

The bridesmaids' dresses, in yellow silk organdie over taffeta, were also made at Neiman Marcus.

Lingerie came from Los Angeles, where one press report vividly described her purchase as, 'wispy thin silk, lace edged nightgowns, negligée and foundation garments in pink, peach or black.'

Other under-garments, including nylon stockings, came from New York. So did her every day dresses, purchased from an unnamed Manhattan wholesaler.

Her shoes were brought at Delman's on Fifth Avenue. 'Not too high in the heel', the papers said. While her hats – a travel turban of white silk jersey, a delicate yellow straw toque plus a white tulle creation cut in baby tucks for the crown and veiling for the brim – were made by Mr John, a well-known New York designer.

But the best frock of all came straight from MGM.

As a gift, the studio not only gave her all the clothes she wore in *High Society*, they also asked their Academy Award winning chief costume designer, Helen Rose, to create her wedding dress.

Six weeks of work by three dozen seamstresses went into the ivory, Renaissance style regal gown made up of 25 yards of heavy taffeta, 25 yards of silk taffeta, 100 yards of silk net and 300 yards of Valenciennes lace for the petticoats.

The train was three and a half yards long.

The long-sleeved, rose, point-lace bodice was re-embroidered to hide the seams. The gown fastened down the front with tiny lace buttons and fit over a silk soufflé, flesh-tone under-bodice. The overskirt was bell-shaped without any folds in front. The fullness at the back was laid in pleats at the waist, flaring into a fan shape at the bottom. The underskirt was actually three petticoats in crepe and taffeta.

The bride's veil, embroidered with rose point-lace and sewn with several thousand tiny pearls, was specifically designed to keep her face on view. It was paired with a juliet cap of matching lace with a wreath of small orange blossoms and leaves fashioned from seed pearls. Appliquéed onto the rear of the veil were two miniature lace love birds.

Grace also carried with her a prayer book covered in taffeta to match her gown, with the cross on the prayer book embroidered in pearls.

As for Rainier, he decided to wear a uniform which he designed himself, based on the uniform of Napoleon's marshals. The trousers were sky blue with a gold stripe down the sides. The jacket was black with gold oak leaves on the lapels and gold braid over his right shoulder.

*   *   *   *

On the night of 3 April 1956, Grace Kelly dined with her parents at the Ambassador Hotel in New York.

She had to go out for dinner because she was moving to Monaco the next day and, even though there was still last-minute packing to do, her Fifth Avenue fridge was empty. She couldn't even make a cup of coffee for herself early the next morning before she left for Pier 84 on West 44th Street.

There was a light drizzle that morning.

Still, a good-sized crowd of well-wishers were waiting at the pier when she arrived in a limousine.

The press also came out in force.

She'd previously agreed to meet them for 20 minutes inside the ship's Pool Cafe. The idea was that reporters would be allotted some time with her, then a session with photographers would take place. Just before the ship sailed she would appear on deck for television and newsreel cameras. But because of the weather all the three groups jammed into the room at the same time.

Nearly 250 people fought for space in a bar that was meant to hold 50.

'This is frightening,' she gasped as microphones were shoved into her face and flashbulbs went off, non-stop. 'I'm flattered at all this attention but I wish all of you would be more considerate of one another.'

Questions were hurled at her from all sides of the room, rapid-fire, one right after another.

Q: 'Miss Kelly, Miss Kelly, will you now give up your career?'

A: 'I feel I am starting a new one.'

Q: 'Miss Kelly, does that mean you won't make any more movies?'

A: 'Right now I'm too interested in my marriage career to think about the movies.'

Q: 'Miss Kelly, will you love, honour and obey?'

A: 'Whatever His Highness wishes is fine with me.'

Q: 'Miss Kelly, what will it be like to be a princess?'

A: 'I intend to take each day just as it comes.'

Q: 'Miss Kelly, Miss Kelly, please, will you wear something old, something new, something borrowed and something blue?'

A: 'Yes, I hope so. But I haven't figured out exactly what, yet.'

Q: 'Miss Kelly, has the Prince called to wish you a *bon voyage*?'

A: 'We haven't talked by telephone but we we hear from each other every day by letter.'

At precisely 11 a.m., with a blast of the ship's horn and the tug boat's sirens, with a ton of yellow confetti and a thousand coloured streamers thrown from the upper decks, and with the sound of a band playing dixieland jazz on the promenade deck, the SS *Constitution* slipped out of her berth into the Hudson River, swung downstream and sailed for Monaco.

Grace had booked the bridal suite. A combination living-room and bedroom with a veranda on the high sun deck, it was the ship's most luxurious cabin. A party of 70 friends and relatives were sailing with her. So was her French poodle, Oliver. The only thing she inadvertently left behind was the key to one of her large steamer trunks. The ship's carpenter had to chisel off the hinges.

However, almost as soon as the *Constitution* left New York, with the Statue of Liberty in her wake, Grace discovered she had a lot more ship-mates than she'd originally bargained for.

It was when the captain called a lifeboat drill.

An announcement came over the public address system instructing everyone on board to don a lifejacket and proceed immediately to the designated station nearest their cabin. Each lifeboat on the *Constitution* was intended to accommodate 150 people. But this was the cruise taking Grace Kelly to Monaco to marry Prince Rainier and there wasn't a single person on board who didn't want to meet her.

When she got to her lifeboat she found nearly 300 people also claiming it as their own.

A whole slew of reporters sailed with her, although they were in tourist class and rules forbid tourist-class passengers to enter first-class territory. Still, they wired daily reports back to their papers. She even broadcast a short speech by ship's radio to the people of Monaco, in French, saying how much she was looking forward to meeting them, promising that she would try her best to be a worthy princess.

Meanwhile, in Monaco, the Prince was frantically busy with all of the last-minute preparations. He didn't have much time for the press so the reporters gathering there had to find something else to write about.

It didn't take them long to discover the best interview in town was the leprechaun priest from Delaware.

'She knows that she's making history,' Father Tucker told reporters, 'and that she has a tremendous duty to these people here. She will not, I am sure, interfere politically, not more than any American girl would whose husband were a Republican and she a Democrat.'

When asked how the Prince was taking the wait for his fiancée, Father Tucker assured them, 'He's as nervous as any bridegroom. He's pretending to be calm but underneath he's just like a jubilant boy.'

And when they questioned him about his own role in arranging this, the self-proclaimed matchmaker insisted, 'Grace was really the Prince's choice. I was just a kind of consultant.'

Eight days after she left New York, the *Constitution* slipped into the Bay of Hercules off the coast of Monaco.

Rainier, aboard his yacht *Deo Juvante II*, pulled out of the port to fetch his future bride.

The sky was dull and overcast and the seas were slightly choppy. The Prince's yacht came up alongside the ocean liner and, surrounded by a flotilla of small boats with photographers and camera-men at the ready, he waited for Grace to appear.

His heart was pounding.

Hers was too.

And then, suddenly, she was there.

She came down the gangplank.

He helped her step onto his boat.

Sirens and ships' horns blasted their welcome.

More than 20,000 people lined the streets surrounding the port, waving flags and cheering and applauding as the *Deo Juvante II* brought her ashore.

Now there were more horns and more sirens.

And now cannons boomed and planes flew overhead and parachutes appeared and flares went up.

It was her greatest entrance.

Only one thing marred it. She'd worn the wrong hat. It was too big and the brim hid her face.

The entire population of Monaco had come out to see her.

But all most of them saw was the brim of her hat.

What they missed was the joy and wonderment and excitement and tears of happiness in the then most famous blue eyes in the world.

*　*　*　*

Their wedding was a complicated affair.

Because it so captured the imagination of the world, over 1,600 reporters and photographers showed up – nearly three times the number of journalists, photographers and broadcast crew members who reported on the marriage of Prince Charles and Lady Diana. As if that's not statistic enough, consider the fact that there weren't 1,600 reporters and photographers at any one time covering the entire European Theatre during all of World War II.

The problem was that no one in Monaco had the experience to deal with so much press.

The principality had never known anything so grand.

There were lunches and dinners and parades and appearances and great galas where everyone danced on into the night.

There were eight days of festivities that both Rainier and Grace agreed were not quite the way they would have wanted it had they been given a choice.

Today Rainier manages to chuckle when he recalls what he and his bride had to go through. 'But it wasn't fun then and in the middle of the turmoil Grace kept saying, maybe we should run off to a small chapel somewhere in the mountains and finish getting married there. I wish we had because there was no way either she or I could really enjoy what was happening.'

It was, he feels, simply too big an event for its time.

'There's no doubt about that. It was very over- publicised. The press showed up en masse and because so many of the events were private, they had nothing much to do. One day we went to have lunch at my sister's villa at Eze. Afterwards we were driving back to Monaco and one of the photographers who'd followed us lay down across the road. He actually lay down, flat on his back. I wasn't driving quickly and saw him from far away so when I got close I stopped. That was my mistake. All his friends started shooting pictures. The next morning in the papers it looked as if I'd knocked him down. They'd have done anything for a photo.'

Caroline adds, 'Mother once told me that those eight days were so awful, that she and my father felt so uncomfortable, they couldn't look at the home movies of the event for more than a year afterwards.'

The guest list had to be compiled with several thoughts in mind. Of course they both wanted their friends and family to be present. But then there were other European royals to be invited and political protocol to be considered.

Queen Elizabeth was invited, but declined.

Distantly related – the Queen and Rainier are, to be precise, 15th cousins – their common line is traced through Monaco's Prince Albert, who married Scotland's Lady Mary Victoria Douglas Hamilton, who in turn was related to Henry VII, the first Tudor king, and Elizabeth of York. In fact, most of the ruling houses of Europe are related through that same line. It ties Rainier to the Swedish, Norwegian, Danish, Belgian, Dutch, Luxumbourger and Greek royals, to the Queen Mother and also to Winston Churchill.

Anyway, while most of the other royals accepted, the Queen declined. Whatever her personal reasons were, the public reason was a matter of protocol. As she'd never met Rainier or Grace, neither she nor any member of her family could attend the ceremony. She did, however, send the couple a gold serving tray.

Cary Grant gave them an antique writing desk. SBM gave her a diamond and ruby necklace. And the people of Monaco gave them a Rolls-Royce. Friends in Philadephia gave her a Cinemascope screen and two 35mm projectors to create a movie room in the Palace so that she wouldn't miss American films. The local American community presented the couple with a solid gold picture frame, the local German community offered them a fine porcelain table-service and the French government presented them with a matching pair of decorated helmsman wheels for their honeymoon yacht.

When she finished making *High Society* the cast and crew sent her home with a loaded roulette wheel.

A wedding list was not posted so there were duplicates. Though they only received one lion for the Prince's zoo, there was plenty of gold, silver, glass, paintings, antique picture frames and a lot of jewellery.

Just as welcome, and perhaps in some ways the most touching of all, were the gifts that flowed in from people who didn't know either Rainier or Grace but simply wanted to send a little something, people who somehow wanted to feel a part of this wedding. There were dozens of objects people made themselves, whole cheeses and cured hams. There were cookbooks, pot-holders, shamrocks, wall-plaques, knitted goods and all sorts of knickknacks – ash trays, ceramic animals and plaster-of-Paris angels – many of which are still today scattered around Palace shelves.

Each gift was logged by Grace in a white satin volume.

By the time all the gifts were accounted for she'd filled a dozen of those bride's books.

The press, somewhat indelicately, estimated the value of all the gifts at well over $1 million.

If putting a price tag on the gifts wasn't embarrassing enough, the story of the National Council's gift certainly was.

A few weeks before the wedding the Council sent one of their elders to a jewellers in Paris where he selected a necklace worth 39

million francs – then about $72,000 or £30,000. He advanced the
jeweller 12 million francs and brought the gift back to Monaco. As
far as he was concerned it was wonderful.

Unfortunately, it was awful.

A heavy, multi-jewelled, absolutely grotesque object, there
was no way that anyone with taste could imagine this might be
suitable for a modern, 26-year-old woman. When the Prince saw
it he supposedly found it so hideous that he doubted it would even
be worthy of the Dowager Empress of China.

Adding insult to injury, it then came out that the National
Council's representative had lined his own pocket with a five
million franc commission from the jeweller.

To cover themselves, the Council immediately rushed over
to the local Cartier's and bought Grace an even more expensive
parure – a matching necklace, bracelet, ring and earrings set. They
then tried to return the original necklace to the Parisian jeweller.
But he said no, refused to refund their money and demanded that
they pay the remaining 27 million francs. The Council said it
was out of the question and threatened the jeweller with a court
action. Immune to their threats, the jeweller would not take the
monstrous necklace back – it was really so terrible, who could
blame him? – and even instructed his attorneys to try and block
the Prince's assets in Monaco and the United States in order to
force payment. That failed. The Council, in fact, did take the
jeweller to court and won. But they lost in the press as the papers
turned the affair into a front-page scandal.

At the time, Rainier described the business as, 'sordid'.

Today his opinion has hardly changed.

'It was very embarrassing. But it was entirely out of our reach.
The National Council chose the jeweller, they settled on the price
with him and that was their gift to Grace for the wedding. We
couldn't interfere at all. Grace wasn't asked nor did she ever
volunteer to them, or to anyone else, that she might have preferred pearls to diamonds or emeralds to rubies.'

Unlike all other marriages in Monaco, no banns were posted
for Rainier's and Grace's, presumably so that no one could object
to it.

Not that anyone would have objected. But as their wedding day
approached, signs of nervousness and tension began to get the best
of everybody.

Rainier grew especially short-tempered with the photographers and cancelled a photo session that was supposed to re-enact the couple's signing of the marriage register.

During the rehearsal, Grace looked strained and Rainier bit his fingernails.

The civil ceremony took place on 18 April.

Held in the Palace throne room, it was for immediate family and a few very close friends only, although the television cameras were there so that all of Europe could watch too. Grace wore a pale pink gown and carried a bridal bouquet. Rainier wore a black morning suit with grey striped trousers. Both were obviously suffering from stage-fright and neither of them smiled. The room was hot, filled with powerful lights for the television cameras and also for MGM's cameras who had the exclusive film rights to the ceremony. The bride and groom sat a few feet apart on a pair of red velvet chairs, Grace with her gloved hands in her lap, Rainier nervously fingering his moustache. As a member of the sovereign family may only marry with permission of the ruling Prince, the ceremony began with the senior judge who conducted the ceremony, totally in French, first asking Rainier's permission to hold the marriage. He said, 'Oui.' And 40 minutes later Rainier and Grace were legally man and wife.

In most cases, couples only have to suffer such an ordeal once.

But this wasn't most cases.

Rainier and Grace had to do the whole thing a second time, re-staging it for the sake of MGM.

Later Father Tucker told reporters, 'They wouldn't go through this again for the world.'

But the toughest part was still to come.

The next morning, the religious ceremony was viewed by 30 million people in nine European countries and a full house in Monaco's Cathedral.

It was a very crowded, strictly white tie, event.

Rupert Allan found himself seated next to Ava Gardner. But on the other side of him there was an empty seat. It turned out to be the only empty seat in the Cathedral.

Puzzled, Allan one day got around to asking Grace, 'Who didn't show up'

She told him, 'Frank Sinatra.'

Allan was shocked. 'You put me in the middle of Ava Gardner and Frank Sinatra?' Their publicly turbulent marriage had gone sour a few years before and Allan couldn't believe that, had Sinatra shown, he would have found himself literally at the centre of their first meeting since the break-up. 'You wanted me to sit between them? Who knows how they would have gotten on?'

Grace smiled, 'I knew you could handle it.'

Actually the reason Sinatra stayed away had less to do with Ava Gardner than it did with his affection for Grace.

He'd flown to London from Los Angeles a few days before the wedding to have final fittings for his white tie and tails. One of the first things he saw in London was that the newspapers were filled with Gardner's arrival in Monaco. She was attracting a lot of publicity. He knew that once he arrived the press would be on him too because of their bitter divorce. So he phoned Grace to say, 'I won't be there.' She wanted to know why. He told her, 'I'm not coming, because this is your day.' And he stayed away.

Grace later confided to Allan that she always thought Sinatra was the only man Ava Gardner ever loved. She said, 'They were right for each other. I put them on either side of you because it seemed like a good way of trying to rekindle the flame.'

The religious ceremony was held with great dignity.

White lilacs and lilies-of-the-valley filled the ancient Cathedral, contrasting with the red silk drapings and a red carpet that stretched from the altar to the front steps.

Bright late morning sunshine poured through the stained glass windows.

Men in morning suits and women with colourful hats took their places.

Then all heads turned.

Grace walked in, very slowly, on her father's arm.

Rainier joined her at the altar.

The choir sang Bach's *Uxor Tua* and Purcell's *Alleluia*.

There was an awkward moment as Rainier had trouble getting the ring on Grace's finger – she had to help – and both were still so nervous that their vows were whispered only loud enough for the Bishop to hear.

She fought back her own tears.

He stared tensely straight ahead.

And then it was over.

The Bishop declared them man and wife.

Now there wasn't a dry eye in the house.

He kissed her.

And the Cathedral's bells rang out to signal that they were, in the eyes of God, one.

Six hours of parades, receptions and balcony appearances later, they boarded his boat and left for a one-month honeymoon cruise around the Mediterranean.

They literally sailed off into the sunset.

Hollywood couldn't have done it better.

Although the show-business newspaper *Variety* announced the wedding with the headline, 'Marriages – Grace Kelly to Prince Rainier III. Bride is film star; groom is non-pro.'

⋆   ⋆   ⋆   ⋆

6

The Taming of SBM

ONE MORNING in 1951, while casually strolling through the streets of Monte Carlo, Aristotle Socrates Onassis noticed that the old Sporting Club was boarded up.

In those days his Olympic Maritime empire – 91 ships, of which 70 were oil tankers – had its headquarters in Paris.

But French taxes were killing him.

He thought that a building like the Sporting would suit him very well, all the better considering Monaco's no-tax politics. So he asked around, discovered that the place had been empty for some time and went to see SBM, hoping he could rent it.

Their answer was no.

He asked why not.

No one came forward with any explanations.

He offered to buy the building.

They said no.

He offered to buy the building and the ground under it.

They said no again.

He increased his offer.

And still they said no.

He asked why they were being so stubborn.

They showed him to the door.

They wouldn't sell him the building, so he bought the company.

*   *   *   *

Honoré-Charles' mother was the one who got her son thinking about bringing new businesses to Monaco.

She was the one who got him thinking about the barren hill across the port, in those days called Les Spelugues.

Under her guidance the Prince formed a company called *La Société de Crédit de la Région Méditerranéenne*, intending to build a health spa on the hill, with a beach club, a sanitorium and a collection of private villas. But he was unable to raise the necessary capital and the plan seemed doomed.

Being widely travelled, Caroline knew that many European spas combined bathing facilities with a casino. A good example was Bad Homburg in Hesse-Homburg, a tiny sovereign state just north of Frankfurt. Gambling was the main attraction but it was billed as nothing more than a sideshow. In other words, Bad Homburg, like the even more famous Baden-Baden, was not really so much a spa with a casino as it was a gambling resort masquerading as a spa.

As games of chance were illegal under the Sardinians' rule there were no casinos in the south of France. So in 1855, Caroline encouraged her son to form the *Société des Bains de Mer* and open a casino.

The company's first group of backers included a pair of Parisians, one of whom was, at the time, bankrupt. They agreed to build a bathing establishment and a hotel, and to develop both sea and road communication with Nice. In exchange, they were granted the right to 'provide amusements of every kind'.

At Caroline's insistence, however, the casino would have to operate as far away from Le Rocher as possible so the natives wouldn't be tempted. Even today, Monégasques are not permitted to enter the casino and the sovereign family is never seen there.

Honoré-Charles assumed the title Prince Charles III in mid-1856 and the first roulette wheel spun under his reign in November of that year in the converted Villa Bellevue on the slopes of Les Spelugues.

But the venture was doomed.

Monaco was too isolated and the few people who showed up couldn't support the expense of keeping the place open. During the week of 15 March 1857, for example, records reveal that only one punter played at the casino and he won two francs. The following week two visitors lost 205 francs.

Within three months, barely still in business, the Parisians

sold out to another Frenchman who moved the casino to a hotel
nearer the Palace, hoping that might provide some glamour. Before
the end of the year he sold out to a Parisian gambler who tried to
economise by cramming two roulette tables and one trente-et-
quarante table into a single dingy room. By then the best of the
casino's clientele was a meagre collection of reprobates exiled
from the German spas.

The following year foundations were laid for the permanent
home of the casino on the top of Les Spelugues. But as construction began, the mountain underneath gave way. The original
architect quit, payments to his workers trickled to a halt, the
concessionaires' funds dried up and the rights to gambling in
Monaco were sold yet again.

A new group took over in May 1859, pouring money into the
project, only to see building stop for the Franco-Prussian War.
Once Austria was defeated, their casino was opened in a villa on
the Rue de Lorraine.

Still, serious gamblers stayed away.

Getting to Monaco was just too difficult.

There was a boat between Nice and Monaco but the printed
daily schedule bore absolutely no relation to the captain's own
irregular hours. There was also a footpath from Nice along the
coast, where the Basse Corniche now runs, plus a road high above
the principality linking Nice and Italy, where you find the Grande
Corniche. But the lower road was filled with highway bandits.
And to get to Monaco from the upper road you either had to make
your way to Roquebrune and double back or leave your landau at
La Turbie and come several miles down a dangerously steep and
winding path. The Grande Corniche is where Grace Kelly and
Cary Grant did their famous driving scene in *To Catch a Thief*.
The dangerously steep and winding path down from La Turbie,
now the D37 road, is where Princess Grace lost her life.

Having seceded from the principality, Roquebrune and Menton
were considered 'free towns', although under the 1861 Treaty
of Turino, which ended the war with Austria, they were now
annexed to France. As a gesture of compensation from France for
the loss of those towns, Charles received three million francs –
about $750,000 or £300,000 – a promise to build both a coastal
highway from Nice to Monaco and a railway a few dozen yards
inland along the same route, in addition to a guarantee to maintain
his throne.

By now Charles was growing impatient with the casino's owners. Gambling had not yet added so much as one *sou* to his treasury. He told the consortium that unless the casino was completed by the end of the year he'd withdraw their concession. Unable to make good, the major shareholder of the group set out to find someone else who might be interested in taking over.

That man was François Blanc.

Owner of the gambling concession at Bad Homburg, a bounder and convicted fraudster, it was Blanc who, with the showmanship of P. T. Barnum, literally invented Monte Carlo.

Born in 1806, he grew up in Bordeaux where he left school at the age of 14. Often bragging that he had a head for numbers, he played the French stock market so successfully that by the time he was 21 he owned his own brokerage house. His skill at tipping shares was legendary.

At least until the bubble burst.

Where the Rothschilds used carrier pigeons to bring the news from the Paris bourse back to Bordeaux, Blanc and his brother found it more efficient to bribe telegraph operators at a local post office into providing prices before they were relayed to other brokers. When the Blancs were caught out, they were charged with fraud and bribery and sentenced to seven months.

Leaving France as soon as they could, they wound up in Luxembourg where they managed a casino. A few years later they convinced Count Philipp von Homburg to sell them the gaming concession at Bad Homburg.

Now catering to the crowned heads of Europe, the Blancs covered the casino's walls with oriental silk and the chairs in fine Moroccan leather. They billed their establishment as, 'The rendezvous of travellers, the elegant and fashionable retreat of people of taste, leisure and wit and a peaceful oasis visited yearly by whole caravans of tourists who may well be called the pilgrims of pleasure.'

It was at Bad Homburg where François Blanc learned the lessons of the gambling business – the hard way!

Prince Charles Bonaparte, Napoleon's nephew, arrived one night with more cash in his pocket than Blanc had in his safe and broke the bank. Blanc publicised Bonaparte's run of luck because he knew how one winner will always bring in a hundred losers. But to protect himself against punters as wealthy as a Bonaparte, he decided the house must always have more money than the gamblers and from that night on he stocked his coffers accordingly.

Next, a small syndicate wiped out his profits for two seasons by continually doubling bets whenever they lost. Blanc understood how doubling narrowed the odds, so he established betting limits to ensure that infinite sums of money could not be wagered against him.

No one had to tell him that with so much money being played every day he had to maintain strict surveillance of the croupiers. But as the reputation of Bad Homburg grew, he decided he also had to keep an eye on the gamblers. So he created a special team of physiognomists, security guards with a trained memory for faces, whom he posted at every door to keep out cheats and other undesirables.

Blanc's rules are the backbone of every working casino in the world today.

He bought Monaco's gaming concession for 1.1 million francs – about $280,000 or £118,000 – in April 1863 and renamed SBM the *Société des Bains de Mer et Cercle des Etrangers* – the Sea Bathing Society and Foreigners' Club. In exchange for an annual remittance to the Prince based on the profits, plus Blanc's promise to pay for some of the expenses involved in completing the new road from Nice, SBM was granted an exclusive 50-year lease on gambling.

Blanc refurbished the gaming rooms, making them truly elegant, and used his influence to hasten construction of the Hôtel de Paris on the Place du Casino, intending to create a hotel which could rank among the most luxurious in the world. Prince Charles agreed that Les Spelugues could be named after him, although by this point he was almost totally blind and never saw the new casino. The railway was eventually completed, arriving in the principality on 19 October, 1868.

And with the trains came the punters.

Right from the start Blanc believed that Monte Carlo must be about fantasy, wish fulfilment and show business. He promoted the idea that anyone who stepped through the casino's doors could be the one to break the bank. To keep the myth alive, whenever the casino lost heavily, he ordered a table to be covered in black as if the place was in mourning.

Even today, tourists come because Monte Carlo is less about respectable gambling than it is about the past, about being seen, about hoping that the aura which surrounds Europe's 'beautiful people' will somehow rub off. Because Blanc created Monte Carlo to be the playground of kings, it forever attracts mere subjects who, with little more than a short pile of 20 franc chips can, at least for one evening, pretend to have walked through the history of another, more madcap, more bejewelled world.

To spread the faith, Blanc paid a legion of tame journalists to place stories for him about the principality. For instance, when a Polish gambler lost his last penny at the tables and in desperation shot himself, Blanc installed him at the Hôtel de Paris and insisted the man be attended to by the best doctors. When the man recovered Blanc also paid his fare home. Newspapers throughout the world covered the story, reporting that Blanc would offer 'journey money' to any client who could prove that his gambling had left him destitute. Not that Blanc did it for charitable reasons. It simply generated a lot of good press.

But then Blanc was not only crafty, he was also extremely lucky.

By 1872 the German and Belgian casinos were shut and the only other casino in Europe, at Saxone-les-Bains in Switzerland, was about to be closed. Without lifting a finger, Blanc found himself owning the European monopoly on roulette wheels.

Thanks entirely to Blanc's casino, Monaco in the mid-1870s boasted four major hotels and 200 smaller inns with rooms to let.

In fact, Blanc was such a highly respected entrepreneur that he even married off one of his daughters to quasi-royalty. In 1876 Louise Blanc wed Prince Constantine Radziwill, which ironically makes Blanc an extremely distant relative by marriage of Jackie Kennedy Onassis, whose sister is a Radziwill and whose second husband would also one day own SBM.

When Blanc died a year later, one journalist suggested that his tombstone should read, 'You can play red or black, but it's always Blanc (white) that wins.' There must have been some truth in that because the ex-felon from Bordeaux left a personal fortune worth nearly $60 million or £23 million.

* * * *

The reins of SBM passed to Blanc's son Camille who only occasionally shared his father's flair for showmanship. It's true that the company made money but he came close to seeing his gambling concession dissolve into thin air at the hands of Monaco's first American princess.

Alice Heine was born in New Orleans in 1858, the great-granddaughter of Solomon Heine, a Hamburg banking rival of the Rothschilds. Her mother was a Miltenberger, from a prominent Louisiana family. Two weeks after her 17th birthday she married Armand, Duke of Richelieu, head of one of France's most famous families. She bore him two children before he fell ill and died, leaving her a widow at the age of 22. Retiring from Paris to the Portuguese island of Madeira, she wanted to quietly mourn her husband's death.

Prince Albert happened to be there at the time conducting deep sea diving experiments.

A friendship blossomed and when they returned to Paris, only to discover they were neighbours, that friendship turned into romance. But Albert's father refused them permission to marry. Instead they lived together until Charles III died in 1889. And then they were wed.

Disembarking in Monaco in January 1890, Princess Alice created a great deal of excitement with her open, relaxed manner.

One chronicler of the times wrote – as others would, using almost the exact same words 66 years later for Monaco's next American Princess – 'She was as intelligent as she was pretty. Her blonde beauty lit up the Palace.'

Her only fault, as far as the Monégasques could tell, was that she felt gambling was immoral, often said so and urged her husband to put an end to it.

It certainly wasn't what Camille Blanc wanted to hear, especially as Albert was prone to consider his wife's suggestions.

The dowry he'd received from his first wife and the fortune that Alice brought with her gave him more than enough power to take on SBM. But there could be no denying that, because of the casino, the Monaco he'd inherited was considerably better off than the Monaco his father had inherited.

In the end he decided that gambling should continue.

Not one to give up easily, Alice believed that music, opera and ballet could rival gambling.

Her plan was to turn Monaco into a major European centre for the arts and put an end to gambling that way.

Again she lost.

Yet thanks to her, Raoul Gunsbourg, an impressario with an international reputation, was appointed director of the Monte Carlo Opera. He was not only the first to stage Wagner outside Bayreuth, he was also the man who brought Diaghilev and the Ballet Russe to Monte Carlo. He worked in Monaco for half a century and stamped an indelible cultural tradition on the principality.

Just as a brief aside, while Alice did not join Albert in his passion for maritime exploration, preferring to stay at home rather than suffer chronic sea sickness – another trait she shared with Monaco's second American Princess – she encouraged him in his passionate but decidedly unpopular defence of Captain Dreyfus.

In 1894, an anonymous letter containing sensitive military information was passed from a member of the French general staff to the German military attaché in Paris. Word of it reached the French and Dreyfus, the only Jew on the staff, was accused of treason. Despite any real evidence against him, Dreyfus was found guilty and sent to Devil's Island for life. A huge wave of anti-Semitism swept across France, followed by the indignation of men like Emile Zola who protested Dreyfus's obvious innocence.

Having maintained a friendship with Wilhelm II, Albert travelled to Berlin to ask the Kaiser – who was, after all, in a position to know – whether or not Dreyfus had been a spy. Without naming the real spy, the Kaiser swore that Dreyfus was innocent. Albert brought that news back to President Felix Faure in Paris who was so shocked by it that within 30 minutes he suffered a stroke. A new trial was ordered.

Convinced that justice would win, Albert wrote to Mme Dreyfus that he would be pleased to receive her and her husband at Marchais, 'As soon as the sacred work of Justice has been accomplished. The presence of a martyr, towards whom the conscience of humanity turns with anxiety, will honour my house.'

In response, the French accused Albert of meddling in their affairs and directed anti-Semitic slurs at Alice.

Making matters worse, the re-trial turned out to be as much of a farce as the first one. Dreyfus was again found guilty.

However, public opinion created the desired effect and Dreyfus was eventually granted an official pardon. Six years later the highest French court reviewed the case, ruled that the evidence presented against Dreyfus had been forged and nullified his court martial.

Their stand for Dreyfus gave Albert and Alice high profiles in Europe.

Unfortunately Alice's high profile did not necessarily please other monarchs.

When Albert learned that Queen Victoria was on holiday in Nice he requested an audience of courtesy. A note returned saying that Her Majesty was busy and suggesting he write again at a later date. Refusing to accept the snub, especially as he and Alice had an ongoing friendship with the queen's son Bertie, a second request was dispatched. This time Victoria conceded that she would be willing to receive the Prince, without ever mentioning the Princess.

Sadly, their marriage was doomed to failure. His research took him out of the principality for increasingly long periods. Alice in the meantime concentrated on the opera and in particular championed the works of a new-found friend, a young British composer known as Isidore de Lara but whose real name was Cohen. As a result of Albert's lack of interest and Alice's affair with de Lara, they separated in 1902. Yet they never divorced. Alice became one of the leading socialites of London and Paris and after Albert's death lived her remaining years as the Dowager Princess.

*   *   *   *

Camille Blanc saw SBM through the next 20 years.

He continued making money with the company right up to World War I.

But life changed radically on the French Riviera after the Great War.

New boundaries put a dent into the ranks and purses of the monied classes.

The Russian grand dukes were either dead or penniless in exile.

The Habsburgs were no more.

The kings of Italy, Spain, Albania and Yugoslavia were only just holding onto their crowns.

Most of the other royal houses were in tatters, their finances a shambles.

Yet Americans had money.

And now, as tourists, they re-conquered Europe.

For them, July and August were the calmest months to cross the Atlantic. They didn't care that the Riviera was supposed to be a winter resort. They didn't pay any attention to the old adage that a sunburn was a tell-tale sign of the working classes

At the same time, remote mountain villages in Switzerland and Austria looked for economic salvation by transforming themselves into ski resorts. Winter on the slopes became the European craze.

To cater to these predominantly middle-class summer crowds, resorts developed along the coast, each of them with their own casino – from Menton east of Monaco, to Beaulieu, Nice, Juan-les-Pins and Cannes on the western side. For the first time, Monte Carlo had some real competition. And the Monégasques couldn't cope.

Prince Albert now cast a wary eye towards SBM and the man who ran it.

As far as he was concerned, Camille Blanc was more interested in ladies than in SBM.

So the Prince, anxious to see fresh money and new ideas poured into the company, turned to one of Europe's wealthiest, shrewdest and most mysterious men.

Basil Zaharoff, a Greek from Constantinople, lived in Monaco in a state of conspicuous adultery with a married Spanish noblewoman.

The world's most important arms salesman, he was the major shareholder in Europe's largest armament manufacturers in addition to having diversified interests in shipping, oil, metals and banking.

Albert wanted him to take control of the casino.

But Zaharoff was a cautious man who first needed to be assured of Monaco's independence. Possessing considerable access, he personally discussed the matter with French President Georges Clemenceau. Within a matter of months – some people say entirely due to Zaharoff – France signed the 1918 Franco-Monégasque Pact which re-enforced the sovereignty of the principality.

Zaharoff advanced $5 million, telling Albert he would assume control of SBM at his own convenience. He then secretly began setting up a string of dummy companies to buy SBM shares. As soon as Albert was dead in 1922, Zaharoff called an emergency meeting of the board, dethroned Camille Blanc and set about managing the company.

A few months later, when word from Spain reached Zaharoff that his noblewoman's legal husband had passed away, Zaharoff and his mistress were married.

He then put the second part of his plan into action.

Even though he was by this time well into his 70s, Zaharoff tried to coerce Louis into selling out so that he could install Señora Zaharoff on Monaco's throne.

Louis refused and the ferocious battle that followed was played out in local newspapers. Accusations of fraud and mismanagement were flung back and forth. Zaharoff purchased a local newspaper to use just to insult the Prince, so Louis purchased a rival local newspaper to use just to insult Zaharoff.

That's when the fight ended, oddly enough, as abruptly as it had begun. Señora Zaharoff died and with her so did Zaharoff's interest in Louis' throne. Zaharoff simply sold his SBM shares to a bank in Paris and faded away.

However Monaco was still in bad shape.

Exploring all the possible solutions, Prince Pierre, acting on Louis' behalf, invited Elsa Maxwell to Monte Carlo.

She'd been the so-called 'public relations consultant' who'd turned Venice's Lido into a playground for the newly discovered beautiful people of summer. In 1925, Pierre and Louis hoped she might be able to do the same for Monaco.

A dumpy, unattractive, asexual nickelodeon piano player who'd worked her way up to Broadway music halls and London's West End, Maxwell was born in Iowa in 1883. While in England, she side-stepped her way into society and earned a reputation as a woman who gave good parties, knew how to bring people together and could organise a successful charity event. For the rest of her life they called her a 'society hostess'. In reality she was nothing more than a super-successful freeloader who house-guested and name-dropped her way through European capitals, staying with the Windsors in Paris and the Douglas Fairbanks in London.

Monte Carlo was a natural place for her to ply her trade.

Put on the payroll to help bring Monaco into modern times, Maxwell reported back to Prince Pierre that Monte Carlo had come upon bad times for obvious reasons. She said the casino was too gloomy, too much of a dump, and the Hôtel de Paris was too old-fashioned. She also felt it was incongruous that a company called the Sea Bathing Society did not have a beach.

To help her cause, she even announced to American reporters

that the Monégasques were building a rubber beach. She said – supposedly off the top of her head because it sounded like a story that could get headlines – SBM was laying down huge strips of rubber over which sand would be poured. The reaction was so positive that a plan for a rubber beach was actually discussed, at least until someone in Monaco realised that the sand would immediately wash away and salt water would then eat through the rubber.

Next, she decided SBM should acquire the land at the far eastern end of the beach, which happens to be in France, to build a huge blue-tiled swimming pool and what is now the beautiful tangerine-coloured, California-style, Old Beach Hotel. She also encouraged the construction of the Monte Carlo Tennis Club.

Perhaps best of all, Maxwell was responsible for the Summer Sporting, which opened in 1927, the only casino in the world where the ceiling rolled back so that gamblers could play under the stars.

When it first opened, there was a restaurant along a terrace just above the casino. One night a lady dining there dropped a 100-franc piece onto a roulette table. When the roulette wheel stopped she was a winner. The lady asked for her coin to be returned and it was, along with 3,500 francs. Shortly thereafter a small roof was built to cover the tables.

Finally, it was Maxwell who started the tradition of Friday night galas featuring major European stars. She filled the stage with the likes of Grace Moore and Maurice Chevalier and stocked the audience with celebrities such as King Gustav V of Sweden. Although, typical of Maxwell, she regularly confessed to friends that whenever Gustav was around, two concessions had to be made. 'You had to pretend he didn't peek at your cards at the bridge table and you had to brave his lisp that sprayed you when he spoke.'

Thanks to Maxwell, Monaco's treasury found itself healthier than it had been for years. SBM reckoned that each visitor to the Casino averaged a loss of £3.

* * * *

Rainier settled into his role as ruling Prince.

And SBM showed him the face of a force he'd have to reckon with.

By the early 1950s Rainier realised the time was long overdue for a show-down with SBM.

'As the biggest employer here,' he begins, 'SBM was always trying to exert their influence. But I felt they interfered too much with the running of the principality. A lot needed to be changed, or at least to be redefined. For example, until I looked into it, SBM's payment to the government for the monopoly on gambling was very mysterious. During my grandfather's reign there was always talk about envelopes being passed under tables. It was an unacceptable way of running a business.'

Under Louis, one part of SBM's contribution was paid to the government and one part was paid directly to the Prince. Rainier now ordered SBM's entire contribution be sent to the government. He then established a Civil List – today it is nearing the $10 million or £6 million mark – a lump sum voted by the National Council which the Prince is then free to spend any way he chooses for salaries, including his own, expenses and household costs.

That organised, he turned to the question of SBM's political influence in Monaco.

But these were times of great uncertainty, with the government of the France's Fourth Republic changing every few weeks. What's more, it was no longer true that wealth and exclusivity were synonymous. The world was now a place where a lot of exclusive people were no longer wealthy and a lot of wealthy people were not very exclusive.

On top of that, SBM had still not recovered from the war.

Tourism in Monaco had ebbed to such a point that in 1951 every SBM employee was docked a month's salary because the company simply did not have enough money to pay everyone. The 1952–53 season went on record as being SBM's worst, showing an $850,000 or £300,000 loss.

So Rainier got it into his head to find someone who could inject both money and enthusiasm into the company.

The man he was looking for came in the guise of a shabbily dressed Greek millionaire bearing thick black-rimmed glasses.

Ari Onassis was born in Smyrna in 1906, but was forced to flee at the age of 16 when the Turks ravaged the village and murdered his father, a successful tobacco broker. He found a ship bound for South America, jumped on board and headed for Buenos Aires with just $60 in his pocket. To avoid being sent home when he got there, he lied to the authorities that he was 21. To buy food once he settled there, he worked at night as a telegraph operator.

Even as a young man Onassis showed the keen eye of a world-class opportunist.

When he noticed tobacco was in short supply he became a broker and later parlayed that into a factory. When he saw tobacco ships leaving empty for the return trip, he became an exporter and made a fortune by filling their holds with leather and grain. He soon took over a small fleet of old freighters, negotiated a commercial treaty between Greece and Argentina and got himself appointed Greek Consul General. He used his title to build up his freight business, which he then diversified into whaling and a fleet of oil tankers. When he bought 20 former American Liberty ships after World War II at knock-down prices and changed their registry from the US to Panama, the Americans said he was in breach of his purchase agreement and fined him $7 million. But Onassis was such a natural wheeler-dealer that, while paying the fine, he actually convinced the Americans to offer him a $14 million loan to build himself 20 more ships.

If he wasn't yet the wealthiest man in the world in 1946, when he married 17-year-old Tina Livanos and honeymooned in Monaco, he was fast becoming that.

'I knew Onassis was always looking for interesting places to visit,' Rainier continues, 'so I convinced him to come to Monaco as a sort of a super-tourist. He and Tina started spending a lot of time here. He based his shipping company here. And his yacht, *The Christina*, usually wintered here. After a while he began to think of Monaco as something of a second home.'

Stupefied by SBM's attitude when he tried and failed in 1951 to rent and then to buy office space for Olympic Maritime in the old Sporting Club, Onassis took a closer look at SBM and discovered the company was losing money.

He also learned that Rainier was not happy with the way things were being run.

Because it was a public company, Onassis had no trouble in establishing the fact that the ruling Prince held only about two per cent of SBM's shares, the remainder of which were freely traded on the Paris bourse. At under 1,000 francs per share –

less than $2.80 or £1 – Onassis concluded that SBM was under-valued.

Proceeding slowly, much like Basil Zaharoff 30 years before him, Onassis used front companies to acquire small blocks of stock. Over the next two years he managed to obtain 300,000 SBM shares and hide them in various portfolios before anyone in Monaco realised what was happening.

It was a costly exercise that put a strain on his cash flow but then, whenever he was short of cash, he simply turned for help to Stavros Niarchos, the Greek ship-owner who'd married Tina's sister.

Niarchos later swore to Elsa Maxwell, 'I bought Monte Carlo with Onassis. But when it came to a settlement I was out. Oh well, that's my brother-in-law.'

Maxwell then said of Onassis, 'His manners are hardly those of Beau Brummel. In fact the only person he treats with real respect is his friend Winston Churchill. But he has enormous physical attraction.'

When Onassis's interest in the company finally surfaced, he boasted, 'I have bought between 300,000 and 500,000 shares in the casino. I forget the figure. I just know I've enough to do what I want.'

And the first thing he wanted to do was move Olympic Maritime into the old Sporting.

Next, he set out to convince Rainier that the future of SBM was safe in his hands.

As the Prince held the right to certain vetoes, Onassis assured him that he was going to modernise the company, add rooms to the Hôtel de Paris and build a grill restaurant on the top floor.

He promised Rainier, 'I will spend millions and make the place a world cultural and tourist centre.'

Obviously, Rainier liked what he heard.

'In the beginning I thought Onassis could be useful to SBM even though he had some slightly odd ideas, like tearing down the opera house. A Greek architect he'd hired told him that the sound was bad and the best thing would be to rip it down and put up a huge shell.'

Almost right from the start SBM made money under Onassis, partly because he and Tina were at the centre of the European jet-set – their clique had loads of money to spend – and partly because of a general upturn in French economy.

But then, as the 1950s wore on, Onassis spent less and less on the company.

Instead of making good on his original promises he adopted the tactic of 'benevolent obfuscation'.

Knowing that all governments, even small ones, are administered by bureaucrats and that bureaucrats can be counted on, at least to some extent, to be bureaucratic, when the Prince tried to push him into building the new Summer Sporting, Onassis directed his people to ask the government what their plans were for electricity, roads, sewers and gas. The bureaucrats took a predictably long time to answer that they'd provide electricity, roads, sewers and gas based on SBM's plans for the site. But SBM said they couldn't proceed without knowing what the government intended. It went back and forth like this until the bureaucrats finally came up with blueprints. Then SBM questioned technical aspects of those blueprints. The government had to answer those questions. And when they did, SBM posed more questions. Onassis generated a massive, nonsensical dialogue with the government because as long as it was going on he didn't have to spend any money.

Rainier was both disappointed and troubled by Onassis's attitude.

'During the years that he was majority shareholder, none of the big investment programmes he'd spoken of were carried out. He patched up whatever needed patching up and left the rest. All right, he built the Grill on the top of the Hôtel de Paris. He did it because that interested him. And he painted some of the gaming rooms. But he didn't spend money on things like renewal of the company's activities or the creation of new activities. I didn't find the same enthusiasm in the man once he took over the company as I'd expected.'

To be perfectly fair, it wasn't just down to Onassis and his enthusiasm.

Rainier might have been Monaco's Prince but, Onassis owned the casino, and that made Ari the next best thing.

He loved to cater to his jet-set friends while the Prince wanted to cut Monte Carlo into that increasingly important middle-class tourist market.

Some people have over-simplified the problem by saying that Onassis wanted caviar and the Prince wanted sausages.

That's not quite true either.

Onassis merely saw SBM's assets in a different way. The casino was a kind of big kid's toy. Like his yacht, it was something he enjoyed telling people he owned.

Rainier was anything but amused by this side of Onassis and, when he didn't agree with certain construction plans, he used his princely veto to quash them. At one point he threatened not to renew the lease on Olympic's offices. Onassis objected to Rainier's interference and in turn threatened to leave Monaco. The Prince didn't want things to go that far so he backed off just a bit.

Then in 1959 Onassis dumped Tina for Maria Callas and truly became an international superstar.

Whether Rainier would have wanted to admit it in those days or not, having Onassis and Maria Callas in Monaco was very good for business. Except that by this time Onassis was thinking of SBM as little more than a real estate investment.

And now, when Rainier learned what Onassis had in mind, it frightened him.

'I had certain indications that definitely scared me. I was led to believe that one day he might try to sell off part of the property. He was a very intelligent man and terribly tough to do business with. But when it came to running SBM the way I'd hoped he would, it was almost as if he was too busy with other things.'

Eventually Onassis got to the point where he said he wouldn't put any more money into SBM except for the small things like upkeep and the redecoration of rooms in the hotels.

'Even then I didn't like what he was proposing. He said he wanted to find some famous decorators and give them each two rooms to do any way they wanted. I couldn't believe it. It would have been a mess. There would have been no harmony. Two people in two different rooms would never have thought they were staying in the same hotel. We had lots of meetings, just the two of us, trying to find a solution. But we got to a point where there was no way out.'

Trying to force a solution in November 1962, Onassis gave Rainier a 90-day option to pick up his holding at nearly $30 per share while the quoted price was about half that.

At that price the option was left to expire.

A little while later Onassis announced that he was splitting the company into three groups, one for gambling, one for the hotels, restaurants and the beach facilities, and one for real estate. He said he might even sub-lease the gambling concession so that he could concentrate on the main holding company and the real estate.

That was the last straw.

Around the Palace the drastic step of nationalisation was discussed. And for the first time in many years Rainier had the National Council behind him.

'Onassis and I did not quarrel,' Rainier insists. 'We just both dug our heels in to maintain our positions.'

However, the Prince was quoted at the time as saying, 'Mr Onassis is nothing more than a property peddler with no real interests in the welfare of Monaco.'

Finding no equitable way out of the situation, Rainier ordered – as was his right by law – that the company's capitalisation be increased by 800,000 new shares. Those shares were then sold to the state and Onassis was deprived of his majority.

The story they love to tell around the principality, romanticising the shoot-out between the two into a sort of Monégasque OK Corral, is that Rainier offered Onassis $14 a share, when Onassis had paid between $2.80 and $5.60. Onassis demanded $19. So Rainier took Onassis to the government printing plant and showed him SBM's new share certificates rolling off the presses. Onassis supposedly said, 'That will ruin me, that will drive my shares down to under $5.' Rainier supposedly said, 'Either accept $14 gracefully or try to find someone else who'll give you more than that for your reduced holding.' And so Onassis accepted Rainier's offer.

Except it didn't quite happen that way.

'That's not my style,' Rainier says, although he admits the new share certificates were printed and that Onassis did see them. 'There's no doubt that the law permitting me to print those shares was a huge economic sword to hold over his head. But we didn't nationalise SBM. We bought those shares and paid Onassis a fair price for his. Now, it's interesting that once Onassis lost his majority holding, once he no longer had this personal interest in SBM, he became more reasonable and much more involved. He held onto a nominal shareholding, had a representative on the board and took a real interest in what the company was doing.'

Of course the instant Onassis saw those new share certificates he understood what was happening. Despite the Prince's explanations, Onassis screamed nationalisation and went to court to try to stop it.

Unfortunately for him this was an away game as the only court
with jurisdiction was in Monaco.

He lost.

But then he didn't exactly walk away penniless.

The 51 Panamanian companies he used to hold his total of
650,000 SBM shares came out with a profit of more than $7 million,
something like five times his original stake. Still, when he heard of
his defeat in court, he barked, 'We were gipped.'

Rainier won't accept that.

'The Onassis affair ended as well for him as it did for Monaco.
Today the state permanently holds 1.2 million shares, which is a
majority stake in SBM, so that one man can never again own SBM.
At the same time he made some money on it. But that wasn't really
the important thing. He never would have said so but I think he
liberated himself from something he'd gotten into which wasn't
really in his waters. I sincerely believe that because as soon as the
deal was completed our personal relationship improved. On the
contrary, it was even better than before because there was nothing
to get in the way.'

Their friendship continued until Onassis's death in March
1975.

'I liked him a lot. He was a very human man. Of course the
tragedy in his life was the death of his son in a plane crash in the sea
off Nice in 1973. The son was working with him and would have
succeeded him. I don't think he ever got over that. Nor do I think
he was ever very happy in either of his marriages. I'm convinced
the only woman who brought him happiness was Callas.'

Rainier and Grace sailed on several occasions with Onassis and
Callas on *The Christina*, giving them a chance to see those two
up close.

'There was a very good rapport between them. They understood
each other. After all, they were both terribly Greek. They both had
international reputations. They were both self-made. Grace and I
agreed they were really meant for each other. We thought that
Callas was fun. She was forever playing jokes on him. She was very
easy to get along with, except that every morning she annoyed the
hell out of him by vocalising. He absolutely hated that. She'd run
through her scales and he'd run around the ship turning up all the
radios to drown out the sound.'

In the end, however, Rainier says he will always remember
Aristotle Onassis as an intensely lonely man.

'I can recall the first time he showed me around *The Christina*. The ship had 12 cabins and I remarked what great cabins they were. He looked at me and confessed, "But they're always empty." I asked why. And he said, "Because I don't know 12 people I'd like to have with me."'

*   *   *   *

7

Teamwork

*I*N OCTOBER 1971, Rainier and Grace flew to Iran as guests of the Shah to join in the celebrations marking the 2,500th anniversary of the founding of the Persian monarchy.

Estimated to have cost anywhere from $100 million to $1 billion, it was to say the least, quite a party.

After gathering in Tehran and going on to Shiraz, the Shah, his Empress Farah and their 600 closest friends – including 37 heads of state and representatives of 69 nations – moved in armoured convoy to Persepolis, ceremonial capital of the ancient Persian empire.

That night's feast was held in the huge state banqueting tent at the centre of the spectacular canvas village that had been built in the middle of the desert especially for the occasion.

Cooked by 180 chefs from Maxim's in Paris, the Hôtel de Paris in Monte Carlo and the Palace Hotel in St Moritz, the first course was quails' eggs stuffed with golden imperial caviar and served with champagne and Château de Saran. Next came a mousse of crayfish tails with an Haut Brion Blanc 1964. Then there was roast saddle of lamb with truffles served with Château-Lafite Rothschild 1945 and followed by a sorbet of Moët et Chandon 1911. After that, waiters paraded in carrying silver platters with 50 peacocks, their tail feathers put back in place and surrounded by roasted quails. That was served with a salad of nuts and truffles and Musigny Conte de Vogue 1945. Fresh figs with cream, raspberries and port wine came next, as did Dom Perignon 1959, coffee and Cognac Prince Eugène.

The only substitution on the menu went to the Shah who had artichoke hearts because he didn't like caviar.

With so many dignitaries in one place for the first time ever, it was an opportunity for all of the Shah's guests to mingle with people they might not normally have a chance to be with on such an informal basis. At one point Grace spotted somebody she wanted to meet, walked up to him and said, 'Good evening, I'm Grace of Monaco.' Such was the tone of the evening that he simply extended his hand and said, 'Good evening, I'm Tito.'

Rainier and Grace were two the 94 guests seated at the Shah's long zig-zag head table. Rainier was next to the Duke of Edinburgh while Grace sat next to an Eastern bloc prime minister. She and the gentleman chatted amiably over dinner in French and German but when he followed dessert with a cigar and inadvertently blew a huge cloud of blue smoke in her direction, Grace sneezed.

Really sneezed.

She popped some of the buttons on the back of her Givenchy gown.

And the dress opened.

Horrified, her lady-in-waiting rushed to the Princess's aid.

So did the Prince.

But they were both too late.

Neither of them could do anything more than stand by helplessly while Grace — who figured that popping buttons after a meal like that had to be the perfect ending to a perfect evening — instantly doubled up in great convulsions of laughter.

★   ★   ★   ★

Royalty is something of an odd concept this late in the 20th century.

More often than not it's based on somebody's questionably related marauding ancestors having once stolen large tracts of land from the previous owners and accordingly then spent much of their newly claimed wealth defending their right to that land from others.

In most countries around the world where you find royals, their very existence depends on a mass of subjects willing to suspend belief and – even if only for those few moments that it takes to salute the 'Godflag, troop the colour or sing *God Save the Queen* – accept the concept that all men and women are not, as it happens, created equal.

However, in many of the places where royalty exists and has done so for a long time, such a suspension of disbelief can be the glue that holds together the national character, keeps the people united through difficult times, ironically lends credibility to the concept of democracy and often gives stature to many of the activities that make up the social climate of a nation.

Royal warrants and royal patronage are frequently the frosting on the cake that takes an event out of the ordinary and makes it that much more special.

Royalty also helps to sell postcards.

In Monaco, at any given time of the year, there are no fewer than 212 different postcards on sale with pictures of one or all of the Grimaldis.

That Monaco's sovereign family has become the principality's most important business is not by chance.

There are other casino towns in Europe, like Divonne, Evian and Deauville. There are also other city-states in Europe, like Andorra, Liechtenstein and San Marino. What makes Monaco special is not the fact that the casino is world famous. Las Vegas is world famous too. It's all about Rainier, and it was all about Grace, and it's still all about Caroline, Albert and Stephanie.

Other city-states are just city-states.

Other casino towns are just casino towns.

Monaco is in a category all by itself.

As Louis de Polignac puts it, 'There's something special about a monarchy. I recall seeing Marshall Tito in a parade in Paris and the people stared at him as if he was an animal in the zoo. It's sort of the same with presidents. But I also once saw Queen Elizabeth proceed down the Champs-Elysées and the streets were filled with cheering crowds. Anyone can become a dictator or a president but to be a king or a queen or a prince or a princess is something one dreams about. Now, there are other monarchies, like in Scandanavia, but they're not often in the public eye, at least not outside Scandanavia. The English royal family is the top, of course. But Monaco's royal family is something unique. There's no doubt whatsoever that it was Rainier and Grace who made this little vest-pocket country known throughout the world.'

It was very much a team effort.

Grace's cousin John Lehman explains that he's watched that team effort since his first visit to Monaco in 1965.

'Monaco in those days was like something out of Central Casting. Dowager Russian princesses and out-of-work Balkan kings. Monaco was a very stodgy watering spot for European millionaires and down-at-the-heel aristocrats. But you could see changes starting. Rainier was determined to bring Monaco into the 20th century while still maintaining a certain dignity. He didn't view himself as the prince of the millionaires. He wanted to breathe life into the economy, to provide jobs and create a more wholesome environment for the people. Today it's the most remarkable achievement. Rainier and Grace accomplished it together. They were the most totally complete marriage I've ever witnessed. They were very different personalities but you can't separate them. Rainier's vision of Monaco was the guiding force. He clearly wore the pants. But she was no shrinking violet when it came to her own views.'

Like any good team aiming to reach a common goal there was a separation of responsibilities.

Grace never concerned herself with matters of state, politics or government. That was left to him. She dealt with anything that had to do with the arts, their social life, the running of the Palace and what might be called human relations.

There were times, the Prince says, when he spoke to Grace about affairs of state. But Grace once told her press attaché, Nadia Lacoste, that when he did mention such subjects it was almost as if he was merely thinking out loud. She acknowledged, 'I never give him any advice unless he asks for it.'

Not that she necessarily hid her opinions.

When François Blanc brought pigeon shooting to Monte Carlo in the last century he used live birds. When Grace moved to Monaco and saw how birds were being slaughtered, she begged her husband to abolish it. And he did. Later, when the new convention centre was being built and the question came up of a name for it, she proposed that it be named after him. The Prince's response was, 'That sort of thing isn't important to me.' Grace held her ground and in the end won out. But, as he's not the type of man who seeks self-promotion, it wasn't easy.

Like all couples they changed each other.

Nadia Lacoste suggests that Grace helped Rainier open up more. 'Because she was confident and supportive, she gave him confidence in himself. In turn, he helped her grow into her role as Princess. Within a few years she'd got to the point where she had nothing to prove to anyone anymore and was comfortable with that.'

Adds Gant Gaither, 'Rainier has a terrific sense of humour and I think he also helped develop that side of her. She was a very witty woman. But she did not have that same sense of humour as a young girl. It developed after her marriage. So did her interest in self-improvement. She was always studying something or other. I wouldn't have been surprised to find out she was trying to learn Chinese or hieroglyphics. She was always trying to improve herself.'

SBM might have been the principality's single most important business as far as employment is concerned but Rainier and Grace quickly became the principality's most visible and most important export. The marketing of that team was very much the marketing of Monaco and no one understood this better than Rainier and Grace themselves.

As a team they directed the rejuvenation of the Monte Carlo orchestra and brought world-class artists to perform there. Grace, as President of the Monaco Red Cross, convinced her Hollywood pals to come to the annual summer gala, which made it the biggest social event on the European calendar. They encouraged the revitalisation of SBM's hotels, built an addition to the hospital, sponsored races, rallies and regattas, oversaw vast improvements in the public utilities and communications, championed construction of the new golf course at Mont Agel and built the public swimming pool at the port. They travelled, appearing together at all the right places because being seen helped to bring tourists to Monaco. They worked hard to create a public image for themselves and the principality.

Grace turned out to be the magic Monaco had lacked since the *belle époque* dissolved into dusty volumes on library shelves.

'She showed a quality of belonging that I've found to be rare in people who suddenly rise to such a position,' Elsa Maxwell observed right after their marriage. 'And she made certain that what they did they did together.'

Notes the former Minister of State, André Saint Mleux, 'Perhaps one of Princess Grace's greatest achievements was to understand how to market Monaco to the outside world without ever once giving the impression that she was selling something.'

Not that their team work was confined to the selling of Monaco. Together they designed a new Palace projection room and the sky-blue, oval-shaped swimming pool in the Palace gardens. They bought the farm at Roc Agel and surprised a lot of people when word got out that Rainier was planting the gardens and the orchard himself.

Those early years were especially difficult for her because she was the one who'd made the biggest change.

She'd given up her career, right at the top, and in her mind there would always be a distant question mark over what might have been had she stayed in the business. She'd also given up her friends. Apart from Rainier, she didn't really know anyone else in the entire country. Then, she'd moved from comfortable rented houses in California and a well-appointed flat on Fifth Avenue to a huge empty Palace in the south of France that hadn't been lived in for any length of time in many years.

'The Palace itself was very beautiful,' Grace used to say. 'It was enormous but it was also a bit sad. It was uninhabited most of the year. But we planned to live in it all year long, to make it our home. So I threw open the windows, opened them all the way, put flowers in the pots and got a legion of people to sweep away the dust.'

Little by little, the two of them turned the Palace into a home.

They brought specialists from Italy to do stone-work and craftsmen from France to put the woodwork into shape. They spent a fortune restocking the period rooms with the correct furniture and tapestries. At the same time, they tried to make the most of their own fairly small private apartments. They lived in a terrace, off the main courtyard, Pullman car style, with all of their rooms in a straight line. There was a drawing room, dining room, study, the master bedroom, a dressing room and the children's room. You walked through one to get to the next one. Their three children were born in the study, which was converted for the purpose into a delivery room. Caroline and Albert shared a room with a sliding partition down the middle that could be closed at night.

When Stephanie came along she moved into Caroline's side of that room. But as the children got older, Rainier and Grace decided the arrangement wasn't very convenient so they built a wing onto the Palace and together they designed new private apartments.

Today, just over 100 people are employed at the Palace, including maintenance staff. Most of the 225 rooms are offices. There are only eight guest apartments. The Palace household staff numbers around 20, including cooks, valets, footmen and maids. These days, however, only a few of them work in the private apartments where Rainier lives alone with Albert.

*   *   *   *

Within a week of their marriage, Grace was pregnant.

She spent much of the summer of 1956 nauseous with morning sickness.

That autumn they sailed to the United States. It was Grace's first trip home as a Princess. It was also her first trip to the White House.

'We went to Washington and called on Eisenhower,' Rainier says.'He was a glorious figure but a bit dull, the way all military men are when they're out of their element.'

They returned to Monaco with two tons of white lacquered nursery furniture, a wicker crib and toys. The theme for the baby's room would be bushy-tailed rabbits.

Caroline Louise Marguerite was born in the rain on the morning of 23 January 1957.

It was a good sign.

According to the local superstition, a child born in the rain has health and character and brings prosperity. She was called Heiress Presumptive as she would lose her right to succeed her father if a boy came later. Still, all of Monaco rejoiced because Rainier had an heir, because the line was secure, because the child born in the rain had assured their continued freedom from the dreaded French tax man.

Towards the end of that year they took Caroline to meet her paternal grandmother.

Grace wanted to patch up the strained feelings between her husband and his mother. Charlotte had turned much of Marchais into a half-way house for ex-convicts. She'd given them shelter in the 100-room castle and found them work on its huge grounds with a three mile moat. Rainier felt it was too dangerous having such types around and he argued with his mother about it. Grace hoped the baby could somehow heal the wounds. This was not Charlotte's first grandchild. But Caroline would always hold a special place in her grandmother's heart. Just as 'Mamou' would in hers.

Within five months of Caroline's birth, Grace was pregnant again.

Albert Louis Pierre, now the Hereditary Prince of Monaco, was born on 14 March 1958.

Eighteen months later Rainier named Grace regent, issuing a decree that she would rule in the case of his death until Albert was 21. In the meantime, he'd given up sports car racing and skin-diving.

The children now occupied much of their free time. They still travelled but Grace flew with Albert in a separate plane from Rainier and Caroline. They began dividing summers between the Kelly house on the New Jersey shore and Roc Agel, where they moved into all 14 rooms and stocked the stable with two horses and a donkey.

They also did a lot of sailing although Grace was never much of a sailor. She convinced Rainier it might be better if he replaced the *Deo Juvante* with something that didn't rock back and forth quite as much. So he bought a handsome 40-year-old Spanish cargo boat. But that didn't exactly solve the problem because, as he put it then, 'Without bananas in the bottom it still rolls.'

She found she much preferred *The Christina*.

In 1962, Rainier and Grace joined Onassis on his boat with Maria Callas and a small group of friends for a cruise to Palma, Majorca. Rainier had taken a financial interest in the Son Vida Castle hotel there. Other friends were waiting for them when they arrived, including the inimitable Elsa Maxwell.

At this point pushing 80, Maxwell was living out her final years in *grande dame* style and loved to tell anyone who bothered to ask how she was the first person to say the Riviera should become a summer resort. She'd made it her life-long business to know everybody who was anybody and often bragged that in 1923 she included among her best friends, Sergei Diaghilev, creator of the Ballet Russe, and the Aga Khan, then probably the richest man on earth.

Diaghilev's company, housed for part of the season in Monte Carlo, featured one of the greatest dancers of all time, Nijinsky. He was an inarticulate, sombre man whose temperament bordered on schizophrenic off-stage. But Diaghilev knew how to bring out his unbelievable talent on stage and convinced all the great composers of the day, including Stravinsky and Debussy, to write music for him. By also commissioning painters like Picasso, Matisse and Chagall to design sets and costumes, Diaghilev spent money faster than it came in, even though his houses were usually always sold out. Despite the constant stream of debt-collectors at his door, he often said, 'I spend nothing on myself. My tastes are simple. The best is good enough for me.'

In honour of Maxwell's 40th birthday, Diaghilev staged the premier of not one, but two ballets. Because it was her night, he asked if she'd mind if a young Russian pianist played during the intermission. Maxwell, fearing an amateur, said it might be out of place. Diaghilev beseeched her. Maxwell agreed but then turned to the Aga Khan who was sitting next to her and apologised that she didn't have a choice. The young piano player's name was Vladimir Horowitz.

Now, in Majorca, it was Maxwell's turn at the piano.

Rainier and Grace and Onassis and Callas and the rest of their party had taken over the bar at Son Vida Castle. In the mood for music, Onassis begged Maxwell to play. She tried to back out. To encourage her Onassis announced, 'If you play the piano, Rainier will play drums and I'll sing.'

Callas immediately grabbed a set of maracas and Grace appointed herself the orchestra leader.

The ad hoc combo made music into the early hours.

A few days later they all went to a privately staged bull fight. In the middle of one corrida, Rainier jumped into the ring and grabbed a cape.

Elsa Maxwell later wrote, 'His footwork was splendid, almost professional, and he emerged from the ring without a scratch. When he popped back into his seat beside his wife, she turned, grinned at him, and clapped him roughly and affectionately on the back.'

On that cruise with them was their Lebanese friend, Khalil el Khoury.

'In a small group of intimate friends like that you could see how comfortable Rainier and Grace were together. He was 100% Latin and she was 100% American and, in spite of their differences of upbringing and culture, they functioned like a team. It was when they were forced to show themselves in public that they were sometimes under strain. Especially the Prince. She made him see more people than he might have tended to. But most couples are this way. They change each other. He became more sociable. She made him realise the virtues of public relations. The world became fascinated with Monaco's image and the family's image. He understood it and did it gracefully. I wouldn't say he loved every minute of it because he's the sort of man who prefers getting to know people on a one-to-one basis. His is the more reserved approach to life and people. But he did it because it was right for Monaco.'

Rainier and Grace also knew it was right for Monaco to encourage all sorts of well-known people to associate themselves in one way or another with the principality.

They sponsored celebrity tennis tournaments and convinced American television to tape shows there. The weekly galas attracted bigger and bigger names. So did the orchestra, the opera and the ballet. But they didn't just limit the stars to show business. They wanted celebrities in every field and sought out writers, artists, scientists and politicians.

Once again, Monaco became a place to be seen and that in turn attracted people who wanted to see.

There were times when you could walk down the street and bump into almost anyone, from Henry Kissinger – Rainier says, 'He stayed with us once in the Palace. He was very professorial. You'd ask a simple question and he'd answer with the entire university-level course' – to Albert Schweitzer. 'He gave a lecture here and the principality donated an operating-room, with all the equipment, for his hospital. I found his attitude to be a very noble one. I don't think enough has been said or written about him. Maybe he's even been a little forgotten. That's too bad. He set a great example, all the more so because what he did had no political resonance at all. He was far above that. His was pure human kindness and concern for people, with no other considerations.'

There's never been any doubt in Rainier's mind that having well-known people come to Monaco is always good for business.

'That's one of the reasons I encouraged Onassis to come home here. It was good for Monaco because his presence here was a great pull, especially for the jet-set. He was an attraction, if you will.

When Frank Sinatra stays at the Hôtel de Paris, business in the hotel and in the bar booms. Although these kinds of people are becoming more and more scarce. Cary Grant is gone. Winston Churchill is gone. How many are there left?'

Gone but hardly forgotten.

Churchill often came to the principality in the years before the war and just after the German surrender he returned for the first of several 10-week visits to the Hôtel de Paris.

Alex de Taglia, who retired in 1976 as the hotel's doorman, was then a floor valet. Because he spoke some English he was assigned to Churchill as his personal valet.

'For the most part Churchill stayed alone. Although he made daily visits to see his chum Lord Beaverbrook at Cap d'Ail. Sometimes I'd be straightening up his suite and he'd ask me to stop and chat with him. I got to see the two faces of Winston Churchill. He was very pleasant and open with me but when other people were around he was very serious and formal. Once I admired his paintings and he gave me a brush. He also once gave me a cigar, one of those really long ones. By the way, he never smoked the entire cigar. I'd see them when he crushed them out. He usually left at least half.'

Just as a brief aside to history, the reason he didn't smoke all of those really long cigars was because they weren't very good cigars. According to his London cigar merchant, Churchill didn't smoke good cigars until very late in life. And even then he hardly ever paid for them. Before the war he couldn't afford good cigars because he didn't have any money. Somewhere around the middle of the war the Cubans offered him a gift of 10,000 top-quality cigars. At that point he was smoking ten a day. Towards the end of his life he was forever being given cigars by friends and admirers. He only smoked those very large cigars in public to keep up his image. In private he smoked smaller, much better brands.

As Churchill spent his mornings reading and writing and his afternoons painting, his only real companions in those days were his dog and his parrot.

And one afternoon the parrot escaped from its cage and flew out of the window.

Churchill, believing that the bird was gone forever, was grief-struck.

He kept calling for the bird from his hotel window.

De Taglia rushed downstairs to inform the management, who duly dispatched most of the staff to search every corner of Monte Carlo.

They finally located the bird perched in a palm tree.

But no one could coax him down, so they rang for the fire department.

A huge hook and ladder arrived, sirens blaring, and a few minutes later the bird was duly returned to its owner.

Churchill immediately ordered champagne and asked that everyone involved with the rescue be brought to his suite for a drink.

'Many years later when he stopped here and I was the doorman', de Taglia recalls, 'I'd go to help him down the stairs but he'd push me away, saying he could manage. He was a very proud man.'

Rainier adds that he got to know Churchill fairly well, 'But I'm not sure anyone could have gotten to know very well. He came here a lot when Onassis was here. He was a great character. I found out that he loved to see films so Grace and I used to invite him to spend the evening with us. We'd built a projection room in one of the old stables and once or twice a week we'd show a film and serve a buffet supper. Except that he was such a stickler about food he'd eat dinner first at the Hôtel de Paris. He liked coming to us for movies because there weren't too many people and we'd always put a bottle of cognac next to him. I remember one of the films he saw with us was *Lawrence of Arabia*. Afterwards he was very excited and couldn't stop telling us, "I knew that man."'

Another Monaco regular was Cary Grant.

As handsome as ever, tall and tanned with snow-white hair, he always stayed in one of the guest rooms at the Palace. First with his daughter and later with his last wife, Grant returned year after year as a judge at the Circus Festival, giving the event that little extra touch of sophistication.

But of all the names associated in any way with the principality – besides Rainier and Grace and their family – the biggest draw since the early 1970s had to be Frank Sinatra.

There were some years when he'd only come for the Red Cross Ball.

Other years he'd show up for a month.

He'd take the big suite on the eighth floor of the Hôtel de Paris, play tennis at the Country Club, go to the Beach Club and hang out at some of the better-known restaurants. But he was most visible every evening when he held court in the hotel bar.

And, like Rainier said, when Sinatra was in residence, business boomed.

For the most part the years had mellowed him.

At least in Monaco his famous temper only got the better of him a couple of times.

Known for his contempt of the paparazzi, his bodyguards never hesitated when it came to shoving photographers out of the way. But it was a rare occasion when he did anything about that himself – like the night someone took a photo of him in a club and he decided he didn't want his photo taken so he grabbed the camera and smashed it on the floor.

It turned out the photographer was merely a hapless tourist.

Then there was the night that Sinatra and some of his chums were in a club and one of them had a pocketful of fire crackers.

They started throwing them around the room.

One of the fire crackers landed on the table of a certain Cuban woman who didn't think it was all that funny. She walked over to Sinatra's table and voiced her objections.

When no apology was forthcoming, she hauled off and slapped Sinatra.

That wasn't especially well received and she was slapped in return.

Storming out of the night club, the woman raced home and told her wealthy Cuban husband about the incident. He immediately grabbed a shotgun, got into his large American convertible car, put the top down and spent the night driving around Monaco like a Dodge City sheriff looking for Old Blue Eyes.

Discretion being the better part of valour, Sinatra left Monaco that very night for Nice airport where he chartered a dawn flight to Biarritz.

The 1970s was also the decade that the Arabs discovered serious money and beat a path to Monte Carlo to seek as much western decadence as their petrodollars could buy.

Among the most visible was Adnan Khashoggi, in those days said to be one of the three or four richest men in the world.

'He liked to think of himself as part of the jet-set,' Rainier explains, 'but he wasn't really. And anyway his star has faded a lot in recent years.'

Typically, Khashoggi loved to gamble for very high stakes.

But Khashoggi also wanted to gamble in a private room, either alone or with a few pals like the then Crown Prince Fahd of Saudi Arabia.

Anything is possible in Monaco, so Louis de Polignac, as Chairman of SBM, made the appropriate arrangements. However, he soon noticed that Khashoggi and Fahd only played roulette long enough to win. They then stopped.

Now, one of the basic rules of the casino business is always to get as many people around the table as possible. Otherwise, the punter is gambling against the house and not, as is preferable, against the other punters.

It's a simple insurance policy.

If there is one big winner at a crowded table then there will be lots of small losers and the casino will still come out ahead.

When Khashoggi and Fahd wanted to play alone, the casino was faced with a risk that whatever they won would not be offset by losses.

In reality, Khashoggi and Fahd were asking SBM to gamble against them.

Polignac told them, 'If you continue winning like that you'll bankrupt us. That's why I've given instructions that as soon as you lose a large enough sum we're going to close the table.'

Fahd was incensed. 'You can't do that. You're a casino so you have to let us play as long as we want to. It's not your choice to stop, it's ours.'

Polignac answered, 'But you're playing alone against me. You're richer than I am and the reason we're in business is so that we can win and you can lose. If you stop whenever you win, I can't continue. Therefore I have to stop when I win.'

Fahd argued that wasn't possible.

So Polignac proposed a deal. He said they could come to play in the private room, all alone, at any time of the day or the night. But once they were there they had to stay until 6 a.m. when the game would stop, no matter what the score was.

'You know what?' Polignac says, 'They played by those rules. They agreed to our deal. That's when they started losing and we started winning back the money they'd won.'

As crown prince, Fahd was well known as one of the highest rollers in Monaco.

One evening, around midnight, he and his entourage hit a roulette table at the Summer Sporting, betting as heavily as the house limits would allow. By 5 a.m. they were $2.4 million ahead. Two hours later they were $1.4 million in the hole. In 120 minutes the roulette wheel had turned around $3.8 million.

That's $527.70 or £310.41 per second!

'Those were the days when we used to get a lot of the Arab royals coming here,' Polignac comments. 'Some of them walked into the casino literally with suitcases full of money. I don't understand why because I can't see where they got a kick out of gambling. I don't think winning or losing ever meant much to them.'

An Arab royal Polignac found particularly odd wasn't even a gambler.

He flew in from London one afternoon with his daughter in his private Boeing 727 and explained to Polignac that he wanted an appointment with Prince Rainier so he could arrange for his daughter to become friends with Princess Caroline.

'I tried to explain that he'd arrived unannounced and it wasn't possible to get an audience for him. He never understood that, in spite of the bejewelled necklace he wished to bestow on Caroline to secure her friendship with his daughter, Prince Rainier and Princess Caroline simply weren't available. He got furious with me and left. He took his daughter and his necklace, got into his private Boeing 727 and flew away. I'd never heard of him before he arrived here and I've never heard of him since. Curious, no?'

Just as that gentleman packed his camel bags and stole away, many other Middle Eastern visitors to Monaco have since found greener pastures. They now seem to prefer Cannes.

'The reason why is simple,' Polignac continues. 'When they first came here – I'm talking about the important Arab royals – they all wanted private audiences with Prince Rainier. They'd come to me to arrange meetings with him, which I always tried to do. Naturally he'd receive the very important ones. But he simply didn't have time to see all of them, especially those distant relatives who called themselves princes. They got annoyed and took their business to Cannes.' Polignac shrugs, 'Au revoir.'

*   *   *   *

Grace brought teachers into the palace for Caroline and Albert when they were of kindergarten age, starting them off in school together. But she quickly decided that wasn't very wise even though they're only a year apart.

For much of his youth, Albert suffered from an awkward stutter.

And some people think it might have stemmed from that period.

Whatever the cause, it was a great concern to his parents.

Like both his parents, Albert was naturally shy. His speech problem only added to his timidity. But as he grew older he realised he could overcome it. Today there is no trace of the stutter left. He speaks slowly and at times very deliberately but the problem that haunted him during his childhood is gone.

Caroline, perhaps because she was that year older, became the outgoing one.

She was the one who always organised him and their friends into games. Her favourite game as they grew up was playing school. Albert and the others had to be the students. Caroline, of course, was always the teacher.

On 1 February 1965, after Grace had suffered a pair of miscarriages, Stephanie Marie Elisabeth joined them.

'The thing about them as a family', says Nadia Lacoste, 'is that they were just that, a real family. The Princess would read to her children in the evening. The Prince would balance all three kids on his shoulders or get down on his knees and play with them. They were a team at work and a team when it came to raising their children. They shared the feeling that it was important to be close, to be together. You know, to stick together. The Prince and Princess both wanted to make certain that their children had a happier childhood than they had.'

Rainier and Grace raised their family with some simple rules, like teaching them to believe that good manners are a virtue because everything rare is precious.

They were strict parents by modern standards, approving of old-fashioned manners, insisting on basic courtesies like 'please' and 'thank you' and generally rejecting any arguments in favour of what used to be called the 'permissive society'.

As Grace once put it, 'If one doesn't impose some discipline on one's children at an early age then life will impose it later on perhaps but with a great deal more brutality than any parent could be capable of. There was a time when religious institutions used to take over a child's education if the parents were too weak. Or boys would go off to the army. But the church seems to be falling to pieces and discipline in the army is out of favour.'

She used to say that she stressed certain moral principles with her children but agreed that getting any child to believe in such things was a struggle.

'You explain certain eternal values, in which you yourself believe implicitly, only to see everything you teach them contested and made fun of by newspapers, films, television, books and the theatre. I've also tried to treat my children in accordance with their different personalities. I've always respected in them the adults which they will one day become. I've never lied to them because I feel that would be tantamount to treating them as inferiors. At home I've insisted that they respect the rules of life which my husband and I have established. And when it comes to those rules, we are inflexible. He and I are both convinced a child senses that the discipline you subject him or her to is nothing more than a reflection of the love you have for that child. A child left to himself is an abandoned child. And abandoning your child is the worst injustice I can think of.'

While Rainier and Grace desperately wanted to raise their children in a normal way, like other children, there was never any doubt that Caroline, Albert and Stephanie were more privileged than most. Even if they couldn't be allowed the same freedom that average children know – they had to grow up with a bodyguard nearby – at least Rainier and Grace stressed that privilege should be earned and not simply expected.

Caroline was the first to realise they were not like other children.

'I was maybe 14. It wasn't a complete shock finding out that we were different from other kids because we'd sort of gotten used to certain things, like people taking our picture all the time. But that's when I started to see there were a lot of things my friends could do that we weren't allowed to do. Our parents were very strict with us. We weren't allowed to go the beach every day. They wanted us to stay home and read and take our school work seriously. We had to dress properly all the time. My mother didn't want me to wear a two-piece bathing suit when I was a teenager. She thought it would be more proper if I wore a one piece even though other girls my age were wearing bikinis. Like I said, mommy and daddy were very strict with us. We had to have somebody walk us to school and back. We couldn't just hang out with the kids. We didn't understand it then and I'm not sure I understand all of it now. I'm not sure all of it was necessary.'

She says, for instance, it wasn't always easy to have friends.

'When I was 12 it was a big deal to go and sleep over at a girlfriend's house. Everybody else did it but mommy wouldn't let me do it, except for a couple of times when she really knew who the people were. And we couldn't just ask friends over to the house. First we had to ask mommy. I'd come home from school to ask if so and so could come over and maybe she wouldn't be there or she'd be in her office so we'd have to wait and the day would go by. Then the next day I'd ask if my friend could come over and play and she'd say, maybe another day. When you're eight years old and want to play with your girlfriends and your Barbie dolls, it's not always easy to accept being told, maybe tomorrow. Mommy always used to say, "Maybe." She said it so often that I used to imitate her telling me, "I said maybe, and that's final." I guess what I'm saying is that we were a little too protected.'

Albert has the same reaction.

'I couldn't bring just anybody home either. I had to ask mom and dad and they always wanted to know who he or she was. It was sometimes hard to handle. But Caroline broke the ice so by the time she convinced our parents that it was sometimes all right to bring friends home, I was able to do it too.'

At least in that area, Stephanie appears to have had it easiest of all.

'I didn't have that much of a problem because I went to school in Paris and lived there with my mother. The rules weren't as tight at the apartment as they were for the Palace of Monaco. I could almost always bring girlfriends home or have a girlfriend stay over. Everything was more relaxed in Paris.'

Asking each of them who was stricter, mother or father, they laugh and answer in exactly the same way.

They each say, 'It was pretty even.'

But Caroline and Albert both contend that, of the three Grimaldi children, the one who got away with the most was Stephanie.

Being seven years younger than her brother and eight years younger than her sister, they claim that Stephanie was always the baby in the family and that generally meant she was the one who could do what the other two couldn't. Being freer than they were to bring friends home with her was just one example.

Says Albert, 'Stephanie learned very quickly how to wrap my mom around her little finger. And probably my father even more so than my mother. But don't tell him that.'

Stephanie however doesn't see it quite the same way.

'I was the smallest one so maybe it seems to them that I got more attention than they did. They were close enough in age that they had many of the same friends. They played a lot together. I was more alone at home. Then they went off to school and Caroline got married and I found myself the only one left at home with my mother and father. That's why they think I could wrap them both around my little finger. But there wasn't much of a contest because I was the only kid in the house.'

However, she admits, at the time she thought her parents were particularly strict with her.

'I remember when I was 15 or 16 thinking to myself that my father was the only father in the world who was that strict. I kept saying to myself, why are my parents giving me such a hard time? I always thought they were after me. Of course every teenager goes through that. I didn't realise until lately how lucky I really was. Looking back, I see now that it wasn't me being able to wrap them around my little finger as much as it was them being very understanding parents who helped me grow up. Every kid, at one point or another, thinks their parents give them a hard time. But when I look back I can see they did everything possible for me.'

Both her parents stressed the importance of developing true family values in their children. It was, she says, a central theme.

'We were raised to respect each other and to be honest with each other and above all to communicate with each other. We were raised to understand that we were a family. When any of us had a problem we'd bring it out, we'd talk about it with each other instead of just keeping it inside. We do it to this day. We've always done that.'

Early on both girls were exposed to music, opera and ballet, while Albert was encouraged to pursue his interest in sports. His father even set up a soccer net in the garden so he could play there. Caroline still maintains a very active interest in the classical arts and Albert still plays soccer and tennis and races power boats. They've both competed in events like the Paris–Dakar Rally while Albert is also an international class bob-sledder and a veteran of the 1988 Winter Olympics.

Stephanie is somewhere between the two.

'I did ballet when I was very young but stopped and went into swimming and gymnastics. I liked that. For a while I was even in training to be on the French national gymnastics team. I didn't make it though because I was too tall. I still read a lot but I can't say I read very intellectual books the way Caroline does. She reads philosophy and history. I like a good love story. We both love music but there again our tastes are hardly the same. I can't stand opera. On the other hand, I'm not sure she'd enjoy sitting through a *Guns N' Roses* rock concert.'

Where the three are very similar is that they were each raised to be multi-lingual.

They spoke English with their mother and their nanny but French with their father and the household staff. While they were still very young, Rainier and Grace also encouraged them to learn other languages. Today Caroline, Albert and Stephanie speak absolutely perfect French and equally perfect English with slightly east coast American accents. They each also speak German, Italian and some Spanish.

Rainier and Grace mostly spoke English together.

Grace however perfected her French, as she used to say, 'Because the children demanded that I do. Whenever I made mistakes they'd make fun of me so I had to learn to speak it well.'

Throughout the 1960s, Rainier and Grace stood side by side as battles raged with de Gaulle and Onassis.

In 1964 Rainier's father passed away.

Six months later Grace's father died.

In July 1967, while visiting Expo 67 in Montreal, she suffered her third miscarriage. She and Rainier wanted another child but it wasn't to be.

The 1960s became the 1970s and the decade dawned that might one day go down in Monaco's history as the greatest in modern times.

Rainier and Grace were totally in sync with each other.

And it showed in the easy way they appeared in public.

They were photographed driving in the vintage car rally from London to Brighton. It was too chilly for Grace so she cheated a bit, driving most of the way in a comfortable modern car and only getting into Rainier's 1903 de Dion-Bouton in time to reach the finish line.

And they were photographed at masquerade balls – Rainier with a bald wig and a huge black moustache and Grace with a fat-cheeked rubber mask and her hair in braids under a straw hat.

They were raising their children to be totally comfortable both as young royals at official ceremonies in Monaco and in the middle of touch football games every summer at camp in the Pennsylvania Pocanos.

'I don't think there is any formula for handling children,' Grace told a women's magazine when pressed to come up with an easy solution to the problem. 'All a parent can do is play it by ear and hope for the best. That and raise them with a lot of humour and a lot of love.'

No one who's ever seen them up close can doubt the love.

But one of the things that bothers Caroline about the way her family is often depicted in magazines and books is that the humour is never shown.

'They don't show us laughing, which we did a lot. My mother had a terrific sense of humour and so does my father. No one ever writes about that. Meal time was a time to tease each other. My parents always made sure that we'd have at least one meal a day together as a family. And when we did we laughed a lot.'

The story most people know is the one about Grace, Alec Guinness and the tomahawk.

It started when they worked together on *The Swan*.

Grace discovered that Guinness had received an over-adoring fan letter from a woman whose name has since been lost to time. For the next few weeks, wherever Guinness was, she'd have him paged, leaving a message from this woman. It drove him crazy, much to Grace's delight. To get even, he took a tomahawk that someone had given him and paid a hotel porter to sneak it into her bed. A few years later the same tomahawk mysteriously turned up one night in London between the sheets in Guinness's bed.

Guinness waited a few years before managing to have it put on her pillow while she was in the States. In 1979, when he returned to his Los Angeles hotel after having received a special Oscar, the tomahawk was in his bed waiting for him.

It went back and forth like that over the years without either of them ever mentioning it to the other.

It was their running gag.

Stephanie was with her mother one night when she discovered it in her bed and recalls, 'I never saw my mother laugh so much.'

But Caroline says that's only one of many stories because, as a family, they were always playing tricks on each other or inventing funny things to do.

For example, there was the time they threw a birthday party for the dogs.

'I was maybe about 11. Mommy and I realised it was one of the dogs' birthday so we decided to throw a party for him. I guess there were 10 or 11 dogs that came. They weren't all ours, of course, we invited some from the neighbourhood. You know, our dog's friends. Because this was a birthday party, we wanted to do it right. So we had party hats for the dogs and a paper table cloth on the lawn. We also had games for them to play and gave the winners prizes. We gave them bones. We had dog biscuits and cookies they could take home and even baked a chocolate birthday cake which we brought out to them with candles. They loved it. But then who doesn't love a birthday party?'

In 1957 Rainier and Grace hired a young English girl named Maureen King to be Caroline's nanny. When Albert came along she took charge of him too. At about the same time, Grace hired a young American woman named Phyllis Blum to be her secretary. And right from the start both Phyllis and Maureen found that their sense of humour melded well with Rainier's and Grace's.

Following one trip to the United States, Rainier returned with some dress shirts that he was very proud of. Maureen vaguely recalls that there was something new and special about them, like being his first permanent pressed shirts. Anyway, Phyllis's office was under the portico at the Palace, literally in the family apartments and Maureen was often given the extra chore of ironing the Prince's shirts in a little room next to the office. The Prince, being so fond of these shirts, kept reminding Maureen to be careful with them. She and Phyllis got the message. So they found an old sheet, burned holes it in and waited at the ironing board for him to check on Maureen's progress. The next time he poked his head through the door, there was Maureen ironing what appeared to be scorched remnants of his shirts.

They thought that was pretty funny.

Once they convinced him it wasn't really one of his new shirts, so did he.

Then there was the night that Rainier and Grace went out for the evening and Maureen stuffed their bed. She took Grace's nightgown and Rainier's pyjamas and filled them with pillows. The nightgowned pillow was reading a magazine. The nightshirted pillow was looking at a picture of Brigitte Bardot. To make the scene complete, she turned the lights way down so that at least on first glance it appeared that there really were two people in the bed. At the same time, Grace had just acquired a new puppy which hadn't quite been house-trained, so Maureen bought some plastic dog droppings and sprinkled them around the bedroom for good measure.

She went to bed hysterical.

When Rainier and Grace returned they could be heard shrieking for miles.

Maureen repeated the joke one night with Caroline.

They took an old shirt and some trousers and stuffed them to look like a body. They then snuck out of the Palace and hid it under some shrubs.

They thought it was a riot.

Unfortunately the security guards who found it weren't nearly as amused.

As Maureen says, 'It didn't go down terribly well.'

Not that Maureen or Phyllis escaped unscathed.

In Switzerland one evening, on a family ski trip, they were dining at a table on the other side of the room from Rainier and Grace. The waiter asked them what they wanted to drink with their meal and they jokingly answered, 'Whatever the Prince sends over is fine.'

The next thing they knew a bottle of Chianti arrived with a note that read, 'And you'd bloody well better drink it.'

They each had a glass or two.

Later that night the half-empty bottle showed up in their room with another note attached. This one read, 'Please finish.'

On another ski trip, Phyllis and Maureen left their window open to have some fresh air as they slept. But no sooner were they asleep than the attack began. Rainier and Grace were outside, pelting them in bed with snow balls.

On yet another trip, a ski lodge piano player smiled at Phyllis while Rainier was watching. He teased her about it, insisting that a romance was obviously on the cards. She protested her innocence. No sooner had they returned to Monaco when flowers arrived for

Phyllis from the piano player. The flowers were followed with notes swearing undying love and affection. She didn't know how to turn off the piano player, until she found out that Rainier was behind the whole thing.

Being raised in the confines of a Palace was not always easy and there were times when Caroline and Albert were less than pleased that their parents chose to attend official functions rather than have dinner with them. The two were especially peeved the night King Constantine was invited to dinner and they weren't. Instead of letting them pout, Maureen simply organised their own formal dress gala in the nursery. She attired Caroline and Albert in whatever finery they could find in their parents' closets, then called the butlers to serve dinner on silver trays.

Caroline so adored Maureen that years later the two still kept in touch. She even asked Maureen to be nearby for the birth of all three of her children. So Maureen was in Monaco for Andrea's and Charlotte's births and actually in the delivery room for Pierre's.

'I was right there,' she says. 'Even though I've had two of my own, I'd never really seen a baby being born. Well, I'm afraid I must have gotten a little queasy because I found myself having to go outside to get some fresh air. I waited until I felt better and then went to see Caroline in her room with the baby. I knocked on the door and the Prince opened it. He took one look at me and said right away, "They're just getting your bed ready for you now, dear."'

*　*　*　*

On Rainier's 25th anniversary in office, all 4,500 of Monaco's citizens were invited to a picnic.

And there was a lot to celebrate.

He'd ensured the principality's economic transition, multiplying the country's business turnover in a quarter of a century by nearly 200 times. Almost 700 firms were now doing business in Monaco, employing 18,000 people.

SBM's importance had been diminished and accounted for only about 30 per cent of the total of Monaco's business activities.

They were a rich, healthy and handsome family and, except for the constant pressure from the paparazzi, life was great.

Grace was even named by a magazine poll, 'World's Most
Youthful Woman', beating both Jackie Kennedy Onassis and
Sophia Loren to the finish line.

They bought a new apartment in Paris and fell in love with
Ireland.

Grace began collecting Irish books and Irish music and together
they bought the ancestral Kelly home. Those Irish books became
the basis of what is now the Princess Grace Irish Library in
Monaco, perhaps the most important collection of its kind outside the Emerald Isle.

Caroline went off to school in Paris and later Albert went off
to school in the States. Grace now spent part of the year in Paris
while Stephanie was at school there. Then Caroline announced her
engagement and the family was less than thrilled. There were tears
at the wedding but those might have been for the serious doubts
Rainier and Grace shared about their new son-in-law. Eighteen
months later they stood by their daughter as the marriage broke
up.

In the summer of 1981 the family decided to take a cruise
together.

Stephanie didn't join them because she was at summer camp
in the States.

But Rainier and Grace and Caroline and Albert and a few old
family friends, like Louis de Polignac, boarded the French ship,
Le Mermoz, and sailed up the coast of Norway to the North
Cape for a look at what was left of the late-summer midnight
sun.

Typical of all cruise ships, the *Mermoz* entertainment programme featured a costume night. The Grimaldis dressed as
pirates and joined in the fun, although they insisted that Louis
de Polignac go in drag as a little girl troll with big braids.

A few nights later was the ship's magic show.

Caroline and Albert had already met the magician and befriended him. So he invited them to be part of his act. Without
saying anything to their parents, on the day of the show, the two
of them snuck off to rehearsal.

That evening the magician announced that his grand finale
would be to saw a woman in half.

He asked for a volunteer.

Suddenly he yanked Caroline out of the audience.

Rainier and Grace gasped.

Caroline lay down in the box as the magician pulled out some very long knives.

Rainier and Grace were in a near state of shock.

After making a point of mentioning how the trick sometimes goes wrong, the magician sawed her in half.

Much to everyone's relief he also put her back together again.

Rainier now says he figured out right away that she must have been a part of the act. He was merely hoping that she'd do everything she was supposed to when she was supposed to do it.

Even today Caroline still laughs about that night. 'It was pretty hilarious.'

Then, a few weeks later, Grace got killed.

And everything changed.

*   *   *   *

8

Midday

E *VERY* parking meter in Monte Carlo is taken.

In the summer, the public beach along the Avenue Princess Grace is packed with people lying on inflatable mattresses or on huge towels, baking in the sun. Young men with flat stomachs and gold chains around their necks play backgammon. Young women, the tops of their bikinis casually tossed aside, rub oil on themselves as small beads of sweat trickle down between their toasted breasts. Children sit at the water's edge where the gentle ebb and flow of the sea covers the pile of smooth pebbles they've used to build a castle.

A helicopter flies in from Nice airport.

To the east, just past the border into France, the very private Monte Carlo Beach Club is like something out of Hollywood in the 1930s with rows of pinkish-coloured cabanas covered by green and white striped awnings and an old-fashioned wind sock stuck on the end of a tall pole so the driver of the boat that yanks people into the sky on a parasail knows which way the breeze is blowing. There's a small wooden pier that goes out from the rock beach – there's no sand here – to the lake-like sea. And further out there are two small docks floating on pontoons so that if you can swim that far you'll have a place to rest or sunbathe or simply collapse.

A waiter sets tables at the Café de Paris.

Facing the port, on the sundeck below the Hôtel de Paris where the indoor pool is heated all year to a constant 82.5 degrees, old men with paunches, gold Rolex Oysters on their wrists and spotless white terrycloth robes hanging loosely around their shoulders, walk barefoot to the bar where they order another glass of champagne for themselves plus another Kir Royal and a $35 or £20 Niçoise salad for the no-longer-so-young woman in the stylish one-piece bathing suit with the matching gold Rolex Oyster on the next chaise longue.

The man who runs a small supermarket around the corner from the railway station starts taking in his wooden baskets of peaches and green peppers and oranges and onions and lettuce so that he can close for a three-hour siesta.

In the winter, the public beach gets only the truly hearty types, who take a daily dip no matter what. The Monte Carlo Beach Club is closed. But the Health Club is open all year round and, if you know someone who rents one of the private sauna rooms, you can meet your lover there for what is called here – as it is in much of the world – an 'early matinée'.

In Monaco, a melon for lunch with a small piece of Parma ham on top can cost upwards of $40 or £27 depending on the restaurant.

Chinese waiters on one of the larger yachts in the harbour set out a buffet for the owner and his 20 guests, who will board the ship soon for a two-hour cruise to nowhere, consuming $6,800 or £4,000 in fuel, while the men in white slacks and blue blazers talk business and the women in their summer dresses discuss the price of shoes at the boutiques in Monte Carlo's newest shopping arcade.

An architect sits hunched over his drawing board desperately trying to finish the final designs on a small block of flats where a miniscule studio-flat will sell for $255,000 or £150,000 – and for that you still have to lean over the balcony, stand on tip-toe and twist your neck to get a glimpse of the sea.

Less than a hundred yards away, an old woman in Beausoleil, just across the Monte Carlo line in France, who always dresses in black and lives in a narrow, two-storey villa with a breathtaking view of the sea, draws her green shutters to keep the afternoon sun out. Then she shuffles towards the rear door, across her polished linoleum kitchen floor, pushing her slippered feet on top of a dish cloth so as not to dull the shine. Outside, in one corner of her narrow yard, there's a chicken coop. She bends down to fetch an egg and bring it back to her butane stove where she drops it in an old pot and boils it for lunch.

In Monaco, on any given day at noon, between omelettes, Niçoise salads, soufflés, quiches, flans and pastries more than 2,200 dozen eggs are cracked and cooked.

*   *   *   *

9

Grimaldi Inc.

*I*N *THE EARLY* 1800s the United States was heavily involved in naval commitments along the coast of North Africa.

A pair of costly expeditions against Libyan pirates gave rise to the feeling in Washington that the US Navy could use a refitting and supply station somewhere in the Mediterranean.

Florestan supposedly learned of America's interest, knew that his country's most valuable natural resource was its deep, protected harbour and considered negotiating the sale of his principality to the United States.

It was not such an outlandish idea.

The Russians later tried to buy nearby Villefranche to use as a base for the Czar's fleet. And Florestan's grandson, Albert I, would one day entertain a similar proposition from the Swiss.

There's no telling how history might have been changed had Florestan gone ahead with the deal.

Perhaps Monaco would today be the 51st state.

Then again, anyone who's ever witnessed bus-loads of American tourists climbing the steps of the casino to play the five franc slot machines might be excused for thinking the sale had indeed been concluded.

*   *   *   *

One hundred years ago gambling in Monte Carlo accounted for 100 per cent of the state budget.

Forty years after Rainier assumed office, the casino accounts for only about four per cent of the state budget.

The Prince brags, without any hesitation, 'We make more money on stamps than we do on roulette.'

Wearing grey slacks and a custom-made pale blue shirt open at the neck with his personal crest on the pocket, he's sitting on a couch in front of the huge fireplace in the double-storeyed living-room at the heart of his private apartments which take up the entire, newly built, left wing of the Palace.

It's a bright, airy room with marble floors, enormous French windows overlooking the private gardens and huge leafy green plants climbing towards the ceiling.

'In about 1976 or so,' he says, 'we found a series of old drawings and plans for the Palace and decided to add a wing on the west side of the main entrance. There'd been one here up to the end of the 18th century but it was destroyed during the French Revolution when the Palace was occupied and part of it was turned into a hospice. Sadly the Palace was emptied of everything it contained. We've since found a few of the original pieces – furniture and paintings, that sort of thing – and bought them back. But it would be impossible to find everything. Anyway, we got our architect to re-create this wing and Grace designed the apartment. This was our home.'

Furnished modern, with family photos in silver picture frames on almost every table, there's a small lofted study overlooking the living-room where the Prince sometimes works in the evening. Next to it is the small study which Grace occasionally used.

There's a dining-room and a kitchen leading off the living-room and down the hall there's a second, less formal living-room that doubles as a family room.

Upstairs there's the master bedroom, dressing-rooms and a large bathroom. Albert, Caroline and Stephanie each have a two-room suite there as well, separated by a large communal room where they had their desks and did their school-work.

'Grace was always very concerned with the Palace, in restoring it to its original beauty. She also paid great attention to Le Rocher, which is now an historic monument. The whole quarter around the Palace is protected. In order to build anything here you need a permit based on a very precise plan. You must conform to the traditional style of all the buildings on the Rock. Grace was so concerned with maintaining a sense of historical harmony here that she even changed the colour of the Palace. It used to be a kind of pale yellow. She thought that a pale, salmon pink might be better, more harmonious with the rest of the Rock, so that's the colour it is today.'

Grace's influence on him notwithstanding, some of the men who've worked with the Prince for many years and claim to know him best say that no one can rightfully claim to be his confidant and adviser in all things. They say that one of Rainier's great strengths is his uncanny ability to keep things compartmentalised.

Others lead you to believe that the secret to his success lies in his instincts.

They portray a man true to his Mediterranean heritage, an emotional man, one who relies on his feelings, a man who has come to depend on his intuition.

He is not, they assure you, the sort of man who goes about things in a scientific way.

While he's looked upon as head of Grimaldi Incorporated, a family business which happens to run a country – even he sometimes refers to himself as, 'Chairman of the Board of Directors of a business called Monaco' – he is willing to agree that he is the sort of man who sees opportunities rather than someone who studies balance sheets and worries about decimal points.

'In a way, the principality has become a family business. I don't think it's really Grimaldi Inc. and I'm not certain it will ever turn into that. But it's much more business-like now than it was years ago. The way the world is today, it had to become that.'

But it didn't happen overnight.

He brought about a fundamental change, turning the principality from a company town into an economically viable industrial state, the only way it could have happened, slowly.

'I was born here and I've lived here, basically, all my life. When it comes to dealing with the people, understanding them, that's a major advantage I've had over my predecessors. Perhaps it was less important for the Monégasques that the Prince be born here and live here in, say, my grandfather's day. I don't think it mattered much that my great-grandfather was out at sea six months a year or that my grandfather spent most of his time in Paris or at Marchais. There wasn't the same volume of business or events in those days that you find here today. Now it's become much more important. One can't any longer be a part-time prince because this is a full-time job and the people here know that. They also tell me they feel secure when they see my flag flying on the residence. That's why Grace and I agreed that it was very important for our children to be born here and also to be educated here. I didn't go to school here and I found it was a drawback not knowing my generation very well. Grace and I decided that Albert should go to the high school here and get his pants dirty with the other guys. When he takes over he'll have grown up with an entire generation here. He'll know them all. That's a benefit I didn't have.'

For the most part, the Monégasques are small shop-owners, taxi drivers, croupiers, government functionaries, doctors and lawyers.

Very few Monégasques wheel and deal in international business.

With the exception of the ones who have made names for themselves in real estate, many Monégasques find themselves caught in the paradox of living in a country with one of the highest living standards in the world, yet not always being able to afford it.

'When the real estate boom hit, one of the immediate effects was that many Monégasques could no longer afford to buy an apartment here. That's why I steered legislation through so that there are buildings where flats are sold at cost to Monégasques, who are further aided with generous terms on long-term loans.'

In essence, Rainier literally looks on his subjects as one big family.

He may even be the only monarch in the world who, though he doesn't necessarily know every one of his subjects by name, at least has probably met them all.

Under the state's benevolence, children and old people are looked after. Equally, it's almost unthinkable for a Monégasque to be fired. They live better than their economic and social equivalents in nearby Nice or Menton because the Prince sees to it.

'The younger generation no longer looks towards SBM for employment the way their fathers did. Most of them realise that, having gone to university, there are other possibilities open to them. So the old adage that every Monégasque is born with a croupier's rake in his hand simply isn't true any more. A lot of them are tempted to work for SBM because the salaries are high and the benefits are good. But SBM is no longer the only game in town. We offer good scholarships to our students so they can go into the professions and many of them go on to study abroad.'

Despite the 1962 power-sharing constitution, Rainier's understanding of the special mentality of his people, the respect with which they regard him after 40 years in office, the skills he's developed over those years and his own dogged determination to steer the ship of state mean it's very rare that anything important ever happens in Monaco without the Prince's consent.

He alone is the driving force.

But he can't control everything.

'Of course not. For instance, there is little we can do about the exchange rate of the dollar against the French franc. And when the dollar is weak you clearly see it reflected in diminished tourism. In 1986 the French government insisted that Americans have visas to enter France. That also affected us. Then too, terrorism plays a role. Americans don't travel when terrorism in Europe captures the headlines even though Monaco might well be the safest country on earth. Americans are also very sensitive about international relations. When Jacques Chirac as Prime Minister of France refused to allow American F-111 bombers to use French air space in the 1986 attack on Libya, American tourism slowed in France and consequently slowed here too because the Americans were annoyed at France.'

Nor is this just a phenomenon of the 1980s.

Outside influences have always forced changes on Monaco but rarely have they been more noticeable than in the 1960s and 1970s.

A quarter of a century ago Monaco attracted a certain type of international jet-setter who knew all the other international jet-setters. People like Onassis and Niarchos. And Dino de Laurentis. He always seemed to be there, at least as long as he was in love with Silvana Mangilo.

As a clan, united in wealth and the pursuit of pleasure, they assembled each year at the Hôtel de Paris, threw parties for themselves on each other's boats and gambled together in the *salles privées*.

Thanks in large part to Princess Grace and the publicity she created for Monaco in the United States, Americans now joined the crowd.

There was Henry Ittleson, chairman of C.I.T. Financial, and movie producer Sam Spiegel. There was Charles Revson of Revlon Cosmetics and real estate magnate Bill Levitt of Levittown Fame.

Revson always docked his boat, *Ultima II*, next to Levitt's boat, the *Belle Simone*, and in those days those two boats were usually considered the most beautiful yachts in the world.

There was also a regular band of Italian industrialists.

One in particular started out after World War II repairing bicycles and soon developed his business into the largest refrigeration company in Italy. He had absolutely no interests in life except Italy's national soccer team and occasional weekends in Monte Carlo. He'd show up in his private plane every few months and toss 5,000 franc chips around the casino as if they were pennies. He managed to average about $1 million in gambling losses a year and went on that way for eight or nine years, until he died. But, for those few days every few months, he liked to think of himself as the king of Monte Carlo.

He was, more like it, a dinosaur from another era.

Fiat tycoon, Gianni Agnelli, for example, who'd been a regular at Monte Carlo, eventually told the Managing Director of SBM, 'I can't afford this any more.' He was still probably the richest man in Italy and certainly one of the wealthiest men in Europe but as an industrial leader he was suddenly under the scrutiny of the labour unions. He felt that if they saw him gambling his nights away he wouldn't be able to negotiate with them on a very sound basis.

That quickly diminishing breed of hard-core gamblers, who arrived every summer to stay for a month, divided their time between the Beach Club and the casino at the Summer Sporting.

But by the mid-1960s the Summer Sporting was a slightly seedy place, too small, not air-conditioned, its tropical ambience created by nothing more than a string of harshly coloured lights shining on a couple of palm trees.

Admittedly, the ones who showed up were big players, high rollers, but 75 per cent of the casino's total takings came in during July, August, Easter week and the week between Christmas and New Year. While 80 per cent of the total takings came from fewer than 2,000 known clients.

The rest of the year Monte Carlo was three or four little old ladies sitting in the Hôtel de Paris having tea.

Many hotels, like the Hermitage and the Old Beach, closed for the winter.

There was no young, international, year-round community.

There were hardly any foreign companies in Monaco.

There was limited industry.

Off-season, Monaco was very quiet.

So quiet, in fact, that when Pan Am sponsored a feasibility study to build an Intercontinental Hotel there in 1964 the result was negative.

The state didn't have sufficient funds to back the project and the only other man around who might have been interested, Onassis, didn't see any reason to help a company which would be in direct competition with SBM.

So Pan Am dropped the plan.

They couldn't come up with a single backer who believed in the future of Monaco.

Rainier concedes, 'It was pretty obvious that no company could survive very long on such a short season and with a regular clientele that was actually smaller than the number of employees in the company.'

But then several things occurred, all at about the same time, to change Monaco forever.

It began when Rainier wrested control of SBM away from Onassis.

Up to that point, everything at SBM was still very antiquated. The stoves in the Hôtel de Paris kitchen dated back to 1899. The kitchen staff included men to carry coal to those stoves and one fellow in the basement whose job it was to receive huge blocks of ice, cut them up by hand and send them in plastic bags to various bars around Monte Carlo.

Worse still, most of SBM's personnel lived off the fat of the land.

If they worked in a kitchen, SBM's food was their food.

If they worked in a restaurant, SBM's silverware was their silverware.

Rugs, furniture, glasses, whatever anyone needed at home, they simply helped themselves.

And no one batted an eyelid.

If you worked for SBM, then SBM took care of you for life.

Within a year of the state assuming majority control of the company's shares, strikes and a student revolt crippled France. In solidarity with their French brothers, the unions in Monaco also went on strike. Even the croupiers walked out of the casino, although theirs might have been the only picket line in history where the protesters arrived in Cadillacs and Mercedes.

The 1967 take-over of SBM combined with the 1968 social unrest resulted in a series of sweeping changes which not only included refurbished kitchens and things like a central buying office for the company but also the establishment of a minimum wage for all SBM employees, regularly scheduled holidays and the guarantee of year-round employment.

But SBM still wasn't ready for the 21st century.

A long way from it, in fact.

It would be another 15 years before the company would invest $100 million in a five-year refurbishment programme to modernise the hotels, construct a 1000-space parking lot under the Place du Casino and build a new Café de Paris, in the style of the original 19th century cafe.

They took the American games – craps, slot machines and 38-number roulette – out of the casino and put them in the rear of the cafe, Las Vegas style, so that they could turn the clock back in the casino, making it into the same sort of elegant private club it was when Edward VII and the Russian Grand Dukes played there.

Monte Carlo was finally trying to earn back its reputation as the Mecca of casinos.

The lights might be brighter in Atlantic City and the games might be faster in Las Vegas but if you haven't won or lost at Monte Carlo, you're still in the minor leagues. So the punters began to return to Monaco the way the faithful go to Lourdes. No matter what the result of the visit, at least you've been to the most famous altar in the world.

'You can't really compare Las Vegas or Atlantic City with Monte Carlo,' says Rainier. 'There isn't a lot of elegance in Las Vegas or Atlantic City. Nor is there a lot of charm there either. I would never want to see in Monaco some of the things I've seen in Las Vegas. It was very depressing to see people in wheelchairs stuck for hours in front of the slot machines. The casino at Monte Carlo isn't merely a place for gambling, it's an historic monument.'

The Prince might well like to think so because, in truth, there are very few places in the world where a tiny park like the Place du Casino is surrounded by buildings as architecturally interesting as the casino, the new Café de Paris and the renovated Hôtel de Paris.

Yet, inside the Café de Paris, there are all those five franc slot machines and crap tables surrounded by tourists who've just stepped off a bus that stops in town for only an hour, tourists in bermuda shorts crying out, 'Shoes for baby', as they toss the dice. Only three minutes down the hill, at the Loews Hotel, more tourists are playing the same games at the casino there, where entry is open to anyone over the age of 21.

Both the Café de Paris and the Loews look like Las Vegas or Atlantic City and sound that way too.

The contrast between the old casino and the newest games in town is startling.

Some people say that in order to compete with Las Vegas and Atlantic City, or even just with the casinos along the beach at Nice and Cannes, SBM has had to go down-market, has had to try to come up with a mini-Vegas.

But around Monaco they don't see it like that.

They say they've merely tried to offer visitors two different kinds of things. There are some Americans, for instance, who want to recreate America no matter where they are. So SBM gives them a little bit of America, something modern, something casual. They can even find hot dogs, if that's what they want. Other clients want something more refined so SBM offers them the taste of another era, something very traditional.

But again, none of that happened overnight.

You need a lot of time to change things at SBM.

Consider the fact that it took a 90-minute lecture from SBM's managing director just to get the various hotel chefs thinking about a new dessert menu.

As Monaco moved into the 1970s, Rainier was more convinced than ever that the principality could no longer exist solely on gambling. SBM might generate a lot of business but it was clear that it could no longer generate all of the country's business. So the Prince turned towards a policy of creating light industry.

Two things were involved.

First he aimed to attract very specific types of businesses to Monaco.

'We chose business carefully because we didn't want to ruin the place. The principality was off limits right from the start to any business that would require vast amounts of space, such as an automobile assembly plant. Then, no pollution of any kind could be permitted. No air, sea or noise pollution.'

Next, he had to come up with somewhere to put these new businesses.

'There were severe space limitations. But by 1974 we'd re-claimed about 53 acres from the sea. It enabled us to create Fontvieille, an entirely new quarter where we could house light industry. It meant that we could actively seek foreign investment and take yet another step away from a dependency on tourism. We expanded our borders peacefully. A rare thing these days, no?'

There are currently over 100 factories operating in Monaco, many of them successfully established in Fontvieille where the principality has also built a public housing project and a new three-star hotel.

'The industry here is generally light manufacturing. We looked to bring in industries with a high cost improvement factor, such as pharmaceuticals, perfumes and some electronics. Today we make small electrical components for the Concorde and NASA. Did you know that the shaving razors for the first astronauts were made in Monaco? They were wind-up razors. There are also certain plastic and rubber parts made here for Renault, Citroen and Peugeot. There are pharmaceuticals and beauty products either made here or packaged here. The point is that there is no unemployment in Monaco. In fact, we have to import 4,000 French people and 3,000 Italians every day to work here.'

With the main thrust of the tourist season confined to just over four months of the year, Rainier now looked for ways of filling hotels and restaurants for the other eight.

That was the beginning of Monaco's aggressive policy of attracting conventions.

To cut themselves into the European convention business they first had to provide world-class facilities. There was hardly any-thing suitable in Monaco. The Hôtel de Paris didn't even have a decent room for cocktail parties.

So they built a convention centre that could comfortably take groups of 400 – 1,000 delegates and next to it the Loews Hotel Corporation constructed a 573 room hotel, the largest on the coast. In the past ten years, just over 25 per cent of the visitors to Monaco have come for a convention.

But this was not achieved without a few minor growing pains.

When one of the new convention hotels was being planned, someone noticed that no provision was made to put bidets in the bathrooms. Bidets, the American designers explained, were not used by Americans and this was, after all, the Americanisation of Monaco. No, the local authorities corrected them, this was

Monaco was just a quiet fishing village (*centre left*) until the end of the 19th century when Monte Carlo put the Principality on the map; the Ballet Russe (*centre right*) and gambling brought the beautiful people each winter (*top right*); but it wasn't until the Riviera changed from a winter to a summer resort (*top left*) that modern Monaco was born (*bottom*).

Top photos courtesy of SBM, other photos courtesy of Photo Arch., Palais Princier, Monaco.

L'HIVER à MONTE-CARLO

LES GENS CHIC SONT

L'ÉTÉ à MONTE-CARLO

THÉATRE DE MONTE-CARLO
SOIRÉE DU 19 AVRIL 1911

BALLET RUSSE

Opposite page, clockwise: The original casino at Monte Carlo which failed; Francois Blanc, the man who turned gambling at Monte Carlo into a world class attraction; the opulent setting that Blanc created; the casino today, next to the Hotel de Paris on the Place du Casino; one of the private rooms where opulence is maintained today.

This page, clockwise: In the days when he was flush, Egypt's King Farouk was a major Monte Carlo player; world-class opera was a major attraction, financed by Camille Blanc (*left*) it featured performers such as Enrico Caruso (*centre*) under the artistic direction of the legendary Raoul Gunsbourg (*right*); an unsuccessful gambler.

This page, top to bottom: Prince Albert, the navigator (in dark uniform) at a ceremony with his son Prince Louis II, just before World War 1; Prince Rainier II at his investiture in 1949, seated in between his mother and father with his sister, Antoinette, on the extreme left.

Opposite, clockwise from top right: Rainier aged four years; born with a sense of adventure he has always loved the sea, enjoyed fast cars and motorcycles, and kept wild animals as pets.

All photos courtesy of Photo Arch., Palais Princier, Monaco.

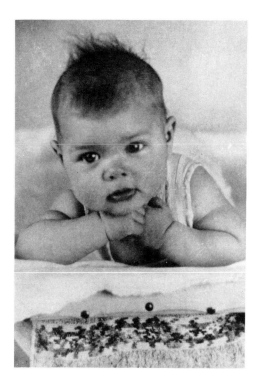

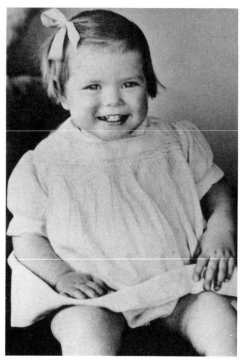

This page, clockwise: Grace Kelly at nine months, at two years and at 12 years. *Opposite*: It was Grace's ice-cold beauty – a new kind of sex appeal in the 1950s –which made her a show-business star at the age of 20 and (*bottom*) at Cannes, the day after she met Rainier.

Photos courtesy of Photo Arch., Palais Princier, Monaco, except bottom far right, courtesy of Popperfoto Ltd.

Bottom left: Romance blossomed between Rainier and Grace with the help of Rainier's Irish friend, Father Tucker. *Top*: The engagement ring marked the official start of the endless Rainier-and-Grace-must-now-pose-for-photographers season of 1956 – they are shown here with her parents. *Bottom right*: Photographers even followed Grace to lifeboat drills, with her poodle on the ship to Monaco.

Photos courtesy of Popperfoto Ltd, except bottom left, courtesy of Photo Arch., Palais Princier, Monaco.

Top: Grace arrives in Monaco to a standing-room-only harbour in April 1956.
Bottom: Only her hat got in the way of the joyous arrival of Rainier and Grace.

Photos courtesy of Photo Arch., Palais Princier, Monaco (F. Picedi).

This page, clockwise: First there was a civil wedding, then there was the religious ceremony in the cathedral. It was a wedding that captured the imagination of the world.
Opposite page: She was a fairy-tale bride.

This page, clockwise: The early years at home, and on holiday – but not all photos of them helped to maintain this happy image – this picture ran the day after John Kennedy was shot and was interpreted as tasteless, although it was taken hours before the assassination.
Opposite page, top: Breakfast with Caroline and Frank Sinatra in the gardens of the private apartments and (*below*) Rainier and Grace on official duties with Caroline, Rainier's father, – Prince Pierre, Albert, and the nannies.

Photos courtesy of Photo Arch., Palais Princier, Monaco (G. Lukomski) except bottom left, courtesy of Popperfoto Ltd.

The family photo album. *Clockwise*: Monaco's most famous Red Indians, Black Eagle and Pink Pearl, on the warpath; cowboys at the Roc Agel corral; Rainier at home with Caroline; Grace at the beach club with Caroline and Albert.

Photos courtesy of Photo Arch., Palais Princier, Monaco, except top left, courtesy of Maureen Wood.

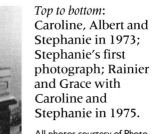

Top to bottom:
Caroline, Albert and
Stephanie in 1973;
Stephanie's first
photograph; Rainier
and Grace with
Caroline and
Stephanie in 1975.

All photos courtesy of Photo
Arch., Palais Princier,
Monaco.

Left: Out on the town. *Right*: At the finishing line of the
London to Brighton Vintage Car Rally in Rainier's 1903 De
Dion-Bouton. The Grimaldis started and ended the race as a
family, but for most of the race Grace, Caroline and Stephanie
sacrificed glory for the warmth of a modern car.

Photos courtesy of SBM (left) and Popperfoto Ltd (right).

Faces seen in the Monte Carlo crowds.
Clockwise from bottom left: Grace with Maria
Callas; at the Red Cross Ball with Sinatra;
Rudolf Nureyev, Margot Fonteyn, Grace
and Maria Besobrasova; Aristotle
Onassis.

All photos courtesy of SBM.

Top: David Niven lived just down the beach and was a family friend.
Left: Anthony Burgess still lives in Monaco and helped Grace establish the Irish Library. *Right*: Winston Churchill painted the Riviera whilst living for months at a time at the Hotel de Paris.

Above: Caroline with her husband Stefano, sons Pierre and Andrea and daughter Charlotte. *Below*: with her son Andrea and *opposite*: with her dad.

Photos courtesy of Photo Arch., Palais Princier, Monaco; Popperfoto Ltd and Frank Spooner Pictures Ltd respectively.

Opposite page, anti-clockwise: Albert as a child with his father, as a teenager with his mother, and as Monaco's young hereditary prince.
This page, clockwise: Running out of luck at the Paris-Dakar rally, jogging during his university years at Amherst; and these days, at his father's side.

Photos courtesy of G. Lukomski, Photo Arch., Palais Princier, Monaco except this page top left and right courtesy of Frank Spooner Pictures Ltd.

Opposite page, anti-clockwise:
Stephanie, as a child with Grace;
grown-up with her mother at the
Red Cross Ball; and with her
father, walking the dog in Paris.

Photos courtesy of Jacques Haillot, Photo Arch.,
Palais Princier, Monaco; Popperfoto Ltd; and
Gilles Merme, Frank Spooner Pictures Ltd
respectively.

This page, top to bottom: As a model
Stephanie could demand
enormous fees for a day's work –
this advertisement ran in the
States; but she gave up
modelling for a singing and
acting career and has already
produced a smash-hit single and
album.

Photos courtesy of Frank Spooner Pictures Ltd
and Popperfoto Ltd respectively.

This page, clockwise: In quieter moments Rainier spends time at his Roc Agel workshop and sailing, but he considers his responsibilities as Monaco's sovereign to be of primary importance. *Opposite page*: Grace loved needlepoint and wrote a book about flower-arranging.

All photos courtesy of Photo Arch., Palais Princier, Monaco (G. Lukomski).

Top to bottom: Reading poetry – here with actor John Westbrook – was the closest Grace could get to a show-business comeback; Diana's first public appearance after the announcement of her engagement to Prince Charles was at a Princess Grace poetry reading. Grace was especially sympathetic to Diana's discomfort at the public attention she was suddenly exposed to.

Photos courtesy of Photo Arch., Palais Princier, Monaco and Reg Wilson, Opera Press Office, respectively.

Top to bottom: Grace's last Circus Festival, in December 1981, with Cary Grant, Caroline and Rainier; her final Red Cross Ball, in July 1982.

Photos courtesy of Frank Spooner Pictures Ltd and Popperfoto Ltd respectively.

Gracia Patricia, November 1929 – September 1982.

A family in mourning.

Rainier and his family today.

Photos courtesy of Photo Arch., Palais Princier, Monaco (top) and Popperfoto Ltd (bottom).

not the Americanisation of Monaco and anyway, bidets are a basic necessity in the civilised world. So bidets were duly added to the plans.

It was at about this time that Monaco, and in a particular Monte Carlo, was seized with real estate fever.

Putting the railroad underground paved the way but it took the outbreak of terrorism in Italy, combined with a real danger that the Communist Party could come to power there to send apartment prices in the principality sky-high.

To protect themselves and to protect their assets, Italians flooded into Monte Carlo.

Prices hit outlandish heights.

While you could buy a flat in Nice for FF 15,000 per square metre – $3,750 or £1,800 – or 18,000 FF per square metre in Cannes – $4,500 or £2,200 – there was a firm market in Monte Carlo for flats at FF 30,000 per square metre – $7,500 or £3,600.

Building sites sprouted on every corner.

At one point in the late 1970s there were no fewer than nine major projects under construction, with 85 per cent of those new flats pre-sold.

Such was the craziness of the market that some flats changed hands two, three and four times when they weren't much further along than the blueprint stage.

Everybody suddenly became a real estate speculator.

It was the '49 gold-rush all over again.

Enormous fortunes were made.

But prosperity was not without its price.

Some people think the Prince didn't speak up soon enough or loud enough and that too many unattractive buildings were allowed to change Monte Carlo's skyline. They say it could have been done differently, more tastefully, but because there was so much money involved and because it all happened so fast, controls and checks on the aesthetics of the urban development of Monte Carlo were too lax.

It got to the point that high-rises were allowed to be built along the beach at Monte Carlo, some of them so badly planned that in the middle of the high season, at three in the afternoon, shadows are cast across the beach.

Grace was especially disappointed.

'I agree that it all happened too fast,' Rainier says. 'I didn't necessarily like it either. But what can you do? You can't make regulations that cover everything. As long as the builders are in conformity with the rules you can't say, "I won't allow this because it doesn't suit my taste." However, I don't entirely agree that Monte Carlo has been spoiled. The alternatives were to leave the place as it was or to have a spread of low-level building. And that gets back to a question of investment. People won't put their money into a project if it isn't large enough to make it worth their while. As soon as we realised what was happening we did try to change things. We put limits on the height of a building which any individual could build. But then builders started pooling their allocations in order to build very tall apartment houses. They got around the laws. So we tightened the laws.'

The days of the great building boom are almost certainly over.

What happened in Monte Carlo in the 1970s won't be repeated.

Building permits are less easy to come by and now that there's so little room left aesthetics are a concern.

Yet anyone who thinks Monaco has reached the saturation point doesn't know Monaco.

The Prince says that no more permits to build high-rises will be granted. So the developers have set their sights on the old buildings, especially around the port, that have passed their usefulness. They'll build new ones there and by the time those are finished, the ones that used to be new when the building boom began will be old and have to be replaced as well.

*   *   *   *

For the most part, there are only two things you can do with a postage stamp.

You can stick it onto a letter and send it to someone.

Or you can put it into an album with a whole lot of other stamps and look at it from time to time.

But any stamp paid for and then pasted into an album is a service paid for and never returned in kind. Which is why post offices throughout the world encourage stamp collecting.

Stamps have been used in Monaco ever since they became commonplace in France in 1848. Yet it wasn't until 1885 that Prince Charles III created the principality's own stamps bearing the sovereign's effigy.

Some 1,250 or so issues later, the stamps of Monaco not only trace the principality's history but have also commemorated trains, planes, fish, fauna, flowers, racing cars, boats, local churches, saints, great works of art, animals, radio, television, sport and the circus. In short, anything and everything that might be considered a category for collecting.

There are generally two issues a year, one in spring and one in the autumn, making a total of, on average, 30 new stamps. With some 50,000 subscribers around the world waiting for each new stamp, the Postage Stamp Issuing Office is assured of selling nearly all of the stamps within a few weeks.

Rainier takes an interest in the stamps, approving every new issue, not necessarily because he collects them – although the Palace museum exhibits every issue of the principality's stamps – but because for Grimaldi Inc., this is a very big business.

'We deliberately aim at the collectors' market,' he explains. 'While most other countries use modern offset printing methods, we engrave our stamps because we want them to appreciate in value as an encouragement to more collectors. However, it's a very delicate business. If you bring out too many stamps no one wants them and they lose their value in the market. If you bring out too few stamps you can't make enough money because you don't have the products to sell.'

Monaco's postage stamps are known throughout the world.

On the other hand, Monaco's coins are not.

Through an agreement with France, coins are struck as a symbol of Monaco's sovereignty. The principality has had its own coins since 1640 and today a complete collection would number about 500 different coins. However, the total value of coins now in circulation is under $1 million or £600,000.

French currency is generally used and many visitors aren't ever aware of the fact that they might have Monégasque coins in their pocket. They are the same size, shape, weight and denomination as French coins. The difference is that they bear the face and seal of the Monégasque sovereign.

The coins are legal tender only in Monaco, the Maritime Alps and the Var.

Try using one in Paris and the shopkeeper is likely to throw it back at you as if it was foreign currency, which is exactly what Monaco's coins are intended to be.

*   *   *   *

Monaco doesn't have a prison.

Instead, there are 37 modern cells for people awaiting trial. Divided into three areas to segregate men, women and minors, they stretch along the outer wall of Le Rocher facing the Mediterranean.

But the rumour that this is *la tôle sur mer*, a slammer with a view of the sea, is not true.

The best view any prisoner gets is of the sky.

What makes the place special is that the warden's wife personally does the cooking. So Monaco's is almost certainly the best eating cell-block in the world.

Justice in the principality is rendered in the name of the Prince, who can pardon or diminish sentences. But as the National Council has long since abolished capital punishment, the Prince cannot decree, 'Off with his head'. And, even if he could, Rainier grimaces, he doesn't think he would. 'That's a pretty messy business.'

Yet the Prince can expel someone from the principality.

If he wants to, by agreement with France, he can even order the expulsion to include the three neighbouring French *départements* which are the Maritime Alps, the Var and the Lower Alps.

Not that it happens very often. That's usually restricted to people who are condemned in Monaco for criminal activity, such as cheating in the casino.

'France has the same interest as we do in keeping certain people out of the region,' he says. 'The only exceptions to this are Monégasques. I cannot deprive them of their right to live in Monaco. Otherwise, they'd have no place else to go.'

However, there have been expulsions in the past not confined to criminals.

The most publicised was the 1958 banishment of the infamous 'Champagne' Lady Docker.

Born in the north of England in 1907, Norah Turner came to London in the 1930s to work as a taxi-dancer at the Cafe Royal where she not only acquired a taste for pink champagne – earning her a life-long nickname – but met the first of her three millionaire husbands.

The woman who once admitted, 'I do not think I could have ever married someone poor, not even for love,' married Clement Callingham, who introduced her to the joys of a Rolls-Royce, a Daimler, a weekend barge in Holland and holidays on the Riviera.

When Callingham died in 1945 and left her £175,000, she invested part of it to find husband number two, Sir William Collins. He gave her a 16-bedroomed country mansion and 15 cars.

When Collins died three years later and left his entire fortune to her, she married Sir Bernard Docker.

By far the wealthiest of the three, he dazzled her with a gold-plated Daimler – which she upholstered in zebra skin instead of mink because, 'Everyone knows mink is too hot to sit on' – a 2400 acre estate, an apartment at Claridges, a gilded coach, a family flag which flew from the top of the house whenever the Dockers were in residence and a 214 foot yatch called *Shamara*.

It goes without saying that the Dockers had little trouble attracting the attention they sought.

Though Norah had been banned from the Royal Enclosure at Ascot and usually made a nuisance of herself while gambling at Monte Carlo, the couple were regulars at the Red Cross Ball and had even managed an invitation to Rainier and Grace's wedding.

But in 1958 when she was refused an invitation for her teenage son to attend Prince Albert's christening, she showed her displeasure by cursing the child's fate and ripping a paper Monaco flag into shreds.

When word got back to the Palace, which it did straight away, the gold watch and silver plate the Dockers had offered as presents were returned.

An hour later a communiqué was issued by the Minister of State.

'The Prince's government have been obliged to take an administrative measure of expulsion from their territory concerning Lady Docker, who indulged publicly in demonstrations offensive to the principality.'

Because the ban applied to the three French *départements* as well as to Monaco, the Dockers couldn't return to the Riviera.

Within a month, having been deprived of their playground, a Docker emissary approached the Monaco Red Cross with an offer of seven million francs – about £6,000 – in exchange for a lifting of the order.

But Princess Grace, as President of the Monaco Red Cross, refused to consider it. She said, 'We are not interested in bribes or bargaining.'

That the Dockers ever imagined they could buy their way back into Monaco still infuriates Rainier.

'She went too far. She was a pushy woman, very difficult, usually drunk by 11 a.m. I remember, after the incident, agreeing to see Sir Bernard. I was flabbergasted. Now, I'm not at all a snob but to see a man of that age, whose wife has provoked a very nasty incident, come into my office wearing white trousers, a blazer and white tennis shoes didn't strike me as being very serious. I gave him a very cold reception. He tried to explain her behaviour, although he never once apologised for it. His attitude was one of being on the continent and treating the natives, well, as natives.'

The expulsion remained in force although on several occasions, Rainier says, he tried to give the Dockers a way out. He asked for a public apology, which the Dockers stubbornly refused to do. Instead they took the tack, 'If the Prince won't admit he was wrong, neither will we.'

Norah Docker did not return to the south of France until the summer of 1982, four years after Sir Bernard's death and long after most of their money had faded away.

Her son was living there and Rainier lifted the ban so that she could visit him.

It was her 75th birthday.

*   *   *   *

As Monaco's convention business picked up and light industry developed, the state's dependency on SBM changed.

With that came a change in the government's relationship with the National Council.

'SBM continues to exert a lot of influence on an enormous percentage of the principality's voting populace,' Rainier says. 'Politically, that's a difficult thing to deal with. They constitute a very strong electoral power. Any local candidate has to make his peace with SBM so he can assure himself that reservoir of votes. In turn, that power is reflected on the National Council.'

Today, out of Monaco's nearly 3000 registered voters, almost half have direct ties to SBM, either as employees or as immediate family members of an SBM employee.

That gives SBM tremendous weight with the National Council and a disproportionate voice in the affairs of the government. With such inflated influence, and largely because of it, SBM has always been an incredibly difficult company to run.

It is riddled with empires.

Therefore, simply stated, the art of living and working in Monaco comes down to knowing just how far you can go without pushing too hard.

The most notable of the well-entrenched interest groups is the croupiers, a closed, independent bunch who are downright fearless when it comes to standing up to the management.

Even at the best of times, managers come and go with alarming regularity. Although the company makes money every year, almost inspite of itself.

In light of SBM's influence, and as the National Council was never intended to be a rubber stamp for the government, Monaco's constitutional monarchy is in practice slightly peculiar.

Unavoidably, the tail all-too-often wags the dog.

To deal with that very problem, Rainier has looked to improve the dialogue between the Council and the government.

'There used to be a nasty feeling that the National Council's great enemy was the government and that the only way they could get even was to cut parts of the budget. I'm happy to have helped erase that.'

He instituted a series of small working groups and committees and put the two bodies in closer touch.

'I wanted them to understand each other's problems. Now I must say, touch wood, everything works fine. Okay, the National Council might not vote a certain item of the budget because they don't understand what it's all about or why it's necessary but now, instead of throwing it out, they ask the government to come back with further explanation. There's a real dialogue now. The government doesn't dictate to the National Council and the National Council doesn't act like a barrier to everything the government wants to do. There'd been a tendency towards confrontation and sometimes I think it was confrontation simply for the sake of confrontation. Frankly, every now and then they still trespass on executive powers which don't belong to them. But that happens less and less. The government and the National Council have still been known to come to hard words but in the end there's a dialogue and cooperation. I will take credit for that.'

The new spirit of cooperation smoothed the political climate so that Rainier could turn his attention to finding new ways of attracting more foreign investers to Monaco.

One of the ways that's been done is through the encouragement of administrative companies.

For example, a ship-owner has, say, 20 ships. They each fly a flag of convenience such as Panama or Liberia. But for commercial reasons, each ship is a separate company. It's done that way so that if one ship happens to sink only that one company goes bust. However, if you have 20 ships you have to manage 20 companies. Not many people want to do that in Panama or Liberia so the ship-owner sets up an administrative office in Monaco. That office handles crewing and charter contracts and all the ships' technical services, acting on account of and for a company in Panama or Liberia. The administrative company in Monaco then receives a fee from each of the 20 companies for handling the administrative duties of the group.

That's good for Monaco because it's clean, there's no pollution, the directors and managers are paid a substantial, usually tax-free salary, they're able to enjoy an elevated standard of living, they spend money in the principality and they give Monaco a year-round, high-class population.

'It's a good system for everybody,' Rainier continues. 'Now, you might think, why come to Monaco when you can go someplace, say, like Geneva? The answer is simple. Geneva has such terrible laws when it comes to employment while here it's absolutely open. You come here and if you want to bring your foreign secretary with you, all she has to do is get her work permit. Sure, if you come here and want to hire a secretary and out of five candidates with equal competence one of them is Monégasque then you're obliged to hire the Monégasque. But that's only normal.'

By creating an atmosphere that encourages administrative companies to come to Monaco, Rainier has a unique product to sell on the international market.

Naturally, many countries offer various packages of products to the international business community. Any number of countries have turned 'mail box' companies into a major industry. They allow anyone who is willing to pay the fee the right to incorporate, using nominee directors acting for the anonymous owner who, a long way from the company's post box address, is more often than not using the company to keep money away from a tax man.

Here too, Monaco might be unique – because when it comes to forming a company in the principality, fine lines are distinctly drawn.

'We don't want mail box companies here. That's completely out of the question. I won't allow that. This is neither Liechtenstein nor the Cayman Islands. They've acquired a certain reputation that we wouldn't want here. I don't mean to sound unkind but they've made a big business out of freely allowing companies to set up there. Any company wanting to set up in Monaco is fully investigated. Anyone with a Monégasque company actually runs a company that does something. Otherwise, we close them down.'

He insists on strict guidelines because he believes it is vitally important to be careful with Monaco's reputation.

Of course, Monaco's reputation is, more often than not, that of a tax haven.

But Rainier scoffs at the term.

'Being a so-called tax haven is of no financial interest at all. People live here and buy things here, yes, that's fine. But if someone doesn't pay taxes in England or Sweden, it doesn't matter at all to us. When Bjorn Borg moved here the Swedish Government thought it was such a scandal because he wouldn't be paying taxes at home. But why should Monaco have a double taxation agreement with Sweden? I can't think of any Monégasque living there. Nor can I envision a time when we will tax people here. I don't think the figures warrant it.'

Unlike almost all other industrialised nations in the west, Monaco does not have to spend money on national defence, unemployment, foreign aid, the construction of highways, railroads or airports. More than half its income comes from value added taxes, the majority of which are funnelled through France. The rest derives from corporate profits tax, stamps, cigarettes, alcohol, the SBM monopoly, stamp taxes on all real estate deals and telephone calls. Monaco has the highest telephone density in the world and more than 80 per cent of the calls are international. Even a call next door to France is international.

So there's no reason to impose income taxes.

However, he says, the day might come when Monaco will have to invent a quota for foreign residents.

'It's obvious that over the past several years there's been a north–south movement in Europe. Northern Europeans move south but no one from Nice goes to live in Oslo. With advanced communications, that north–south movement will accelerate and change the entire structure of the region. I think tax advantages will become less and less a factor. If one day we imposed taxes on foreigners, I don't honestly feel it would hurt us, as long as they're still left with a little advantage. Most intelligent people understand that taxes have to be paid somewhere and don't object to that. They do, however, object to official confiscation when a government takes away 80 per cent or 90 per cent and removes any incentive to earn money or reinvest it.'

Then again, he says, come 1992 when the Common Market opens its doors who knows what the world will be like and how it will change?

'Monaco isn't an EEC member but we're inexorably tied to France with our customs union and fiscal treaties. We're not sure what the future holds. For that matter, neither is France. No one is. Now, I personally don't think we should become an EEC member because we don't have the industrial potential. I think Monaco must remain a special entity. There won't be a customs stop between Monaco and France but then there won't be any customs stops between France and Italy either. Maybe the Common Market will need the kind of financial outpost that we can provide to attract foreign investment. Something like a "little Hong Kong of the Mediterranean" scenario where Monaco might have its own fiscal system and its own status.'

Yet he feels there's no sense in doing much to prepare Monaco for 1992 as long as the European Community members themselves haven't decided what they're going to do.

'I don't think 1992 will be a total non-event. But at the same time I don't think it's right to expect that from midnight onward everything is going to change. How are you going to equalise the fiscal systems in the different countries? How are you going to convince the French that they must bring down the levels of their VAT to equal those of the Germans. It's going to be a big blow to a lot of economies if these things aren't done gradually. The French under the Socialists have gone back to a wealth tax. I consider myself just a spectator here but what use will that tax be in 1992 when we'll have the free movement of people and capital? It means you won't be able to stop people from investing wherever they want within the EEC. If France doesn't have the same liberal system, all the money in France will be invested in Germany or Belgium or England. I think Mrs Thatcher's attitude is perfect, allowing people to invest wherever they want, encouraging the free movement of capital.'

Then what about taxes?

'Good question. If a Belgian comes to live in France, where will he pay his taxes? They haven't worked that out. And if you look at the mess that's being created with the agricultural part of it, I may be a pessimist, but they haven't gotten very far yet, have they? So when you start talking about taxation and you tell the English and the Germans and the French that they have to iron out their taxation and make it all equal, who knows what will happen? Does anyone really think there could be a United States of Europe? Never. Who'd be president? Can you image the French allowing a German to be President of Europe? There are too many nationalistic barriers that still exist in Europe.'

Frankly, he shrugs, he can't quite see how 1992 will work.

'They say there won't be any identity controls inside the EEC at any frontier. It's going to be heyday for the terrorists. And for drugs. What's going to happen to the army of customs officers? They'll control other nationalities coming into the EEC but I suppose that's all. I simply can't believe that it's going to be the full event it's supposed to be.'

The one thing he says he can count on in 1992 is the emergence of a special, new relationship with France.

As England has the Channel Islands, as Germany uses Luxembourg and as China will one day be able to use Hong Kong, he's hoping France might well look to Monaco to become an off-shore financial centre.

'The great principles of the Franco-Monégasque relationship date back to the Treaty of Versailles. On this basis they can't bully us or pressure us. Anyway, it's not in their interest to do so. There are a lot of French politicians with a modern view of the word who understand that Monaco's independence can only benefit France. The development of Monaco as, say, a little Hong Kong offers France an influx of foreigners with their foreign capital. We're talking here of investment. Most of the banks in Monaco have enormous capital reserves and those banks in turn look to France to invest that capital. It's fresh money coming into France though this door. I doubt if the French are going to want to spoil that.'

In fact the idea of a little Hong Kong is one that greatly interests Rainier.

'But with certain limitations. We'd have to try to get the good reputation of Hong Kong and not the bad one. For instance, I don't think Monaco could work very well as a free port. We have no frontiers so it would be difficult to control. There'd be too much abuse. As for banking, there are various facilities and advantages for banks here but they're strictly controlled. I would never want Monaco to become the kind of banking haven you find in the Caribbean.'

There are 35 banks operating in Monaco today. But they operate entirely within the French monetary system and are subject to the rules of the Bank of France. This too might change in 1992. It seems that one of the reasons there are so many banks in the principality is because some bankers believe that come 1992 Monaco will play an important banking role as a sort of open door to the Common Market.

'Consider the fact that with computers and satellites, bankers and stockbrokers no longer have to be in the City of London or on Wall Street. They can, the way many Italian stockbrokers do right now, base themselves in Monaco. With modern communications, you don't have to sit in a dingy office in Amsterdam to service your clients, you can do it all from a balcony in Monte Carlo. And I expect that in the next few years a lot of people will be doing just that.'

*   *   *   *

10

Monte Carlo Chic

O N 18 DECEMBER 1933 the Principality of Monaco declared war on the United States of America.

Well, not exactly the entire US of A, just Mississippi.

A series of bearer bonds issued by the state in the 1830s had been stashed in bank vaults and forgotten about for more than 90 years, until the heirs of the original owners discovered them and tried to secure the monies due. With interest, the nominal $100,000 value of the bonds had turned into $574,300.

But Mississippi had defaulted on the loans in 1841.

When the bond holders tried to sue Mississippi they learned that American law prohibited such an action as an individual state may only be sued by another state, by the US Government or by a foreign government. As foreign residents of Monaco, they approached Prince Louis II and made him a deal. They were willing to give him 45 per cent of the action if the principality would assume ownership of the bonds and press the court case.

So on 18 December 1933, Monaco, applied to the United States Supreme Court for permission to file suit against the State of Mississippi. However, because Mississippi had amended its own constitution in 1875 specifically barring all claims against those bonds, the principality first had to prove that the amendment was unconstitutional.

Making the case even more interesting was the fact that several southern states had also defaulted on bonds and a judgement in favour of Monaco would open the flood-gates. The total of monies due by those states, including interest, was over $78 million.

With so much at stake, the Americans feared the start of a lucrative cottage industry in the principality.

Attorneys for Monaco argued that they were giving the State of Mississippi, 'an opportunity to erase this stigma from her reputation'.

Even the *New York Times* came out in favour of the Monégasques.

In an editorial on 19 December 1933, they suggested, 'Surely Mississippians should think kindly of a foreign state which owes the United States nothing.'

Two days later the same newspaper wondered, 'How would it be if Mississippi proposed to Monaco to roll dice for the money?'

Shortly after that, someone named John Alden writing in the *Brooklyn Daily Eagle*, took a jibe at Mississippi in a lengthy poem which included these four lines:

> Monaco, we know, is a sinful old place,
>   Where blue sky's the limit for any who bets;
> But, wicked or not, she has one saving grace—
>   She sticks to the habit of paying her debts.

The United States Supreme Court heard the arguments in January 1934 and immediately ordered Mississippi to show cause why the principality should not be permitted to file suit.

Attorneys for Mississippi now claimed that Monaco was not an independent state. They cited the 1918 treaty with France where Monaco undertook to exercise its rights of sovereignty 'in accord with the political, naval and economic interests of France'. But the French Foreign Office testified that the treaty did not in the least imply that Monaco had surrendered its rights as a foreign entity.

Monaco appeared to be winning at every stage.

Unfortunately for them, it was the last battle of the war that mattered.

Chief Justice Hughes rendered the opinion that the principality, like the original holders of the bonds, did not in fact have the right to sue the State of Mississippi without consent of the state and that consent was neither forthcoming, nor would it be.

The war was over.

Mississippi won.

And the Principality of Monaco has been at peace with the United States of America ever since.

*   *   *   *

You enter the world's most famous casino up a flight of marble steps which lead to a huge lobby with wide staircases on either side.

The opera house is straight ahead.

Upstairs are the casino's offices.

Downstairs are the workshops where the roulette wheels and gaming tables are serviced. Every morning the wheels are balanced, the roulette balls are checked and the croupiers' rakes are examined.

The chips have been specially designed to be as counterfeit-proof as possible, though that hasn't necessarily stopped people from trying. So the six–eight month training course each croupier must take includes lessons on how to spot counterfeit chips and currencies, and how to recognise all sorts of crooks. Plain clothes inspectors also roam the floors. But because Monaco is such a small place, inspectors must regularly be brought in from abroad so that neither the habitual punters nor the casino staff will necessarily know they are being watched by anyone in particular.

The room where the money is counted and kept is at the end of a very narrow corridor, purposely too narrow for more than one person at a time. Should a thief think he can manage a heist by cutting off the power, the casino has its own generator. What's more, the croupiers have a special button they can push which, at the slightest sign of trouble, automatically drops their cash box through a hole in the floor into a basement vault.

Then there is the 'face squad'.

Burly men in ill-fitting dinner jackets stare at everyone coming in to make certain that undesirables are kept out.

The most famous of these physiognomists was a certain M. Le Broq who claimed to have memorised no fewer than 60,000 faces and could put names to nearly half of them. He knew who to let in and who to keep out, including compulsive gamblers who had voluntarily placed themselves on the permanent 'please don't let me in' list, and no amount of begging, promising, cajoling or insults could get their name off that list or their face out of M. Le Broq's head.

The gaming rooms are to the left of the lobby.

These are large, high-ceilinged rooms with extravagant paintings. In one, a panel by Gervais, *The Florentine Graces*, overlooks roulette wheels and chemin-de-fer tables. In another, originally a smoking-room and now a bar, the robust nude women painted on the ceiling by Galleli have cigars between their fingers.

The public gaming rooms are just that – public. Anyone can toss a few francs on red and shout when they've won. Those rooms fill up late in the afternoon with little old ladies who've left their shopping bags with the hat check girl and with bus-loads of tourists who spend two hours losing 100 francs, then wander the streets for the next two hours checking out every cafe and every pizzeria in Monaco to find one with a *prix fixe* menu 10 francs cheaper than any other.

The penny-ante players never get to see the most beautiful of all the 11 rooms because the *salles privées* are where serious gamblers risk – and eventually lose – serious money in a serious attempt to break the bank.

The man who guards the entrance to the private rooms wants to know who you are and insists that you're dressed properly – ties and jackets for gentlemen, dresses for ladies. There's also an entrance fee to discourage the common tourist.

And here no one shouts when they win.

In fact, they say that no one has raised a voice in the private rooms since that night in 1950 when a Greek gentleman playing roulette was betting heavily on number five. Big gamblers attract crowds and the Greek gentleman was no exception. As the evening wore on, the crowd around the table grew to such a size that one of the croupiers got nervous and mistakenly rolled the ball in the same direction as the spinning wheel. The *chef de partie*, which is a fancy name for the pit-boss, noticed the error and stopped the wheel. The Greek gentleman complained. The management explained that those were the rules. Incensed, the Greek gentleman pulled all his chips off the table. And on the next spin, guess which number came up? The incident cost the Greek gentleman forty grand.

For that kind of money, the Greek gentleman raised his voice.

These are the rooms where the Russians Grand Dukes played throughout the latter part of the nineteenth century when they arrived in Monaco looking for mild winters and long afternoons at the tables. They brought strong-boxes filled with gold and silver to pay for their amusements and, as long as they had money to spend, the party went on.

Princess Suvorov, grand-niece of General Suvorov, hero of the Napoleonic Wars, turned up in Monte Carlo in 1869 with thousands of tiny punched cards, arranged by date and containing random numbers compiled from roulette wheels across Europe. True to the form of most players with a sure-fire system, Princess Suvorov spent her first few hours in the casino losing 300,000 francs.

Then, like magic, her system started to click.

Before the casino closed the next morning, she'd won back her original 300,000 and added another 700,000 to it. She returned the following night and repeated her performance, putting the casino into the red for the second time. As a matter of fact, she continued winning for eight consecutive nights until she announced that she'd won enough.

To celebrate, she decided to throw the largest, most sumptuous party ever held on the Riviera.

Her guest list was based on only one criterion – everyone had to be amusing. She didn't discriminate between a prince or a pickpocket, a dowager or a hooker, as long as they were good company.

But that didn't please François Blanc who politely informed her that the Hôtel de Paris wouldn't be able to handle her party.

Shrugging him off, she looked for another place. Someone told her about a huge villa for sale. She approached the owner's agent and asked to hire it for one night. When the agent realised that a party was planned, he refused. 'All right', she told him, 'I'll rent the place for the rest of the season and pay three months in advance'. She also promised to vacate the premises by 8 a.m. The astonished owner's agent drew up the necessary letting agreement on the spot.

Preparations for the party took several weeks.

The Princess hired an orchestra from Paris to play dance music and an orchestra from Budapest to play gypsy music, which was the current fad. She hired the chef from the Hôtel de Paris to cater the affair and bought 1,000 cases of champagne so that none of her guests went thirsty.

Her invitations made it clear that anyone was perfectly welcome to bring as many friends as they wanted, as long as everybody who came was amusing.

Several hundred people showed up that night, the vast majority of whom Princess Suvorov didn't know, had never seen before and never even got a chance to meet.

By 6.30 the next morning, with the party still in full swing, she dispatched a servant to find the agent to explain that she'd never be able to get everyone out at the agreed time. He arrived, saw that considerable damage had been done and insisted her friends be gone within the hour. Realising there was no way that could happen, the princess did the next best thing – she bought the place.

When word of the purchase reached the other guests, a Parisian actress removed her slipper, filled it with champagne and drank a toast to Princess Suvorov out of her shoe.

It was the first time anyone ever did that.

Not long after Princess Suvorov's party, a chap named Blanchard, who'd been a regular loser at the casino, was walking along the promenade on his way to the tables when a pigeon homed in on him and ruined his hat. That afternoon M. Blanchard won a small fortune. He then refused to return to the casino until another pigeon had ruined another hat. When it did, he won again. But as he never managed to position himself under a helpful pigeon a third time, he never again played at Monte Carlo.

In 1891 Charles Wells came to Monte Carlo and won worldwide fame as 'the man who broke the bank at Monte Carlo'.

Inventor of the 'musical rope' – something long forgotten but then very much in vogue in London – Wells hit a lucky streak one afternoon and wiped out a roulette table's cash reserves. Moving on to the next one, his luck not only held out long enough to close that table too but over the course of three days he turned his original stake of £400 into £40,000.

William Jaggers did even better.

A British engineer, he came to Monte Carlo at turn of the century with six assistants to test his theory that it's impossible to maintain a perfectly balanced roulette wheel, that imperfections will cause certain numbers to hit more frequently than others. After months of compilations by his team, he spent four days at the tables and won 1.5 million francs, then roughly $180,000 or £75,000.

Jaggers is the reason that the casino checks and rebalances every wheel every day.

Even Kaiser Wilhelm II tried to break the bank at Monte Carlo.

He arrived on his yacht with a roulette system devised by a mathematics professor from Heidelberg University who'd staked his future at the school on the Kaiser's success.

The Kaiser headed straight for the casino, lost a fortune and left Monaco, never to return. The professor's career dissolved just as quickly.

Chips are the usual currency of casinos although just before World War I many gamblers at Monte Carlo preferred to use gold coins.

As the story goes, a British gentleman was playing roulette one night when he lost a gold button from the sleeve of his dinner jacket. The croupier saw it fall to the floor and asked, 'Red or black?' The British gentleman muttered, 'Always red', not realising that he'd lost the button. He got up before the wheel was spun and walked away from the table. Red must have hit several times in a row because when the British gentleman returned the croupier handed him his gold button plus 25,000 francs worth of gold coins.

Queen Victoria's son Bertie, the Prince of Wales, who would one day become Edward VII, was an annual visitor to Monte Carlo between 1870 and 1901, even though his mother once ordered the curtains drawn on her carriage as it sped though Monaco so that her eyes would not light on such a den of iniquity.

Using various pseudonyms to avoid calling attention to himself, Bertie travelled only with two equerries, his personal physician, a pair of valets and a butler. He occasionally played baccarat but usually preferred to spend time in pursuit of his two greatest loves, food and women.

Staying at the Grand Hotel, he befriended the manager, César Ritz, and the hotel's chef, Auguste Escoffier. Thanks in part to Bertie's patronage, both Ritz and Escoffier would eventually come to the Savoy in London – Ritz to manage the hotel and Escoffier to cook there.

It's often written that one evening while Bertie was dining with a young woman named Suzette at the Café de Paris, a waiter dared to prepare a special dessert for the couple. He soaked some thin pancakes in several liqueurs, which then accidentally caught fire. The dish was immediately named for the Prince's companion.

Sadly, the story isn't true.

The origin of crêpes Suzettes is generally credited to Monsieur Joseph, chef at Le Marivaux in Paris in 1897. He later succeeded Escoffier at the Savoy and that's where the dessert became famous.

Not surprisingly, both of Bertie's favourite companions had connections with Monaco. The actress Lily Langtry holidayed there with him and died there, while he met his English society favourite, Alice Keppel, at a party in Monte Carlo.

But then, Monte Carlo has never lacked for personalities who are the stuff of legends.

One American millionaire, known as Mr Neal, preferred a pistol to the room bell. He fired one shot when he wanted room service and two when he wanted a maid. He also rigged up an artificial moon to shine outside his hotel window and regularly hired 60–80 people to come to dinner parties he hosted for himself at the Hermitage, instructing them that when he entered the main dining room they had to stand up and applaud. In exchange for the free meal, they also had to listen to him make a speech and laugh at his jokes.

James Gordon Bennett, the notably flamboyant owner of the *New York Herald* started a Paris edition of his newspaper – today it's the *International Herald Tribune* – simply because he wanted to live in France and needed something to do. Using Paris as his base, he ventured south. But in those days the Côte d'Azur was a haunt of Europeans, not Americans. To entice his countrymen to that part of the world – mainly so that he'd have some company – he began publishing a Riviera column in his paper.

Before the decade was out his house guests included the Drexels, the Biddles and the Vanderbilts.

Bennett often entertained his guests at Café Riche in Monte Carlo because he found the terrace an agreeable spot for dining. But he arrived there one day to be told that from now on nothing more than cocktails would be served on the terrace. Bennett protested. The management said, take it or leave it. He chose a third option. He bought the place, fired the manager and asked Ciro, his favorite waiter, to run the place on his behalf. Bennett then plugged Ciro in his Riviera column so often that, before long, Ciro was opening restaurants all over Europe.

Steel magnate J. P. Morgan, an inveterate gambler, once demanded that Blanc raise the house limits in the private rooms from 12,000 francs to 20,000. Blanc refused so Morgan stormed out claiming he had no time to lose a mere 12,000 francs.

Morgan's cohort, Charles Schwab, president of Carnegie Steel, also enjoyed Monte Carlo.

When Morgan heard that his friend had amused himself with an evening's debauchery, he chided Schwab, saying that it was beneath a man of his position to behave like that.

Schwab answered, 'I commit my sins openly, not behind closed doors.'

To which Morgan roared, 'But that's what doors are for.'

Monte Carlo not only has plenty of doors, there's also a terrific secret tunnel.

Walk into the Hôtel de Paris and stop at the bronze statue of Louis XV riding high on a horse whose nose and right front leg have been rubbed shiny for luck by several million hands. Then turn left and go to the front corner. A handsome polished bronze and mirrored door hides a lift, which takes you down to a tunnel, which leads under the street to another lift, which brings you up into the casino. Onassis built it so that some of his more discreet clients didn't have to be seen in public, either going to the tables with their pockets full or coming back to the hotel with tears in their eyes.

And then there were the ladies.

Ilona was a beautiful, raven-haired Greek girl who moved into the Hôtel de Paris, all her bills paid by an Englishman named Aubrey, who was using her as bait to blackmail Austrian Emperor Franz Josef.

But Franz Josef, who frequently stayed at the hotel under the guise of visiting his Empress Elizabeth, habitually spent his time avoiding Elizabeth, cavorting instead with his various mistresses. And in this case he was at the hotel with a blonde known as Gussy. It was several weeks before Ilona could manage to get Franz Josef alone. Once she did, Aubrey burst into the room playing the jealous husband. Franz Josef fled home with Gussy in tow and Aubrey on their heels.

While there was little the Emperor could do about Aubrey in Monaco, there was a lot he could do once Aubrey crossed the border into Austria.

Franz Josef ordered him arrested and sent to jail where he languished for half a year while Franz Josef returned to his Monégasque adventures.

Gertrud Margarete Zelle was born in Holland, worked for a while as a nude model in Paris and came to Monte Carlo as a semi-exotic dancer. The rage of Paris and Berlin, she was always known by her stage name – the Malayan word for sunrise – Mata Hari.

Between 1907 and 1915, as the mistress of German intelligence chiefs and French ministers, she plied her trade of selling secrets.

One night in the casino, confronted by an agent from whom she'd stolen papers that afternoon, a distressing scene developed. He apparently tried to force himself upon her. She responded by taking a pistol out of her handbag and shooting him. Witnesses testified that she acted in self-defence, never realising that he was merely trying to retrieve stolen papers she'd hidden under her blouse.

However the queen of them all had to be Caroline Otero, a Spanish gypsy who married an Italian baron at the age of 14 and came to Monte Carlo on her honeymoon. When her husband lost their money in the casino, she walked up to a roulette wheel, took a gold button from her dress and tossed it on red. The colour hit 20 times in a row and they left with a fortune.

She quickly went through both money and husband, then embarked on a career as one of the truly remarkable *grandes horizontales* of the age.

Among her admirers was a German count who, although one of the weathiest men in Europe, was also said to be one of the ugliest men in Europe.

Always proud to be seen on his arm, *La Belle Otero* simply told friends, 'No man this rich can be called ugly.'

She retired to Monte Carlo in 1922 at the age of 45 with a fortune worth nearly £2 million. Sadly, though, she squandered it at the tables and died in poverty of natural causes in nearby Nice.

By the same token, not everyone who loses at Monte Carlo dies of natural causes.

Suicides are an unfortunate part of the principality's past.

Even the great Sarah Bernhardt tried it one night after losing her last 100,000 francs.

She left the casino, went to her rooms at the Hôtel de Paris and overdosed on sleeping powder. She was only saved at the last minute when a friend chanced upon her, realised what had happened and rang for a doctor.

The most famous story of any Monte Carlo suicide is undoubtedly the one about the young man who, after losing all his money, walked out of the casino, went to the sea wall and shot himself.

At least he was found there face down by the casino security staff with a smoking pistol in his hand and blood pouring out of his shirt.

Hoping to avoid a gambling related scandal, the casino manager stuffed the young man's pockets with 1,000 franc notes.

His stake replenished, the young man got up, dusted himself off and went back to the tables to play again.

Although most casinos, and in particular Monte Carlo, will go to great lengths to avoid any hint of a scandal, the often-told 'true' tale of the faked suicide is nothing more than a short story by Alexander Woollcott.

*   *   *   *

In addition to the casino, Monaco attracts tourists with festivals and museums.

There is the Television Festival and the Ballet Festival.

And there is the Circus Festival.

Created in 1974 by Rainier, simply because he loves the circus, it brings together the top talent from the world's circuses to compete for the Silver Clown Awards, the Oscars of the circus world.

There is Prince Albert's Anthropological Museum, and of course his Oceanographic Museum.

And then there is the National Museum, which houses a splendid collection of dolls and automatons, doll's house furniture and a small collection of modern dolls, each dressed in exact replicas of some of Princess Grace's gowns, including her wedding dress.

There is the Prince's zoo, and there are the Botanical Gardens, which is one of Europe's finest collections of exotic plants.

There are tennis tournaments and golf tournaments and rallies for vintage cars.

But the really big draws are the Grand Prix and the Red Cross Ball.

That's when the high rollers come to town.

The Monaco Grand Prix bills itself as the greatest Formula One race in the world. And even if it isn't, it is certainly the best known.

Actually it's a pair of events.

There's the race, which is a sporting event, and there's the celebration of that race, which is one of Europe's major tourist attractions.

The tarmac at the airport at Nice is never covered with as many private jets as it is during Grand Prix weekend. The harbour at Monaco is never filled with as many huge boats as it is during that weekend. The bar at the Hôtel de Paris is never as crowded with as many easily recognisable people as it is that weekend.

And the roulette wheels at the casino spin from dusk to dawn, turning fortunes.

The men who fancy themselves part of the international jet-set arrive for the Grand Prix with their wives or their mistresses, just as some of the women who fancy themselves part of the international jet-set have been known to arrive for the Grand Prix with their own husbands or someone else's.

Almost as if it were orchestrated this way, they move *en masse* from the Hôtel de Paris bar to their private boxes along the Place du Casino where they stuff cottonwool in their ears for two hours while grown-up boys in multi-million dollar toys drive around in circles trying not to get killed. Then they head straight back to the bar *en masse*, because the celebration of that sporting event is more about being seen than it is about discussing torque and all-weather tyres.

The Automobile Club of Monaco is responsible for staging the Grand Prix each year. They pay the Formula One Association about 15 million francs for the right to hold the race and then spend an additional 25–30 million francs setting it up. In all it comes to 40–45 million francs, or $7 million or somewhere around £4.5 million.

For the two-hour final that works out at about $1,000 or £600 a second.

People arrive in the principality all that week, though the festivities only officially begin on Thursday evening. There are dinners and lunches and private parties and hospitality suites on rented yachts.

For the Sunday afternoon final the Monégasque police estimate that there are never fewer that 100,000 people jamming the streets and hanging over apartment balconies.

It puts a strain on everything.

Telephones, electricity, sewers, food, souvenirs, postcards, film, beverages.

The logistics of staging the race are horrendous.

The place is so crowded you can't possibly get from one part of the country to the other.

For those few days in May, Monte Carlo becomes a city under a state of siege.

Begun in 1929, the Grand Prix hasn't always been run on exactly the same circuit but it has always run through the streets of Monte Carlo.

Today, the 3.312 kilometre circuit – about 2½ miles – starts at the port, heads up the hill to the casino, passes in front of the Hôtel de Paris, swings round the Place du Casino, goes down the other side towards the Loews Hotel, down further to the sea, turns back to come through the tunnel beneath the Loews, turns again to swing round the swimming pool and ends up at the starting line on the street in front of the port.

By international Formula One racing regulation, the 26-car race cannot last more than two hours, which usually means 74 – 78 laps. Although that depends on the state of the streets. Rain means fewer laps. Good conditions mean more.

The most difficult Grand Prix to stage had to be in 1968.

Held in the middle of France's student revolt, there were strikes that shut off the principality's electricity and barricades that tried to stop the Grand Prix from taking place. The organisers only just managed to get the cars moving by smuggling fuel into the principality in milk trucks.

But unlike other sporting events where there are distances to measure and clocks for the timing of world records, there is none of that in Formula One racing. Best-time-ever or fastest-speed don't mean much at Monte Carlo because the race is never exactly the same from year to year and anyway the cars have changed radically over the years.

In fact, it's even difficult to find any one race that holds the record for being the greatest.

Ask ten aficionados which was the greatest Monaco Grand Prix of all time and you get a dozen different opinions.

Some of those who can remember say it was in 1933 when Achille Varzi in a Bugatti 51 and Tazio Nuvolari in an Alfa Romeo Monza kept changing place throughout the entire race and Varzi only won when Nuvolari's car burned on the last lap.

Some of those who can't remember 1933 say it was 1981.

At the start of that race, Derek Daly in a Tyrrell climbed above the car in front, landed on the street, lurched forward, then climbed two more cars before spinning out. Miraculously, no one was hurt but the film footage of that accident was shown throughout the world for months.

Unfortunately, it's the accidents that always rest in the memory.

In 1950 five cars collided at a single turning and spread pools of gasoline three inches deep across the streets.

In 1955 Alberto Ascari missed the turn and wound up in the sea. He was fished out by the rescue teams uninjured but was killed three days later while practising for the Italian Grand Prix at Monza.

The Grand Prix of 1967 witnessed Monaco's only fatal accident to date when Lorenzo Bandini in a Ferrari failed to make a gear change, which caused him to miss the turning at the chicane. He careened into the barrier and his car exploded.

Safely standards have changed greatly since Bandini's death. He wasn't even strapped into his car.

These days, in addition to seven jib cranes scattered along the course at key points, there are 630 commissioners, 100 professional firemen, 50 specially trained emergency room physicians, 100 other doctors, 200 emergency paramedics and 50 medical technicians supplied by the French Air Force.

To help maintain crowd control there are 50 police dog handlers with their dogs, 500 French riot police, Monaco's entire 85-man Carabinier and its full complement of 450 policemen.

At the Grand Prix command centre – linked by radio with every commissioner on the course and looking like something straight out of NASA – they have 32 closed-circuit television cameras covering every inch of the course, each one feeding back to a separate monitor, plus one large screen in the middle that can take the shot from any of the 32 cameras. With the help of a computer they have a huge map of the course which shows the immediate location of every member of the safety team plus the locations of the cars.

Including the organisers, the ticket takers and the staff from the Automobile Club, it takes nearly 3,200 to stage the event.

Then there are approximately 1,000 journalists covering the race, not counting the 300 or so television and radio people who broadcast it.

For many years there was also just about every pickpocket in Europe.

Little by little, however, the organising committee and the police have been able to cut down on that sort of thing. Known pickpockets who show up for the event are quickly whisked back to the railway station for the trip home. Plain clothes officers patrol the crowds and on average – with a crowd of 100,000 – there are usually no more than four or five arrests. Interestingly enough, it's rare for there to be an arrest for fighting or public drunkenness.

The Monaco Grand Prix crowd has never been confused with English football hooligans.

'What makes Monaco really special', says Stirling Moss, 'is the atmosphere and the demanding nature of the circuit. It's a relatively safe circuit but it's very tricky. It's a beautiful, exciting place with an enormous amount of character, and the public, for whom you are performing, are very close to you. They're virtually on top of the cars. They can see you and you can see them. When I was racing, I'll never forget there was a very cute girl with pale pink lipstick who always stood in front of Oscar's Bar and every time I went past I'd blow her a kiss. Monaco is one of those sort of places.'

Moss raced in Monaco from 1950 until 1961, winning three times, once in a Maserati 250 F – that was in 1956 – and then back to back in 1960 and 1961 in a Lotus Climax 18.

'It's not only a physically demanding race, it's also a mentally exhausting race. You can't relax your mind at all. Because it's difficult to pass on narrow streets, and probably more so now than it was in my time because the cars are wider, it's very much a strategy race. Also, because you're changing gears so many times, braking so often, zipping up to maximum speed and down again, it's difficult to get positions where you can pass. You've got to be ready to go as soon as there's an opening. Anybody who wins Monaco is usually a pretty thinking driver.'

Jackie Stewart, also a three time winner at Monte Carlo, agrees.

'Unlike other Grand Prixs, the speeds at Monte Carlo are relatively slow and risk diminishes with lower speeds. Coming out of the tunnel under the Loews Hotel you might hit 280 kph' – that's in excess of 185 mph – 'but not for very long because there's a gear change just there. Because of the nature of the race you have to make 28 to 32 or even 34 gear changes per circuit. That used to be exceptional but it's not any longer. There are other race tracks which are just as difficult. Yet, as it takes something like 100 seconds to go around the course, that's an average of one gear change about every 3 seconds.'

That can add up to more than 2,100 gear changes in a 75-lap race.

'It's exhausting to get around. Even seasoned drivers find Monte Carlo tiring. There's a lot of stop and go, a lot of heavy braking, heavy acceleration. That's physically draining for a driver. It gets to your neck and back muscles. Being one of the slowest races it becomes one where mechanical reliability plays a big part. You find you get transmission problems because of all the gear changing and the heavy acceleration. Then, because it's run on a road course, there are a lot of manhole covers and a lot of drainage grills, all the things that normal roads have and most race tracks don't. So little mechanical faults show up in Monaco that wouldn't always, say, in Silverstone. And while it's not as hot there as it can be in places like Rio, it can still get very warm. It's a tough Grand Prix but it's a good one to win. It's a race that every driver wants to win. If I'd never won Monte Carlo there would be something missing from my record.'

Stewart first won at Monte Carlo in 1966 in a BRM P261, the same car that Graham Hill won with in the two previous years. His other victories were in 1971 and 1973, both in a Tyrrell Cosworth.

'Another thing that makes the race different is that communication within the principality that weekend is very difficult. The mechanics are in one hotel, the drivers and the team management are all scatterd around in other hotels. The roads get closed off and the rest of the traffic becomes a nightmare, so to try and get anywhere is just about impossible. You can't get a taxi. You can't even cross the street easily. I always stayed in the Hôtel de Paris and found that the only way to get from there down to the pits was on a scooter or a motorcycle. So for the drivers and the racing teams it can be frustrating. For the mechanics, most of the Grand Prix circuits they go to today have fully established garages where they can put the cars every night. In Monte Carlo they've got to work out of transporters. Logistically it's a bigger problem than any other Grand Prix.'

Still, he says, it has a very important place in the calendar.

'Monaco tends to be one of the first Grand Prix of the European season. It also is, I suppose, the showroom for Grand Prix racing. If I go to one of the major multinationals of this world to try to interest them in motor racing and take the chairman of the board, the president and all the operating officers to Monte Carlo and they don't buy motor racing after that, they ain't gonna buy it!'

That's because, in Stewart's mind, Monte Carlo represents almost everything that Grand Prix racing is supposed to be.

'If you think of the history of motor sport, it was created from road racing around cities or from town to town. Racing through the streets of Monte Carlo is really a legacy of the basic origins of Grand Prix racing. It's also the most glamorous because it has as a back-drop the Riviera, the Mediterranean, the Maritime Alps. It has great hotels, wonderful restaurants and beautiful women. If you think about what Grand Prix racing represents, it's glamorous, it's exciting and it's colourful. Monte Carlo projects all of those elements.'

All the more so, he feels, for the people who come to watch. 'The sovereign family has a lot to do with it. They're one of the ingredients that make up the perfect pie. They attend the race. They're an integral part of it. Members of the British royal family come to the British Grand Prix from year to year but never very often Her Majesty. We have the prime minister of Australia coming to Adelaide. But that's not the same as the reigning monarch. Now add in the most glamorous and richest people in the world. Everybody who is anybody arrives. It's just after the Cannes Film Festival so you get a lot of the wash from that. The Europeans come. The Americans come. The South Americans come up after they've been to Carnival in Rio. They have big yachts or a suite in the Hôtel de Paris. They go to the gala in the Sporting. They eat at Rampoldi's. Maybe they're invited to the Palace on the Saturday night. The Riviera is fresh, it's new, not like it is in July or August when its a mass of people. The grass is still green, nobody's walked on it, the sun hasn't yet parched it. People come down from the mountains. They've had their winter

at St Moritz or Gstaad or Vail or Aspen and they've come over
for the Grand Prix weekend in Monaco. To have a good suite in
the Hôtel de Paris for the Grand Prix is a passport to whatever
you need.'

*   *   *   *

Monaco's other world class event is the Red Cross Ball in August.

It is without any doubt the largest, most spectacular event of
its kind of Europe.

It's not just the stars who perform there, it's the designer
clothes and especially the jewellery. This may be the one night
in the European social calendar when people who have serious
money, seriously wear it.

To say that there is $50 million or $75 million or even $100
million worth of stones and precious metals in that one room on
that one night would be impossible.

You might change those dollar signs to pounds and still be in
range.

The point is that anyone who's ever been there could never
automatically dismiss such sums as being downright exaggera-
tions.

The Monaco Red Cross was formed by Rainier in the late 1940s.
For the first six or seven years the galas mainly featured European
performers, although occasionally there'd be someone new from
the United States, like in 1954 when a young singer named Ella
Fitzgerald had third billing.

But everything changed in 1956 when Princess Grace arrived.
'She took over as President of the Red Cross and gave the ball a
stature it didn't have before.

She realised that, while the Red Cross Ball was a big money
event, it still had to have a popular appeal. A few weeks before
the first Frank Sinatra concert there, a friend went to Grace and
said, 'You ought to up the price for the gala. It's a charity event
and nobody can draw a bigger crowd than Sinatra.'

But Grace said no. 'If we up the price some people I like won't
be able to afford it.'

At the same time she also kept an eye on the show itself.

In the mid-1970s the topless craze finally hit Monaco.

While women could shun half their bikini at the other beaches along the coast, it was frowned upon in Monaco, largely because Grace thought it totally unnecessary.

For Monaco's Rose Ball in 1975, Producer André Levasseur flouted tradition and introduced topless chorus girls in his revue. He argued, it's been like this for years at the Moulin Rouge and the Folies Bergère, Monaco must keep up with the times.

Grace wasn't convinced.

It bothered her, even though she knew that sort of thing was in fashion.

She also knew that if she protested too loudly she'd create a situation the press would jump on to the embarrassment of everyone involved.

So she handled it with typical *savoir-faire.*

She went to Lavasseur and asked him that his dancers not be topless for the Red Cross Ball. She said she felt it would be more appropriate if his dancers did not show their breasts, at least on this occasion.

He hesitated.

She won her case when she reminded him, 'After all, it's a very dressy evening.'

Since 1974, when the new Summer Sporting was officially opened, the Red Cross Ball has taken place there, in the *Salle des Etoiles* – the Starlight Room.

It's the centrepiece of a circular complex of discos, restaurants, showroom, and casino plunked down on a small landfill peninsula of coloured lights and exotic shrubbery that juts out from Monte Carlo's beach. The room got its name because the roof opens and the sides roll back and on a warm night you're virtually dining under the stars.

On a clear summer evening it is spectacular.

On the other hand, when it rains it is decidedly less spectacular, especially if the roof is still open.

That happened at one of the very first shows there. The drizzle began and the roof mechanism jammed. A lot of very expensive hair-do's got very wet. But that's all part of the game because it happened at the old Sporting too.

Jane Powell was the star of the Red Cross Ball that night.

She was on stage singing and dancing when a huge cloud moved into position and dumped tons of water onto the audience. Everyone in the room ran for shelter, except for Rainier and Grace. They showed their true grit and never budged. Waiters instantly appeared with umbrellas and the two stayed right where they were, fixed in their chairs out of respect for Jane Powell, who stayed where she was, singing and tap dancing on a stage covered with half an inch of water.

Because the *Salles des Etoiles* is laid out the way it is, you don't just walk into the room, you make an entrance.

The main door takes you directly on stage, where steps lead you down to the dance floor for all the audience to see.

Later, when the show starts, the stage rolls out onto the dance floor. It comes to the very edge of the tables which are in strict lines, like tombstones in a national cemetery, fanning out to the terrace along the far reaches of the slightly tiered room. Each place on the fresh white tablecloths is set with four knives, two forks, one spoon, two plates and two glasses. There is space enough for 1,000 to sit in relative comfort, if you don't mind an occasional touching elbow.

Tickets for the Red Cross Ball are now nearing the $850 or £500 mark for dinner and the show. But that's cheap compared to tickets for dinners for the Princess Grace Foundation in Los Angeles which can go for twice that.

Even then, ticket sales don't cover the cost of the evening which can run to upwards of $1 million or £600,000. SBM underwrites the event and in recent years has assured the Monaco Red Cross of at least a $200,000 or £125,000 contribution.

However, the Red Cross Ball means that the hotels are full, the bars are full and the casinos are full, so SBM still comes out ahead.

Some of the featured performers are paid for their appearance. Others work gratis. Frank Sinatra, for example, has not only always appeared for free, he's also always purchased tickets for himself, his wife and several of their friends. On the other hand, even performers who work for nothing can be expensive. When Paul Anka sang there he wanted a special lighting effect which cost SBM nearly $60,000 or £35,000 in projectors.

The man who probably knows the Red Cross Ball best is André Levasseur, as he's been creating and producing galas in Monte Carlo since 1954.

'Onassis did a great job of public relations for Monte Carlo. He brought a lot of important people here. He spent money on the shows. It was a sumptuous era. Even though the old Sporting Club only sat about 600, it had its charm, being right on the sea with a huge terrace. Yet, by the mid-1950s it was tired and out-of-date. It also had sound problems. If you were sitting at the end of the terrace you couldn't hear very well and the singers hated it. Judy Garland came to Monaco once and told Onassis, "I'd never sing in a place like this. I'd never sing in the open air like this." The new Sporting is bigger than the old room yet smaller than the big rooms in Las Vegas like Caesar's Palace or the Sands. So the performers who come here from there like it. They find it very intimate.'

They don't, however, necessarily always find the audience an easy one.

'The Monte Carlo public is very spoiled. They get top names from Europe and the States but they have a reputation for being very difficult. Among show people, they say that in Monte Carlo all those ladies, with all their jewels, have trouble applauding. Then again, not all performers who work here are always very easy either.'

Sinatra was probably the most difficult.

At his first appearance in 1980 he wanted extra tables put on the dance floor so that more people could be there. He wanted the orchestra to fill the stage and then announced he didn't want the dancers to do their number. He said all he wanted to do was walk on, do his bit and that would be the evening.

Levasseur spoke to Grace and she explained to Sinatra why they couldn't put the orchestra where he wanted it because that was where people entered the room. She told him it was also traditional to have the dance floor available so that she and Rainier could open the ball.

In the end he agreed to everything except letting the revue precede him.

The Red Cross Ball that year was Sinatra and only Sinatra.

And the chorus dancers who'd rehearsed an entire revue were furious.

They begged Levasseur to ask Sinatra if he wasn't embarrassed that he was refusing to let entertainers work or had he forgotten what it was like at the beginning of his career?

Again Grace stepped in.

She understood how upset the dancers were, so she apologised to them for Sinatra and invited the entire company to the Palace the next day for cocktails around the swimming pool.

'The American stars always come here with their six-shooters drawn,' Levasseur goes on. 'They're the most difficult but they're

also the most professional. In Europe we have a different temperament. That's given us a poor reputation as far as they're concerned.
They don't think Europeans can do things the way they do. It's
only when they've worked here once or twice that they understand we can give them anything they want. That reassures them.
Sinatra's second appearance was much easier. The third time he
played here there was no problem at all. He realised we're profes-
sionals and that he could count on us.'

Out of friendship to Rainier, Sinatra returned with Sammy
Davis Jr for the 1983 Red Cross Ball, probably the most difficult
of any, as it was the first one after Grace's death.

Since Caroline knew she could always count on him, she
phoned Sinatra a few years later when Liza Minelli had to cancel
at the last minute because of a sore throat. That year he took to
the stage with Elton John.

Unquestionably, those three appearances by Sinatra brought
the biggest crowds.

But the Red Cross Ball that stands out as the most magic of
them all was in 1974, the first one held at the new Sporting, when
Sammy Davis Jr didn't show up.

That afternoon Davis suddenly decided he didn't like the way
things were being organised.

He'd heard there'd been a dinner the night before at the Palace
and because he wasn't invited he felt insulted. Then he had a run
in with the SBM people. He finally decided, to hell with this,
climbed onto a friend's boat and sailed off into the sunshine for
St Tropez.

By 9 that night, with the guests beginning to arrive at the gala,
no one had yet come up with a replacement act.

Looking around the room, one of the SBM directors suggested
that as a last resort they simply ask some of the stars attending the
ball to do a couple of numbers.

They spotted Bill Cosby and he told the audience that evening,
'They asked me to fill in for Sammy because they think I look like
him.'

They found Burt Bacharach and he agreed to play.

They hoped Liza Minelli might sing but she begged off.

Then they saw the legendary Josephine Baker.

An SBM director quietly explained the situation to the 67-year-
old French music hall star from St Louis, Missouri and asked
politely if she'd be kind enough to sing a number or two.

She said, 'Normally I'd be happy to but I have no music with me. It might be different if my piano player was here but he's gone off for dinner somewhere.'

The SBM director wondered, 'If we send a car to collect your piano player from the restaurant right now, will you do it?'

She said, 'Sure.'

'Great,' the SBM director said, 'Where did he go for dinner?'

She told him, 'He had reservations at Le Nautic.'

'Wonderful,' the SBM director said, 'Which Le Nautic?'

'Ah,' she shrugged, 'I don't know, just Le Nautic.'

The problem was that every village along the south coast of France boasts a restaurant called Le Nautic and there are a lot of villages along that coast.

So SBM sent cars to every Le Nautic between Menton and Cannes until they found him and raced him back to Monaco.

The show went on and Josephine Baker owned the night.

'It was at the end of her career,' Levasseur says. 'But she was spectacular. She was unbelievable. It was certainly the greatest performance I've ever seen at the Red Cross Ball. I've rarely seen an audience applaud for anyone the way they did for her. It was one of her greatest triumphs.'

So much so that Levasseur encouraged her to take the show to Paris.

The return of Josephine Baker played 17 nights there, to standing-room-only crowds.

And that's how she bowed out.

She died two days later.

*   *   *   *

11

Grace

A PERFECT summer's evening on St Jean-Cap-Ferrat, what now seems like a long time ago.

Grace, deep in conversation with someone, slowly wound her way across the huge, well-manicured lawn, down to the squat stone sea-wall.

The moon was shining on the water.

Strings were playing somewhere in the shadows.

As she moved further and further away from the party, men in white evening jackets and women in long, sleeveless gowns, speaking softly, arm in arm, drinking champagne and eating canapes, drifted that way too, relaxed, almost unintentionally forming a huge semi-circle around where she stood facing the water.

Then very gently, as if someone was deliberately lowering the sound track little by little, everyone else's conversation hushed until the only voice you could hear was hers.

A moment passed.

Aware that something was happening behind her, she turned to find the entire party simply watching her.

Flustered for only a split second, she clapped her hands, organising everyone, leading them back towards the beach house where she announced, 'Let's go swimming,' and lured them all into the water.

The woman could definitely cast a spell.

*   *   *   *

The Monégasques welcomed Grace warmly when she arrived.

They rejoiced heartily with their Prince when he took her as his bride.

They applauded her and fêted her and told her that she was their Princess.

But deep down they were suspicious of her.

When Grace came to live in Monaco, those old women who dress in black and walk through the narrow streets of Le Rocher with baguettes under one arm couldn't understand what this foreigner was doing here.

In spite of her effort to learn the language and make herself understood, her French in those days was barely adequate, so those old women who dress in black asked each other, could not Monseigneur have found a bride right here in Monaco? Their naturally xenophobic nature reinforced by centuries of invaders – now including the non-stop hoardes of foreign tourists – those old women who dress in black asked each other, there were plenty to choose from in France, no?

Needless to say, the mentality of the Monégasques is very special.

Like all small town peoples who band together to protect themselves from outsiders, there's never a shortage of petty jealousies.

'In the beginning,' says Nadia Lacoste, 'people would point at her and say, there's Grace Kelly. I guess it took almost four or five years before they started to say, there's Princess Grace. It's only in the States that they still called her Grace Kelly.'

Realising what she was up against, she deliberately set out to make the change from Grace Kelly to Princess Grace.

'I had so many problems when I first came here,' she once explained. 'To begin with, there was the language. I still spoke very poor French. What I knew of it I'd learned in school. You know, "la plume de ma tante". I was smothered with problems. But I think my biggest single problem was becoming a normal person again, after having been an actress for so long.'

She went on to say that it was also very difficult to learn her new job.

'It was a very hard job that I had to take step by step. Luckily I had the Prince, who was very helpful and very patient with me.

But even so, there were some difficult moments. I got pregnant right after our marriage. Nobody knew this but it meant taking my first steps as Princess of Monaco while being sick as a dog. I didn't let it stop me though. That's the Irish in me. I can laugh at myself. It's a great help. That's a talent I would never exchange for any other.'

She knew she had to be seen, had to earn her acceptance, so she refused to hide in the Palace.

She deliberately set out to create a presence in Monaco.

It wasn't easy at first but, little by little, especially once Caroline and Albert were born, you saw her there.

She became one of the principality's major attractions.

She was visible, not just at official functions when you were supposed to see her, but at normal times when you saw normal human beings.

She'd go shopping.

She'd have tea with friends.

She'd take the kids to school or to the dentist, to buy shoes or to their favourite pastry shop where she'd buy them cakes.

But just as she was winning her way into the hearts of the Monégasques, word spread that she was not very friendly. Some people went so far as to say she was pretentious, snooty to the point where she would walk down the street and not say hello to anyone.

People started asking, 'Who does she think she is?'

A better question would have been, 'What does she think she is?' Because the answer was, terribly short-sighted.

Without glasses she couldn't see three feet in front of herself. She simply couldn't see people across the street to say hello to them. She wasn't snooty at all. In fact, one of the things that made her special was that the average person could relate to her.

She was accessible in Monaco.

People were always coming up to say hello and she was always happy to smile and shake hands.

And she was accessible to people outside Monaco, albeit mostly by mail or through stories in magazines.

Yet even in those magazine stories, her problems, her fears, her dreams were human problems, human fears and human dreams. She might have once been a movie star and she was now a princess but she was also a wife and mother and much of the world saw her as that.

'I think she had fun being a princess,' says Mary Wells, one of America's most successful woman entrepreneurs, head of the Wells, Rich and Green Advertising Agency and an old friend of Grace's. 'In fact, I know she did. But I also think she was a very motherly mother and a very good wife. She was a woman who enjoyed being pretty. Although I know she felt that she had to make a constant effort not to be an outsider in Monaco. After all, she was an American and it wasn't easy for her to be accepted. It took time.'

It also took a special kind of talent.

'Not just anyone could have done it,' Wells maintains. 'She had a very specific talent, a gift. She was larger than life. She was not just a human being, she was an idea. She was an idea that Monte Carlo was a fairytale in an increasingly ugly world. You see, in a world where things were getting more and more difficult, and smaller, and where more and more things were becoming the same, Monte Carlo had a fairytale quality. I think there was something about Grace that gave that to Monaco. It was in the way she did things, the way she acted. She was a real star. And in the world today there aren't a lot of real stars. There are loads of people who are famous, but there are very few real stars.'

As Princess of Monaco, Grace maintained an office on the top floor of the Palace tower, a large room which she decorated in pale greens and pale yellows. Her desk was placed between the two windows from where she could see the port and Monte Carlo behind it. There was a large couch in the office which she'd brought from Philadelphia and on either side of it there were tables with magazines. Plenty of silver-framed photographs of her family were scattered around the room, while on the walls there were paintings and drawings, her favourite being a large oil of New York City.

These days her son uses that office.

Albert has moved the desk round and put his own favourite pictures on the walls. He's changed the room from greens and yellows to Japanese bamboo. The painting of New York is now in his secretary's office.

Her name is Louisette Levy-Soussan and she was his mother's secretary for 18 years.

'The Princess was not just pretty,' Levy-Soussan begins, 'she was beautiful. But she never flaunted that beauty. It was a perfect kind of beauty and maybe that was one of the things that made her so special. Because she was so perfectly beautiful and yet at the same time so simple in her own way, other women were never jealous of her. Of all her children I think that Prince Albert is probably the one who is most like her. They have the same temperament. I look at him and I can see her. I'll tell him something and he doesn't seem to be listening and then three or four days later he'll say something about it. That's exactly the way his mother was.'

She says that while Grace was very easy to work for, she was very strict about certain things.

One of those things was trust.

'Once she trusted someone she would trust them forever. Let's face it, Monaco is a small town and there is always a lot of gossip but once she trusted someone she would defend them and never believe the gossip she'd hear. I remember she once received an anonymous letter from someone obviously involved with the Garden Club because it was about another woman at the Garden Club. It was very nasty. But the princess laughed about it. She said, "I can just see this Woman sitting with a cup of tea writing this letter to poison her friend." She understood.'

Levy-Soussan notes that Grace came to the office every day. She did not, however, keep banker's hours. Sometimes she'd come in early, sometimes she'd come in late. It depended on her appointment schedule.

'Her days were usually very full because she had a lot of responsibilities. There was the Red Cross and the Garden Club and almost all of the cultural activities in Monaco. She was dedicated to what she was doing and wanted everything to be perfect. She was a perfectionist.'

Busy as she kept herself, almost everybody who knew her well is quick to point out that she always seemed to have time for other people.

Says Nadia Lacoste, 'I got the feeling that her door was always open.'

Levy-Soussan insists it was. 'Some people have written about her that she was cold. But she wasn't. She was poised. She kept her feelings to herself, unless she was with friends and then she'd let them out. People who didn't know her sometimes found her, well, maybe the word is guarded. She didn't show everyone the private side of her that she showed to her friends. But she was certainly not cold. She was genuinely kind and very concerned about other people. Once in Paris I wasn't feeling too well, I was a little depressed and she picked up on that right away. That afternoon, when I came back from lunch, I found a small bouquet of flowers on my desk with a note saying. "Go home and change so that you and I can have a lovely tea at Mme Rubenstein's apartment. Would you like that?" She was the kind of person who was there for you.'

In a way, that's why she created the Princess Grace Foundation.

She'd get letters from people who needed help immediately – a mother asking for money for a sickly child, an old age pensioner wanting a new heater to keep warm for the winter, a battered woman looking for shelter, a young boy trying to get off drugs – and, for whatever reason, the Monaco Red Cross couldn't react quickly enough. She'd get desperate pleas from needy people only to find that the group which should have been helping was too tied down in red tape.

So she established the foundation and initially funded it herself.

'I don't need to have an administrative council decide that someone needs an operation or a roof over their head,' she once explained to Nadia Lacoste. 'This way I can say what I want to do with the money.'

Nor did her concern for other people stop there.

When she saw how various artisans in Monaco were struggling to sell their wares, she set up *Le Boutique du Rocher* – the Boutique on the Rock – as a non-profit venture to help local basket weavers and candlemakers and woodworkers earn a living. It proved so successful that the Princess Grace Foundation has since opened a second boutique in Monte Carlo.

Another of Grace's chores was to run the household.

That meant doing the marketing and dealing with the sizeable household staff. She also paid special attention to proper menu planning for the family, to keep Rainier's and her own weight down, and to make sure that the children ate well balanced meals.

'You know what my husband calls me?' Grace once confided in a friend. 'He says I'm his Domestic Affairs Coordinator. Makes me sound like a member of the cabinet.'

During the summer months, when she was at Roc Agel, she'd often work there, preferring not to come into Monaco, asking instead that Levy-Soussan bring her mail to her in the after-noons.

Letters poured in every day.

Totally unsolicited gifts were a regular part of her post, but never more than when her children were born. Then, she was inundated with knitted sweaters and booties.

If something pleased her she'd keep it on a shelf in her office or bring it back to the private apartments.

At other times, she'd donate those endless variations on coffee mugs with GRACE written across the face or ashtrays with her picture on them to charity bazaars.

She also gave a lot of her own clothes to the Red Cross for their jumble sales.

A woman in Genoa so admired Grace that she put together scrapbooks of her newspaper and magazine clippings and sent them to her every year for Christmas. Every year, by return post, Grace would send her a handwritten note to say thank you. Every now and then Grace would also invite her to the Palace for tea.

Then there was the man from Moscow who started sending her Russian stamps. Grace responded by sending him Monégasque stamps and their correspondence lasted for years.

Once a little girl wrote to ask, 'How may hours a day do you spend sitting on your throne and wearing your crown?' Grace wrote back to explain that modern princesses don't do that.

She also liked to keep in touch with friends, at least during the holiday season.

According to Levy-Soussan, Grace had a constantly expanding Christmas card list – 'It got bigger and bigger every year' – and she often added a few words in her own hand.

Clothes were important to her and she dressed well enough always to be included on the list of the world's ten best-dressed women. But if she was going to spend the day in the office and not see anyone, or when she was at home with her family, she dressed simply. Slacks, flat shoes, frequently a scarf tied around her head.

At Roc Agel she often wore jeans and sweatshirt, but it was extremely rare for her to dress that casually in Monaco.

'We live in a palace,' she once commented. 'One is thus a little embarrassed to walk about it wearing blue jeans.'

* * * *

When Grace first arrived in Monaco she had a private tutor to help her with French. Later in life she decided she wanted to speak better Italian so she and a few friends took lessons. As soon as they all felt confident enough, they decided to show off their new-found skills with a private show for a small group at the Palace. Decorating hats and donning masks for costumes, Grace and her Italian class staged a 30 minute all-Italian rendition of Pinocchio.

She loved needlepoint and once did a waistcoat for the Prince. She also did a lot of cushions and got so involved that she went out and formed a local needlepoint club.

'I never saw her idle,' Lacoste says. 'If we had tea in the afternoon, she'd be sitting there knitting or doing needlepoint. If she had some free time, she'd go walking. She adored that. She used to take the small path that follows the sea and walk along the coast. Or she'd walk up the mountain at Roc Angel. She was interested in flowers so she used to carry scissors and a small pouch with her on those walks and stop to cut flowers or pick leaves. When she got home she'd press the leaves and flowers into a book. I don't think you could have pulled a single book off her shelf without flowers and leaves falling out.'

She painted, did collages and for many years went to pottery classes where she made a lot things like ash trays, cups and saucers.

Once she also sculpted a mouse.

The writer Paul Gallico and his wife Virginia lived in Antibes and had become good friends of the family, so much so that Grace named Virginia Gallico as one of her ladies-in-waiting. When Paul Gallico heard that Grace was working in ceramics, he asked if she'd ever been commissioned to do a piece. Grace said she hadn't.

Gallico told her, 'Well, I would like to commission a work from you. But I am merely a humble writer and could not pay you any money for the work. I could only pay you in kind. If you will make a ceramic mouse for me, I will write a story for you.'

Grace said it was a deal and the two shook hands on it.

But months passed and no mouse was forthcoming.

The two would meet at official receptions and, while bowing to her, Gallico would whisper, 'Where's my mouse?'

It was just about a year later that Grace finally finished the piece.

But when she pulled the mouse out of the kiln, it wasn't quite as great a mouse as she'd hoped.

She presented it to Gallico with all sorts of embarrassed excuses.

She said it was smaller than she'd wanted it to be and for some reason it had turned out to be blue, which was definitely the wrong colour for a mouse. Its ears looked more like rabbit's ears and, worse still, its tail had broken off.

'Oh well,' she shrugged, 'now you owe me a story.'

Gallico studied the mouse that evening over dinner and the idea of a mouse without a tail intrigued him.

A year later he handed Grace not a short story but an entire novel that he'd dedicated to her called *Manxmouse*.

It was all about a big-eared, blue mouse without a tail.

Because she ended up with a novel when the deal had only been to pay for the mouse with a short story, Grace decided she had to even the score. She made another mouse for Gallico, called Mrs Manx, and this time she made sure it had a long enough tail for two.

*   *   *   *

As the years passed and her family grew up, she found herself at times longing for some of the creature comforts she'd known in America.

She never hid the fact that she was American and for a long time she and all three of her children held American passports. Eventually they let them go for practical reasons – the United States is the only country in the world that taxes anyone holding an American passport on his or her worldwide income. Still, she missed certain things about the States and tried her best to re-create them in Monaco.

She brought American furniture with her when she moved to Monaco, used an American interior decorator to help her re-do the family apartment and fitted an American kitchen and American bathrooms. She was a member of the American Book of the Month Club, so she received a lot of history books through the mail. She also subscribed to *Architectural Digest* and the *International Herald Tribune*.

But, most of all, she was especially fond of the *New Yorker* because of their cartoons.

She believed there was always a cartoon that was just right for someone she knew.

So, every week, as soon as the magazine arrived, she'd flip through it from cover to cover searching for appropriate cartoons. She'd sit at her desk, grinning from ear to ear, with the magazine and a pair of scissors. Whenever she found one that suited her purpose, she'd cut it out, put it into an envelope and, with great glee, mail it, usually anonymously, to whomever it fit.

* * * *

Once the Monégasques got used to her as Princess Grace, they were very reluctant to allow her to return, even for a little while, to being Grace Kelly.

'Grace's films were shown here,' Rainier says. 'They've been in the local cinemas and on television. We've also shown them in the Palace. Grace got a hold of some 16mm copies from MGM.'

Although, he points out, she only managed it after a lot of effort.

'It wasn't very nice on MGM's part because they were so difficult when she asked for them. They could have been a little more cooperative. They could easily have made a collection of her films available to her but when she asked if she could get copies of her own films all they did was tell us how many problems she was causing by asking. In the end they said we could have some but we had to sign a paper promising that we'd never show them in public. That discouraged her a bit and I don't think we have all of them.'

Watching her films was one thing.

Acting in films was something else again.

The moment their engagement was announced, one of the first questions anyone asked was, will Grace still make movies?

The answer was no.

Rainier told reporters months before their wedding, 'Grace and I have agreed that she must give up her career. She could not possibly combine her royal duties with those of an acting career.'

Right after her marriage, Dory Schary approached her asking if she'd star in *Designing Woman*. She was interested in the film but never really contemplated doing it.

Yet as the years wore on Rainier became less dogmatic about her retirement.

She'd agreed that her film career was over, though she never hid the fact that she missed Hollywood. She was always glad to spend an hour hearing the latest news and gossip from anyone in the film business who found themselves coming through Monaco.

She even regaled her children with stories from Tinsel Town.

'It was great having an actress mother,' Stephanie says, 'because instead of growing up with stupid bedtime stories, my mom would tell me what was going on in the studios and all the latest Hollywood gossip. She'd sing and tap dance and tell me all about her movies.'

Only one of her 11 films was usually left out of polite conversation, a 1954 adventure about emerald mining in South America called *Green Fire*. Grace thought it was 'A dud'.

Then, in 1963, Alfred Hitchcock sent her a screenplay called *Marnie*.

He was hoping to cast her opposite Sean Connery, who was at the time the hottest male property in the business. He'd broken all the box office records with his portrayal of James Bond in *Dr No*. Hitchcock planned to release this film in between two other James Bond epics, *From Russia with Love* and *Goldfinger*. He wanted Grace to play the role of the compulsive thief caught by Connery and given the choice of either marriage with him or prison.

It was powerful stuff and Grace wanted to do it.

But there could be no question of making another film unless her husband approved.

'She and I talked about it,' Rainier says. 'We also talked to Hitchcock about it. She was very anxious to get back into the swing of things. By that point I didn't see anything wrong with it so I suggested we combine her work on the film with a family vacation. They were supposed to shoot somewhere in New England over the summer. I proposed that we rent a house nearby and go with the children. She said, "If that's your idea of a vacation fine, except working on a film is not what I'd call vacation."'

Hitchcock announced that Grace was coming back.

But not everybody in Monaco liked the idea of their Princess returning to the screen.

Rumblings of discontent soon reached the Prince's ears.

'The appeal of *Marnie* was Hitchcock. He was, I think, very fond of both of us and we both trusted him. Grace would never have considered a film with just anybody. But this was Hitchcock. He was totally in charge and I can't imagine that he would have ever done anything or allowed anything to happen that might have in any way belittled the principality or Grace's position as Princess.'

That might be, but when the question of her fee hit the papers, rumours spread through Europe that Grace was only returning to films because the family was broke and needed the money.

In response, Grace announced that her entire fee would be put into a trust to help needy children.

MGM added their two-cents worth by announcing that if she made a picture for anyone other than MGM she would be in breach of her contract which, MGM claimed, they still controlled.

Then the French newspapers criticised her for concocting the whole thing just to annoy the French President.

As this was happening at the same time that Rainier was battling with Charles de Gaulle, the papers wrote that Grace's return to films was merely Rainier's way of showing de Gaulle that the Prince and Princess of Monaco would do whatever they pleased.

That was followed by a letter from Pope John XXIII personally asking Grace as a Catholic Princess not make the film.

The Monégasques banded together and petitioned their Prince to put an end to this.

'The Prince couldn't see why there was such a public reaction against Grace making film,' comments Nadia Lacoste, who was soon knee-deep in press criticism of the plan. 'I told him that to be an actress was a trade, a profession, and that maybe being Princess of Monaco was also a profession, but a completely different kind of profession. I asked him how he'd see the posters for the film. I wondered if he thought they'd bill her as Grace Kelly or Princess Grace or even Grace Grimaldi? I had the feeling that he hadn't thought about that before.'

Lacoste tried to make him understand that if Grace went back to do a movie it would obviously be as Princess Grace.

'The Prince looked at me and said, "You're so old fashioned." He pointed out that King Albert of Belgium used to climb mountains. I said, "But climbing mountains is a sport, making movies is a business." I just don't think he realised the implications until he thought about what the posters would say.'

Now, with the benefit of hindsight, Rainier feels that Grace's billing would not have been a problem.

'How would they have publicised the film, starring Princess Grace or starring Grace Kelly? It would have been as Grace Kelly because that's the name she worked under. Come on, if Ronald Reagan did a film now, would the posters say, "*Snatch Me Molly*, starring Former President Reagan?"' He suddenly starts to laugh. 'There's a thought to ponder.'

In the end, public opinion won out and Grace announced that she would not do the film.

'I must say', Rainier goes on, 'that she made her decision without any influence from me. I thought it would be great fun for all of us, especially the kids. And I knew she wanted to make more films. It would also mean working again with Hitchcock, whom she adored. Oh well.'

Hitchcock's long-standing girlfriend, Tippi Hedren, got Grace's role and, in spite of panning reviews when it opened in 1964, it is today considered one of Hitchcock's darkest masterpieces.

Grace accepted defeat reluctantly.

'Yes, she missed performing,' Rainier recalls, 'very much so. But mostly she missed the stage, not the movies. That's why she did the poetry readings. She could do it without attracting much criticism. Although people are sometimes such idiots that they even criticised her for reading poetry in public. With some people you can never do anything right.'

Some time after the *Marnie* incident, Rainier and Grace found themselves in Hollywood. She told friends in California that she'd pretty much given up any ambition of ever making another film. She visited a set with her family and after a few minutes started shaking her head. She told her old friend Gant Gaither, 'It's all changed so much. I couldn't work like this.'

However, two years later, Rainier and Grace agreed that she could appear in a documentary about drug addiction for UNICEF.

Included in the cast were Rita Hayworth, Trevor Howard,

Angie Dickinson, Jack Hawkins and Yul Brynner. And just so that there could be no repeat of the *Marnie* incident, it was well publicised that her appearance was for charity and that her salary was $1.

In 1970 she stepped in at the last minute for an ailing Noël Coward as host of a major charity gala at London's Royal Festival Hall.

She followed that in 1973 with a British television appearance in a show called *The Glories of Christmas*.

All of this was fun for her and it didn't raise too many eyebrows in Monaco, but deep down she knew it wasn't really show business. That's one of the reasons why in July 1976 she accepted a seat on the board of Twentieth Century Fox.

By then Grace was living most of the year in Paris while Stephanie went to school there. Paris had rekindled her need for the cultural bounties of a world-class city, although she often said that she was getting anxious for Stephanie to finish school so that she could move back to Monaco.

'I'm not as fond of Paris as I used to be,' she admitted to close friends. 'I'm lonesome here. I guess I'm just a small town girl at heart.'

Yet that small town girl still wanted to return to performing.

There were always film offers. And she could have commanded an enormous fee. A Grace Kelly comeback might have been the biggest box office draw of the decade. There's no telling what kind of money a producer would have paid for that sort of coup. If Marlon Brando, Jack Nicholson, Dustin Hoffman, Barbara Streisand, Sally Field and Jane Fonda could get $1 million for a picture in those days, it's fair to assume that the return of Grace Kelly might easily have been worth two, three, five, ten times as much. She probably could have named her price and got it. But *Marnie* had put a damper on any hopes she might have had.

'Acting in a film again might have been in the back of her mind,' remarks Lacoste, 'but she had a lot of other priorities. Don't forget, she came along before the women's movement, before women wanted to prove they could do anything men could do. In her mind she was the Princess of Monaco and the mother of three children and her job was to deal with that. I once asked her if it had been very difficult to give up Hollywood. After all, she quit at the top. But she said, "No." She answered very clearly, "To me, marriage has always been more important than

my career." Of course, there were times when she thought about
the old days and maybe even missed making movies. She loved to
talk about movies, about who could play this part or another part.
But to say she was sorry she wasn't still in the movies, no, I never
heard that. I never felt that.'

Now Grace's thinking began to change.

Motion pictures were one thing.

Performing on stage might be something else. It was less visible. It was also more in keeping with the serious tradition of the
legitimate actor. Rainier says he was supportive of her and agreed
that, if she could find something suitable, she'd be welcome to do
it. However, anything she wanted to do would have to be carefully
judged and presented in such a way as to be compatible with her
image as the Princess of Monaco.

It was the American bicentennial in 1976 that came to her
rescue.

Celebrations commemorating the Declaration of Independence took various forms throughout the world. Even in Great
Britain – a nation which might be forgiven for suggesting that
American independence was the result of the illegal overthrow
by force and violence of the rightful government – the year was
welcomed with pride and affection. Among the celebrations was
a special series of American music and drama performances at the
highly acclaimed Edinburgh Festival.

In keeping with the theme, John Carroll, who had for years
devised special poetry programmes for the Festival, was asked by
the then director if he would consider staging a programme with
an American slant. Carroll scripted a selection of poems under
the theme of *An American Heritage* but felt that the best way to
present the poems was with American voices. He started thinking
about an American star who might be right for such an event and,
while there were many obvious choices, an old friend suggested
Princess Grace. Carroll said he liked the idea very much. That
friend, who knew Grace, put them in touch.

They met for the first time in Paris.

'I went to have lunch with her and we clicked. She loved the
idea, although she did say she'd have to discuss it with the Prince.
Ten days later she rang to tell me it would be okay. I said that I
thought she should have two actors reading with her and because
the performance was in the United Kingdom at least one of them
should be British. I nominated Richard Pasco who'd been with the

RSC. She promised to think about the other actor and settled on Richard Kiley who'd starred on Broadway in *Man of La Mancha.'*

Before making a final selection of works to be performed, Carroll went to the BBC and listened to recordings of Grace's voice so that he could choose poems that suited her. These included works by Longfellow, Whitman, Frost, Thoreau, Dickinson and one poem in particular by Eleanor Wylie called *Wild Peaches.*

Grace arrived in Edinburgh three days before the first performance so that she could rehearse.

'I'll probably be a bag of nerves,' Grace told one reporter at the airport.

Carroll guided her through two script runs in the sitting-room of her suite at the Caledonian Hotel and one full dress rehearsal in St Cecilia's Hall.

'I was a bit worried about how she'd take direction,' he confides. 'But she was a lamb. When I selected *Wild Peaches* for her I felt it should be done with southern accent. I just wasn't sure I could ask Grace to do it that way. Well, after we rehearsed it the first time she turned to me and wondered, "Shouldn't I do this with a southern accent?" That's how good she was.'

Grace, Pasco and Kiley did four performances in September 1976 at St Cecilia's Hall and the reviews for her were ecstatic. The reception they received in Edinburgh was so enthusiastic, it seemed natural that Carroll should asked Grace if she wanted to recite in public again. He suggested she should appear in Stratford-upon-Avon as part of the 1977 summer Shakespeare Festival. She agreed, and he put together a programme called, *A Remembrance of Shakespeare.* Carroll staged it with Grace, Pasco, English actor John Westbrook and opera singer Sir Peter Pears at Trinity Church where the Bard is thought to be buried.

'We needed to do a full rehearsal,' Carroll continues, 'so the church was closed on the evening before the performance. Grace arrived that night carrying a beautiful, long-stemmed rose. A typical Grace gesture. She brought it to put on Shakespeare's tomb.'

But that was not the only typical Grace gesture of the evening.

John Westbrook recollects that the rehearsal was held up by a bunch of photographers who'd come to shoot pictures of her.

'When they were finished she told them, "Perhaps I should be photographed with Mr Westbrook." I thought that was rather remarkable. Later, when we got onto the platform and took our seats and the lights were arranged, John Carroll said to her, "Is the lighting all right for you, dear lady?" She answered, "It's fine for me but I really think there should be more light on Mr Westbrook." Now, let me say that I've been in this business for a long time and I've done recitals with some of my closest friends from the theatre and not one of them has ever said, "I think there should be more light on Mr Westbrook."'

He was equally impressed by how professional she was.

'She'd been trained in the theatre and that showed. She knew how to command an audience. Her talent was obvious and she was also exceedingly beautiful. The two don't always go together, do they, but she had them both.'

The enormous publicity generated by Grace's poetry readings had two immediate consequences.

The first was an offer to narrate a film called *The Children of Theatre*, a documentary about the Kirov Ballet School in Leningrad.

Grace not only accepted to do the voice-over, she also attended the premières in aid of ballet charities in New York, Lausanne and Paris. She only missed the London première, at which Princess Margaret was the guest of honour, because she wasn't invited.

One British newspaper speculated that the invitation had not been extended to her because it would have proved very embarrassing to Princess Margaret to be upstaged by Princess Grace.

As no other explanation was ever forthcoming from the organisers, it's as good a reason as any.

The second consequence was Grace's first poetry-reading American tour.

The American International Poetry Forum in Pittsburgh wanted her to do the *An American Heritage* programme in the summer of 1978. She asked Carroll's opinion. He said, 'I think going to the States is a wonderful idea but not to do *An American Heritage*. There's an old saying about taking coals to Newcastle. What I think would be nicer is a new programme, written especially for the tour.'

Carroll knew Grace was interested in the World Wildlife Fund so he devised a script with poetry and some prose around the theme of animals and called it, *Birds, Beasts and Flowers*. And, at the end of February 1978, Grace, Richard Pasco and Carroll opened their tour in Pittsburgh.

'Wherever we went she was adored,' says Carroll. 'Although one morning in Pittsburgh I wanted to buy something at a shop near the hotel, mentioned it to Grace and she said she'd come with me. She put on dark glasses and a scarf and the two of us walked arm in arm down the street through the middle of the city. And no one recognised her. She could be anonymous when she wanted to be. It meant she could also relax and just be herself.'

From Pittsburgh they flew on to Minneapolis, Philadelphia, Washington DC, Princeton and Harvard. This part of the tour had been booked by an impressario who paid everyone a fee, including Grace, who donated her salary to the Princess Grace Foundation.

Notes Carroll, 'In several places where we played two performances, they charged an enormous amount for the first one and regular prices for the second. It's much to Grace's credit that she didn't approve of that. She felt the first-night prices were way too high and that they excluded too many people.'

Back in Europe, requests for more appearances poured in. She and Carroll chose the venues with the same care that they chose the poems. She appeared at the 1978 Aldeburgh Festival in East Suffolk, England, with, among other people, Mstislav Rostropovich.

That same weekend, the local cinema got hold of a copy of *High Society* and showed it to packed houses.

Next she did a performance of *Birds, Beasts and Flowers* for charity at St James's Palace in London with the Queen Mother in attendance.

Believing that these recitals were, as John Carroll puts it, 'a compromise between her old career and the dignity of her position', she appeared in 1979 at Trinity College as part of the Dublin Festival, and in London again at both the Royal Academy of Arts and the Lyric Theatre in Hammersmith, now doing a programme called *The Muses Combined*, a series of readings on the arts of painting and sculpture.

Those were followed with appearances at Tatton Hall in Cheshire and the English Theatre of Vienna.

'I didn't realise it at the time,' Carroll says, 'but Grace could speak some German. She learned it from her mother. When she told me that, we added a couple of short verses from Austrian poets referring to the magic of Vienna. Grace recited them in

German at the very end of the programme and absolutely brought down the house.'

Each success brought more offers.

A second US tour was arranged for the end of summer 1980.

Grace returned to Pittsburgh to do the Shakespeare programme there, then performed something new by John Carroll called *Evocations* in Detroit, Dallas, Nashville and Baltimore. It created such excitement that one Dallas paper wrote that there were more millionaires in the audience on Grace's opening night than had ever been seen in one place in the city before.

Between poetry recitals, Grace teamed up with British writer Gwen Robbins to do a book on flower arranging.

Like all best-selling authors, as soon as *A Garden of Flowers* was published, Grace embarked on a publicity tour, suffered end-less interviews for newspapers and magazines, did live radio for the first time in many years and appeared on selected television shows where her hosts were pre-warned not to stray from the subject of the book.

Financially it was huge success and Grace's portion of royalties was soon bolstering the bank accounts of charities such as the Monaco Red Cross.

In connection with that, she also made a film.

Titled *Rearranged*, she wrote the script, supervised the direction and starred in it.

Shot entirely on location in Monaco, she included all her friends in it. There is even a cameo, flower-arranging appearance by her husband.

Never meant to be anything more than an elaborate home movie, a fun project strictly for the benefit of the Garden Club of Monaco, it's only had a few select showings.

When other garden clubs around the world heard about it, there was talk of allowing them to screen it. But Grace's death put an end to that.

Approaches have since been made to buy the rights to the film for commercial, public distribution. One offer went as high as $6 million. But Rainier says that would have entailed re-editing the film and turning it into something it was never intended to be. The print is locked in a Palace vault and Rainier says that's where it will stay.

In 1981, Grace was back in England to do a poetry recital for the Royal Opera at Covent Garden.

She performed at Goldsmith's Hall in the City of London. But this time she had to share the spotlight with a young girl named Diana Spencer.

Her engagement to Prince Charles had just been announced and this was the first time they'd been seen in public together.

Diana appeared in a low-cut, black evening dress that made her look very busty.

The photographers loved it but that only served to send the naturally shy 19 year old deeper into her shell.

Grace picked up on Diana's discomfort right away and moved in fast to lend moral support.

Says Carroll, 'Grace was very motherly with the future Princess of Wales. Diana was terribly nervous. This was her first public appearance apart from posing for pictures with the press in the garden at Buckingham Palace when her engagement was announced. If you remember she was a bit on the plump side in those days. She's slimmed no end since then. But the black dress was *décolletée* and it caused quite a stir. Diana was painfully shy but Grace understood what she was going through. She kept whispering things to Diana. She really was exactly like a mother with her.'

Grace read at the Chichester Festival in March 1982, then went to Philadelphia to accept the home-town honour of a four-day Grace Kelly Film Festival.

In cooperation with the Roman Catholic Congregation of the Holy Cross in New York, Grace agreed to host a series of three half-hour television programmes.

'The Last Seven Words, The Nativity and *The Greatest Mystery* were filmed on location at the Vatican, St Patrick's Cathedral in New York and Chichester Cathedral in England. They featured such varied singers as Placido Domingo and Petula Clark doing spiritual music with choral backgrounds plus British Shakespearean actors doing dramatisations from the Bible.

The only country in the west that wouldn't show them, even after her death, was Great Britain. The BBC refused because they insist on making their own religious programmes, while ITV refused because of the obvious Catholic message.

'Grace was totally comfortable with religion,' Rainier notes. 'She was a practising Catholic and had a very strong, pure faith. She was certainly more rigorous than I was. If we were travelling someplace and it was Sunday she'd insist that we find a church to attend mass. Maybe I wouldn't have always bothered but she made it an important issue. I think it was her Irishness.'

Convinced that poetry readings were the next best thing to being a working actress again, she scheduled further appearances around her official duties in Monaco.

One night, over dinner in a small restaurant in the south of France at the very beginning of September 1982, Grace told Mary Wells, 'I'm so looking forward to this year. I'm coming into a whole new period of my life. The children are grown, Monte Carlo is great, everything is terrific. My responsibilities have changed and I can finally do so many of the things I really want to do. I'm excited about the future. Now is my time.'

Adds Wells, 'She said she wanted to perform more. She said she wanted to paint more. She said she had all sorts of things set up in different places. They were personal, creative projects that she was going to do, as opposed to being a mother and supporting the children and being an image for Monaco. And I looked at her as she was talking and thought to myself, you have never been as beautiful as you are this minute.'

Grace had agreed to read at the Windsor Festival later that month, to do a short series of performances in Austria in March 1983 and to appear at a festival in Washington in June 1983 at the start of her third US tour.

An English actress took Grace's place at Windsor.

The Vienna performance and the US tour were cancelled.

And Nancy Reagan stood in for Grace at the Washington reading.

*　*　*　*

12

Caroline, Albert and Stephanie

*R*AINIER, Grace and their three children have long had an association with the Connaught Hotel in London which has long had a tradition of catering to European royals.

Because some royals are not as stuffy as the Connaught, the two don't always mix.

Very early one Friday morning, with Grace in residence, Caroline and a couple of her friends turned up at the hotel hoping to get breakfast.

They'd been to the famous, pre-dawn Bermondsey antique market, making their way through the maze of stalls armed with flashlights to see the bric-à-brac.Then , still clad in jeans and heavy sweaters, they decided to cap the morning with coffee and croissants at the Connaught.

Walking through the front door, Caroline asked the reception manager where they could get something to eat.

Looking down his nose, he suggested that she and her friends were hardly properly attired for the Connaught.

Caroline explained they'd been to Bermondsey.

He shook his head and apologised, 'Sorry ma'am.'

She said, 'All we want is coffee and maybe some toast or something.'

He shook his head again and said, 'Sorry ma'am, not dressed like that.'

'Come on,' she said, 'You know who I am. We stay here all the time.'

He stood his ground. 'Sorry ma'am, not dressed like that.'

She tried, 'How about if we take a room?'

He wouldn't give in. 'Sorry ma'am.'

'Okay,' Caroline said. 'My mother's here, we'll have breakfast with her.'

She went to the house phone and, despite the early hour, asked for her mother's room. After a few rings Grace picked up the phone. Caroline said, 'Good morning,' and explained the situation. 'Just because we've got jeans on they don't want to serve us breakfast.'

Grace answered, 'Perfectly right, dear,' hung up and went straight back to sleep.

*   *   *   *

Stephanie was the tomboy of the family, raised somewhat in the shadow of her brother and sister.

Like Caroline, she started school in Monaco. Like Caroline, she took piano lessons and attended dance classes. Like Albert, she was encouraged to pursue her interests in sports.

Because Caroline, clearly following in their mother's footsteps, attended a very exclusive, very private convent school for proper young ladies, it was only natural that Stephanie would also attend such a school.

Caroline went to one in England and loved it.

Stephanie went to one outside Paris and absolutely detested it.

It was a dreadful place. But neither Rainier nor Grace realised just how awful it was until they saw it. Once they did, it caused a minor row. Rainier wanted to find Stephanie another school. Stephanie also wanted to find another school.

Grace said no.

At St Mary's College in Ascot, Caroline was taught by young English nuns with a relatively modern approach. Her headmistress was a brilliant woman whom Caroline adored and the two kept in touch for many years.

Stephanie fared considerably less well.

She found herself at a high school where the sisters were older and grumpy and the place was decidedly stale. The setting was also pretty grim, totally isolated in the middle of some woods.

Rainier remembers, 'We took her there by car for the first term, but as soon as we got there I knew I didn't like it. They'd announced a swimming pool but that didn't exist. They'd announced tennis courts but there was nothing more than a mud plot with a net strung across it. It was a real disappointment. By the time we drove away and left her standing there, waving goodbye, she was in tears. I said to Grace, "We've really made a mistake. Let's turn around and go back." But she said no. She was stronger than I was about that. I was absolutely prepared to bring Stephanie home to Paris with us.'

Even today the very mention of the place makes Stephanie wince.

'I thoroughly hated it. I only spent one term there, September to December, but it was more than enough. I'd broken my foot so I was in my room a lot. Can you believe they had bars on the windows and two German shepherd dogs that they'd let loose at night to keep the girls from running away? We weren't allowed to put anything up on the walls or even to have a radio. It was an experience! Frankly, I still don't understand why I was sent to that place. I wasn't that bad, to be stuck there like that. Of course, looking back, I guess it was at the time of my sister's divorce and my parents probably wanted to keep me away from that whole situation. But I left as soon as I could. A week before Christmas break I escaped. I just took my things and got out of there.'

Rainier sympathises, 'The school did have some pretty silly rules. To begin with, the girls had to wear dark blue skirts down to their ankles, with big pleats in them and white shirts with long sleeves. Then, the girls had nothing at all to say in the running of the school, the way Caroline and her friends could voice their opinions at St Mary's. In other words, at this place, the girls did what they were told to or were punished for disobedience. Worst still, there was a limit on the number of showers they could take each week.'

Two!

Only Stephanie's distaste for desserts saved her from that.

'Mom didn't raise us to eat a lot of sweets. None of us in the family like desserts. Albert might have some sweets sometimes but when we were growing up my mom would put fruit or yoghurt on the table for dessert. We didn't get to see a lot of cakes and cream pies. Well, it didn't take me long to find out that some of the other girls were more interested in my desserts than they were in their own showers. So I negotiated away my desserts and wound up with a shower every day. I'd rather be clean and starving than fat and dirty.'

At the end of that one term she transferred to the more congenial atmosphere of a well-known boarding school in Paris, not far from the family apartment.

'That was so much better because I could go home on Wednesday nights and on weekends. I liked that school. I had my own room and there were no convent rules. I took a shower every day without being hassled and still didn't eat my desserts.'

She passed her *baccalauréat* in 1982.

Then the car accident changed the course of her life.

Stephanie promptly dropped out of everything.

Her boyfriend at the time was Paul Belmondo, son of French actor Jean Paul Belmondo. He comforted her. They watched videos together all day long. She stayed in Paris and hid in her shell.

She went through a lot of videos.

Rainier, Caroline and Albert were obviously concerned.

She told them she didn't want to go on to university.

But, after a while, she said she was interested enough in fashion that she might do something with that. It took a year but in the autumn of 1983 she enrolled on a fashion course in Paris. At the end of it Marc Bohan hired her as a design assistant at Christian Dior.

Now the old Stephanie was starting to re-emerge.

One day she showed up with her hair dyed punk orange. The powers at Dior sent her home with orders to wash it out immediately. She did. So the next day showed up with her hair dyed punk green.

'My time at Dior was a great learning experience. I went to work every morning at 9:30, stayed there until I was supposed to leave and had a pay cheque at the end of every month. It was a real job. I had a little apartment in Paris and lived on my own. I was flattered that my father would trust me to do that. After all, I was barely 18. But I learned so much. I learned everything I know about fashion from Marc Bohan. He was great and I'll never be able to thank him enough for taking me in.'

Before long, she traded Paul Belmondo in for Anthony Delon, son of French actor Alain Delon, left Bohan and began modelling.

'Actually, what I wanted to do was create my own bathing suit company. I planned it with a girl I'd met at Dior, but we needed to raise some money. I didn't want to ask my father for it. I have my own pride. I wanted to do it myself. Well, I knew a girl who worked as a model and she convinced me that I could earn enough modelling to start my company. So I became a model.'

Five foot eight, thin, boyishly exotic and with absolutely stunning blue eyes, she had no trouble at all getting work. The fashion photographers loved her and she quickly commanded fees of $5,000 – $10,000 a day, that's £3,000 – £6,000.

'I made the rounds with my portfolio under my arm, just like all models have to. And believe me, it's not a lot of fun. Most models are exploited. I know I was. I worked very hard at it but most of the time photographers were more interested in their camera than they were in me. They didn't care how hot it was under the lights or how long the session lasted. If I complained they simply picked up the phone and asked for another brunette.'

Talk was, at the time, that Rainier was not pleased with Stephanie's modelling but she says that wasn't quite the case.

'If he was really unhappy about it he would have made me stop right away. The truth is that he let me go through with it. I gave it up because I was working so hard that I got ill.'

A US tour had been booked by a New York agency to launch her as a major new face in the States. A lot of money was at stake. But it was cancelled at the very last minute. When satisfactory explanations were not immediately forthcoming from the Grimaldis, the press reported that Rainier was so upset with Stephanie he'd simply pulled the plug on her career and forbidden her to go.

'That's not what happened. The day before I was to leave for the States, I'd been on a job. It was supposed to be done by six that evening but we didn't finish until two the next morning. I was so exhausted from working 60 hour weeks and such crazy schedules that when I got home I passed out. A friend found me unconscious on the floor and rushed me to the hospital.'

Modelling had by this time put enough cash in her bank account to enable her to go into the bathing suit business.

She and her partner brought out a line of swimsuits under the name Pool Positions which they described as 'sexy without being vulgar'. They showed their first collection in Monaco and immediately sold their wares to major outlets like Bloomingdales, Macy's and Harrods.

'It surprised us as much as anyone else that in our very first year we invaded the market the way we did. But I'd like to think that most of our success was based on the bathing suits themselves and not merely on the fact that my name was involved. Sure we did the fashion show in Monaco because that helped. Why not? But in the end you have to please the buyers. If they can't sell the bathing suits in their stores it doesn't matter a damn to them who the designer is. If the bathing suits weren't good they would have said, "This is all very nice but thank you anyway, we'll wait till next year." Instead we had books and books of orders from around the world.'

But the partnership wasn't to be. Personalities clashed. And only two years into the venture the friend she'd started the company with walked out.

'I felt betrayed and hurt when she left because I always considered her to be my friend. Friendship for me is so important and so hard to find. I guess maybe it's that way for everybody. I have one true, true friend in Paris whom I've known for 12 years. He's the kind of person I know I can call any time of the day or the night and if I need him, he'll be there. I just think it hurts more to be betrayed in friendship than it does in business or even in love.'

The company is still active although she did not bring out a 1989 swimsuit collection. She says she simply couldn't find the time to put it together.

It seems music and acting got in the way.

In the middle of her designing career, someone offered her the chance to cut a single, she took it and her song *Irresistible* shot to number one in the French charts.

That might have been expected.

After all, she is extremely well known in France.

To be perfectly honest, her voice is thin and there's no confusing her with, say, Barbara Streisand.

Still, the record sold an impressive 1.3 million copies in Europe in the first 90 days and five million to date.

'Here again I wasn't expecting it to happen like that. I never thought the record would sell the way it did. But given the chance to sing I discovered that's what I really want to do. Singing and acting. It's become my life.'

With the success of the record giving her enough incentive to seek a career in show business, Stephanie found it increasingly difficult to continue living in France.

First there was the terror of having nearly been kidnapped.

In November 1984, a couple tried to force their way into her car and drive off with her.

'That was very strange. And there was a police station just across the street. I was pulling into the garage at my father's apartment when a guy put a gun to my head. I froze. My body was like jelly but my mind was functioning. I kept trying to squirm around in the car. I kept thinking, if he's going to shoot it's better to get it in the arm or the leg and not in the head. So I kept trying to push the guy away.'

Suddenly his girl accomplice appeared at the other side of the car and began yelling, 'Shoot her, shoot her.'

'Out of the blue I said to the guy, "Look, my father is upstairs. If you want to speak to him, let's all go up there and talk it out." I said, "That's the best thing. Let's go upstairs and talk because nobody is going to pay for a dead body." That's when the guy freaked out and left. He and the girl turned and ran away. That's when I freaked out too. I crawled into the concierge's apartment and I was a mess. It was all very weird.'

Next came the jealousy that seems to be one of the inevitable results of success.

'It was driving me crazy. People kept asking me why was I working. They kept telling me that I was taking something away from someone who deserved success more than I did. They hurt me a lot. There was so much crap in the papers about me. They were saying that it was only because I was a princess that my record worked. My answer was, "Selling five million records can't be because it's me, it's because people like the music." Maybe I could sell 100,000 records because I'm me. But come on, never five million!'

She doesn't hide her displeasure when she talks about the way she's been treated.

'It gets down to sheer nastiness. You can be number two and everyone will always love you. However, if you're number one they have to try to destroy you. Did you know that when my record was number one on the French charts, a girl who had a song further down the list purposely tripped me one night while I was going on stage to sing and I broke my ankle? Can you believe that? I would never ever think of doing that to someone. But it doesn't happen like that in America. When I was looking for back-up singers in Los Angeles for my album, George Michael was there and he arranged for me to use his back-up group. He wanted to help me. I decided I couldn't handle things in Europe any more so I moved to America.'

In this case, yet another factor played a part.

The accident.

'There was a lot of pressure on me because everyone was saying that I had been driving the car, that it was all my fault, that I'd killed my mother. It's not easy when you're 17 to live with that. There was so much magic that surrounded mom, so much of the dream, that in some ways she almost stopped being human. It was difficult for people to accept that she could do something so human as to have a car accident. People figured I must have caused it because she was too perfect to do something like that. After a while you can't help feeling guilty. Everybody looks at you and you know they're thinking, how come she's still around and Grace is dead? No one ever said it to me like that but I knew that's what they were thinking. I needed my mother a lot when I lost her. And my dad was so lost without her. I felt so alone. I just went off to do my own thing.'

Stephanie moved to California in October 1986.

Before long she was romantically linked with Mario Olivier Jutard, a twice-married, former waiter from Marseilles who had a criminal record for sexual assault in the United States. He claimed to be a restauranteur and for a time ran a disco in LA.

The romance lasted nearly two years.

'My dad wasn't exactly thrilled about him,' she says, pausing a moment to admit, 'but then nobody was. And I can understand why. But I look at it this way. I did what I had to do and eventually realised it wasn't what I wanted, so I got out of it. Life goes on. I don't regret anything. Dad must have understood what I was going through because I don't think he would have let me go through it for so long if he didn't know I was going to eventually realise it wasn't for me and come out of it all right. Otherwise he would have had me on the first plane back.'

She feels he proved that he believed in her by letting her learn her own lessons.

'He knows me pretty well. Sometimes he says that I'm the one who is most like him. I think it's true. We have very much of the same character although I don't get as carried away when I get angry as he does. I shake when he gets angry. It passes quickly. He doesn't stay angry long. But his voice changes and it gets pretty scary for a few minutes. Then he calms down and he's a sweet little pussy cat. Still, when he starts growling, it's best to get out of the way. He makes his point and you say to yourself, I don't think I want to get him angry ever again.'

It's hardly any secret that the Jutard episode strained Stephanie's relationship with her father.

Yet the door was never closed.

She says they both purposely made every effort, no matter what, to keep it open.

'Sometimes growing up I forgot the door was open and my parents freaked out. It's the same with all parents and their children. I sometimes thought they were the ones closing the door when I was trying to keep it open but I know now that wasn't quite the way it was. I realise how lucky I was because my parents always kept the door open.'

Especially now.

'Yes, especially now, because my father and I are on a different level. We communicate differently now that I've grown up. I don't think he thinks of me as his little baby any longer. He still wants to protect me but it's on a more adult level. I hope I've proven to him that I can do my own thing in life and that I am responsible and that our relationship is a father–daughter relationship based on advice and support. He doesn't lecture me. I ask for advice and he gives it to me without insisting that I follow it. He'll say, "This is what I think, now you go ahead and make whatever you want of it." He and I are much closer than we've ever been, especially with my mom gone. He doesn't feel that he has to look after me in the way that he had to when I was a child. I told him, "I want you to look after me and take care of me by being my friend."'

When her swimsuit company was going through some financial problems, she turned to her father, not for funds, but for business advice. He then instructed his own personal business advisers to look into the situation so that she would get the best guidance possible.

'Okay, I want to do things on my own but I don't want to be completely isolated.'

In Los Angeles now, settling down to take up a music and acting career, she's got herself an agent and has started reading for parts.

'My agent is very tough and won't send me anything if she isn't 100 per cent sure it's absolutely right for me. She says she gets 30 calls a week for me but she turns everything down if it isn't absolutely perfect.'

At the same time, Stephanie spends two hours a day with her vocal coach and meets three times a week with Nina Foch, her acting coach.

Because, as she puts it, she's a night person – 'I can't get up in the morning' – her day doesn't really begin until about 2 p.m.

Coincidentally, that's when her favourite soap opera, *Days of Our Lives*, ends.

'I must confess that I watch that soap every day.' For a very brief moment Stephanie even comes close to blushing. 'It's been running for I don't know how many years but I watch it faithfully. I love it. So, no, my day doesn't usually start until that's over.'

Here she laughs.

'The other afternoon I was with a girlfriend in LA and we stopped at a red light and in the car next to us was the guy who plays Roman Brady in *Days of Our Lives*. I don't even know his real name but he was right there and we both screamed like teenaged girls.'

Does this mean that Princess Stephanie of Monaco can get star-struck?

'Oh God!' Her face lights up. 'The first time I met Peter Gabriel I nearly fainted. It was at the CBS Grammy Awards party. I was talking to Rod Stewart and someone tapped me on the shoulder and there was Peter Gabriel and my legs turned to jelly. I acted like a jerk.'

It goes without saying, of course, that she happens to be one of the most recognisable women in Europe. Which, she explains, is another reason why Los Angeles agrees with her.

'In Paris I get recognised all the time. Although once a woman came up to me in a bakery and said, "It's incredible how much you look like Princess Stephanie." So I answered, "Don't talk to me about her. Every day somebody tells me that. Every day. What do I have to do, cut my hair not to look like her? I have enough of her. I'm really fed up with Princess Stephanie." The poor lady kept apologising and saying how awful it must be to look like her.'

In California it seems that it's mainly French people who ask if she's Princess Stephanie.

'They try talking to me in French and I've found that if I stare at them and say in English, "What? What did you say? What language is that?" they go away mumbling, "No, no, it's not her." Funny, but for Americans I'm not Princess Stephanie, I'm Grace Kelly's daughter. When Americans recognise me that's what they ask, are you her daughter? But what I really like about Los Angeles is that people don't bother with too much stuff like that. I'm just one well-known face among thousands of well-known faces. The average soap star, like the fellow who plays Roman Brady, is much more famous in LA than I am.'

Approaching her mid-20s, Stephanie is probably more settled and together now than at any time in the past 10 years. And part of the credit for that probably has to go to her current boyfriend, American record producer Ron Bloom.

'My father likes him. They met not long ago in LA. He's in his mid-30s, writes music and lyrics, plays 20 instruments and produces my records. He and I have a lot in common. We have a great relationship. He's a very intelligent man, with strong family values and roots. He's someone who's been raised with family values and that's important to both of us. After my break up with Mario, when I might not have been on the best of terms with my father, Ron was the one who helped me realise how important it was to get back on good terms with my dad. He helped me a lot with that. He told me, "The most important thing you have is your family. They love you and will always love you so don't close yourself off from them. Show them that you love them too." That was very important to me.'

These days, thanks in part to Bloom's influence, Stephanie and Rainier have patched up their relationship and are constantly in touch.

'Dad and I speak two or three times a week by phone. At least that. We talk about a lot of things and tell each other the latest jokes. We're very close, all four of us. At one point or another I guess one of us might have drifted off for a while to do his or her own thing but we always come back home. A family is a family and that's the best thing in the world.'

Rainier recently visited Stephanie in Los Angeles and liked enough of what he saw of her life there to stay an extra five days.

Although he slept at a hotel, he arrived at her house every morning at 10:30 and, like so many dads everywhere, showered his little girl with gifts.

The very first day he got there he walked around the house, took note of what she needed and promptly went with some of his friends to a local shopping centre to buy her, among other things, a microwave oven.

So, Bloom seems to have become a long-awaited stabilising influence.

'Before we were romantically involved, while I was getting everything straightened out with Mario, Ron kept saying that he wanted us to have a real relationship but that he also wanted us to take our time. He said he didn't want me falling into his arms because I was under some sort of emotional stress. He kept saying, "I'll be your friend until you're ready for something more." That was the best form of respect anyone's shown me in many years.'

When they both felt the time was right, they decided to look for a house together.

'We lived together for four months in a hotel while we tried to find a place. That's the toughest test I can think of for a relationship. Four months in a hotel room. If you can survive that you can survive anything.'

They eventually found a house in the Valley.

A domestic comes in twice a week to help with the housework and a gardener stops by a couple of times a week to work on the shrubs. But otherwise they have no staff.

Stephanie does the shopping and most of the cooking – just for the record she is probably the best cook in the Grimaldi clan.

But her main interest now is music and acting.

Her first album was released in the United States in spring 1989.

The songs on it were written by her and Bloom.

'It was tough work but it was good work. I loved it and couldn't imagine doing anything else. I love performing. It's weird, I can't stand up and make a speech to people because I get so nervous but when I get up on a stage and sing I'm not nervous at all. And then there's the applause. It sends shivers up my spine. It's really a high. It's the most beautiful thing to have a contact with your audience, especially when you're singing a ballad and everybody in the audience holds up their lighters. It's like a huge birthday cake.'

While she plans to put a band together and go on tour – 'I don't think I'll play Las Vegas just yet. But maybe in 40 years. Vegas is reserved for the oldies' – she is also now finding herself with more responsibilities at home in Monaco.

They are, she insists, official duties that she welcomes.

'I do whatever I'm asked to do and, among other things, I'm on the organising committee for the Circus Festival. The thing is that people tend to forget how young I am. People tend to say, Stephanie doesn't do anything and refuses responsibilities. But it's only been a couple of years that anybody's asked me to do anything and when they've asked I've accepted.'

At the same time, she continues looking for the right film part to come along.

'If I'd have chosen to be a performer while my mom was still alive, I know she would have been proud of me. The only problem is that she would have wanted to go to every reading with me. I don't know where I'll be in 10 years, hopefully living between California, if it hasn't fallen into the Pacific, and Monaco. Maybe I'll be shooting a movie or maybe I'll have two kids. I don't know. What I know for sure is that I'm working very hard now to make something of my life. Something tells me I have to do it for my mom. And I will do it for her. I know that she is with me every minute, that she's looking after me from wherever she is. I want to make her proud of me.'

*   *   *   *

'I played with Stephanie a lot when we were kids,' Albert begins. 'Probably because I love younger kids and even at that age I was kind of fascinated by this little baby in the family. So we always got along great. We've always had a good relationship. I know she went through a lot because of the accident. It affected her more than most people can imagine, maybe even more than we think. She had a very difficult time adjusting afterwards, simply in terms of relating to other people. Hence her chaotic life style. Although I think everything is starting to fall into place now.'

He says that because she has such a high exposure, because the press has been following her and bothering her for years, everything has been blown way out of proportion.

'Because of her age and some of the things she's wanted to do, I think there's been additional pressure on her and worry that she'd get hurt somewhere along the line. I really feel for her. She never asked for any of that. She just wanted to do her own thing for a while and she got caught. My dad and I have had long conversations about it and he's been very worried about her. But that's only normal. I think she's learning who to trust. She's a very sweet girl who puts up a cold, hard front because she's shy and she doesn't always know how to deal with certain people. That's strange in a way because as a family we've been in different situations where we've had to deal with people. But she's always kind of resisted that and now it's working against her. When she does open up to someone maybe she opens up too much. Maybe she's been too easily influenced by the wrong people.'

It is a problem that Albert is finding hardly unique to his little sister.

'I'm discovering that the more I get involved with my job the lonelier it is. Sure you have people around you to help, advisers, but it's really up to you to take the final decisions and I guess the more I move towards a position of power and leadership, the more people I find around me claiming to be my friend. That's hard to deal with. I tend to trust most people but I've been disappointed a lot.'

The problem is in learning to recognise true friendship.

'I don't think there's any clear-cut recipe. You just have to feel the person out. You watch them in certain situations. I was going to say you test them but that's not really what I do. I find it's interesting to see a person's reaction to a given situation. Of course, it's not always fair to define the terms of friendship because a lot of friendships are based on helping each other. But when it starts becoming a one-way street, when that person is asking you for a lot of favours, I suppose that's when you have to start taking a longer look at that friendship. It's not something I find simple to deal with. I know dad had a lot of wonderful friends but many of them have since died so I guess it's especially tough for him. It's difficult for him to make new friends. Even if he has a lot of acquaintances, it's not the same as an old friend he knows and can trust. Although he can deal very well with being alone and working alone and not seeing other people for a certain period of time. But I can't. I need to have people around.'

Like his father, he too is aware of his own visibility.

'Someone told me once that my mom was working a lot more than my dad because she was seen giving prizes and going to charity meetings. They saw her more often than they saw him so they assumed she was working more than he was. Some of the functions that we do, in fact most of the functions we attend, I consider work because I wouldn't necessarily choose to be there if I didn't have to be there. But there's a big difference between representation kind of work and sitting behind a desk. I'm understanding that not everyone makes that distinction for us.'

Albert lives in the private apartments at the Palace.

'Otherwise my father would be living alone. And I don't mind it. It's very comfortable. I do try to spend time with dad, especially when I know he's alone. I try to see him as much as I can. We talk a lot.'

Morning starts for him with a swim or a light workout. He says he tries to get to the gym early every day. However, if there's been a function the evening before he doesn't necessarily get up until 9 and sometimes even later if it's been a long night. He then goes to his office, sitting down at his desk for three to four hours, beginning with the mail.

As a highly visible bachelor – often said to be the most eligible young man in the world – not all of the correspondence that comes across his desk necessarily relates to affairs of state or to his interests in international sport. There is, it seems, the occasional letter from a mother with a snapshot of her daughter to awaken his interest. Better yet, there are sometimes letters from the daughters themselves, with photos enclosed which their mothers know nothing about.

'It's funny, but I've never seen myself as the most eligible bachelor in the world. It still surprises me when I read that. People are always trying to fix me up. I have a whole file of mothers trying to marry off their daughters, complete with pictures. It's hysterical. I also get pictures of girls practically offering their services. But the worst is when an old friend of the family says, why don't you come for dinner because I'd love you to meet so and so. I can't stand that.'

On the other hand, he doesn't hide the fact that for the future sovereign, meeting women on his own is not very difficult.

'At discos or restaurants or at parties or on the beach or even on the street, I say hello to girls. Why not? I like that sort of thing. I haven't yet felt tremendous pressure to settle down, although it's out there. I know it is and it's starting to grow.'

Albert goes to the office every day and, depending on what he has to do, sees an average of two or three people a day about the various associations he's been assigned to deal with, like the Monaco Red Cross. Then there's either a business lunch or lunch with his father, and more meetings in the afternoon. He attends all his father's cabinet meetings and continues to pursue his interest in bob-sled racing. He tries to spend a couple of hours in the late afternoons getting in shape to compete again in the next Winter Olympics.

Above his desk there's a huge colour photo of him with his bob-sled before a race at Calgary.

After attending high school in Monaco, he went on to Amherst College in Massachussets where in 1981 he got a degree in Political Science. He then served six months with the French navy before spending five months in New York with the Morgan Guaranty Trust Company in their management training programme. He followed that with a short management apprenticeship at Wells, Rich and Green Advertising in New York and a training programme in Paris in the marketing department at Moët Chandon.

'The stay at Moët was my father's idea. He wanted me to get a feel for the way a major French conglomerate operated. But the look into banking and advertising was my idea. I then returned to New York in the spring of 1986 to spend some time in a law firm, doing all sorts of para-legal stuff.'

Albert is not only the first Prince to attend the local high school, he is also the first to have been trained in the ways of the corporate world.

'I think banking and marketing are part of what my job is all about, although it's hard for me to give a clear-cut programme or to express my ideas and tell you what I'll do when I take over. They're not necessarily conflicting with the options my dad has chosen in recent years. But if I express them too strongly, people will think that I want to push him aside.'

While he's always been reluctant to be too specific, he believes Monaco will continue developing tourism, light industry, real estate and banking. But he's equally interested in exploring possible new areas of expansion, although he admits he isn't sure what those will be.

'Sure I'd like to see Monaco become a major European financial centre but we have to be careful how we go about that and with whom we're going to do it. I think that we still have enough time to think about those things. Certainly a lot of those questions haven't been addressed yet, especially where Monaco is concerned with the Europe of 1992. I think time is on our side, but for the moment we have to rely on what we've been successful doing in the past.'

Talking seriously about his job, as he does, it's clear that he's taken his training for succession in a serious way.

'It's been an ongoing process for years. I guess I was made aware of my future responsibilities from about age five or six. And it's something that's always kind of scared me because I've seen over the years that there's so much responsibility and so many different problems to deal with. I've come to face some of those problems and to help my dad with the work he does. But it's not easy and I'm not sure if I'm up to it. I mean, I'm fairly confident that I have the right tools to do that kind of work. But I don't know if I can do it as well as he can.'

After saying that, he hastens to add that he's not avoiding the issue, just recognising the fact that he is being called upon to fill some very large shoes.

'I read the papers. I know a lot of the press has hinted that I'm just hanging around and not eager to do any work. Well, I think that's unfair. I'm helping my dad and working as hard as I can. I'm giving my best. Whenever the time is right, it will happen. I don't see any reason why I should press the issue because I'm enjoying the present situation and as long as my dad feels comfortable with the present situation, that's fine. Whenever it's going to happen it will happen. There's no timetable. We'll just both know when it's ready.'

He says he sees his father's legacy as having done more in 40 years than most of his predecessors did in 100.

'But it was a team effort. My mom and dad did more for this principality than anyone else in history. They did it together. They gave Monaco a prestige that no one else ever did or probably ever could have. It's hard for me to put into words but just look around. I guess that's a good indication of what's been going on here. It used to be a kind of happy-go-lucky, half-asleep spot on the Mediterranean that only catered to tourism. Now it's a vibrant, busy little city, much more than just a tourist stop. He and mom have to take the credit for that.'

Having mentioned Grace, he says that one of his fond memories of childhood was discovering that his mother was once a major movie star.

'I was in my early teens and I remember it was a pretty nice revelation. We used to talk about the movies and she used to tell me stories. I'm still interested in films and film making and I've taken a few courses in it. At times I've thought about what I'd like to have done if I didn't have these other responsibilities and doing something in films has come to mind. But it's such a tough business. Anyway, I was never a great actor. I did a few operettas at summer camp. I never acted at school although I was always tempted. Something always held me back. Maybe I'm too shy. But just trying to understand film is fun. Maybe I would have liked to do something behind the camera.'

Once he realised who his mother had been and once he realised who her Hollywood friends were, another revelation started to dawn on him.

'It really amazed me who I was meeting and that I could interact with them. I used to think, hey, I may be the only 14 year old in the world who could pick up the phone and ring Frank Sinatra or Gregory Peck or Cary Grant and actually get them on the phone.'

Now that he understands what access means – and how access becomes power – he says he is careful not to use it flippantly.

'I'm not sure if I always use it the right way. At least I know enough not to ask for favours because the reaction of those kinds of people to someone asking for a favour is the same reaction I have when someone asks me for a favour.'

Yet, he insists he's not shy about picking up the phone when he has to. And in that respect, he claims he's different from his father.

'Dad hates the phone and prefers writing letters. He's a tremendous letter writer. But I'm not a great writer so I call people. He's always after me because he thinks I use the phone too much. As soon as I start dialling he says, "Who are you talking to? Why do you have to call them?" You know what I like best about the telephone? Sometimes I call people I may not know and I tell the secretary, "Hi, it's Prince Albert," and they say, "Yeah sure." It's very funny. I've learned to let my secretary dial calls. Except I really love it when someone tells me, "Yeah sure you are, come on, who is it?"'

Albert feels that being the middle child was not always difficult, especially as Stephanie was so much younger.

But he says that Caroline was pretty bossy and pretty independent.

'I went along with it for a while. Sure she annoyed me a few times when we were kids. Sure we used to fight. All brothers and sisters do. But when I was about 11 or 12, I was taking judo lessons. Once when she was harassing me I did a hip movement and threw her to the floor. Ever since then we've had a good rapport.'

* * * *

Caroline remembers the event well.

'I certainly do. We've always been a very close family and I was especially close to Albert because we're only a year apart. The thing was that he and I used to fight like cats and dogs while we were growing up. I mean we'd fight with the determined intention of causing vast amounts of pain. Well that day, just because he'd been taking judo lessons, he threw me on the floor so hard I knew that was the end of that. There could be no more picking on baby brother.'

As for Stephanie, 'There's eight years difference between us so I guess I always felt responsible for her. I guess I was always playing the older sister. I baby sat for her and watched out for her.'

Caroline's discovery of her mother's fame didn't come about the same way it did for Albert.

'Maybe I was 10. I'd seen some movies when I was seven or eight but when I was 10 we went to California and visited some of the studios. They had some of her films in the archives that they showed us. There was so much fuss and commotion made over us that I started to understand who she'd been. But I don't think it affected any of us too much. Albert and I used to tease her a lot, especially about *Mogambo*. There's one scene where she turns to Clark Gable and says, "I didn't know monkeys climbed trees." It was the silliest thing I'd ever heard. We'd repeat that to her and then break up. Being children, it was difficult for us to understand that she was acting I thought it was just mommy being filmed saying, "I didn't know monkeys climbed trees."'

Even though her mother was a film star, Caroline never shared her sister's ambition in that direction.

'Not me. I didn't want to be in films, I wanted to be a dancer. I never wanted to act. I couldn't even make it into school productions. Or the few times I did it was very silent parts. I was once one of the three kings in a nativity play with a big beard. But I used to get such stage fright. When I danced it was better. But when I had to say something on stage, I'd be sick.'

Nor did she inherit her mother's general outlook on life.

'Mommy was always busy doing something. She got that from her mother who couldn't stand people sitting around doing nothing. So she was always keeping busy. She couldn't just sit back and relax, which of course is miles away from me. I can perfectly well sit back in a chair and not do a thing for two solid hours. But maybe some of my mother has come through to me because when I do sit around like that I feel a little guilty about it. Not that it stops me from doing it, mind you.'

Like Albert and Stephanie, she too has always had problems making friends. It's difficult, not because she doesn't want to, but because there is a little voice inside all of them that asks, what does this person want of me?

Most of her friends these days are old childhood friends.

'The problem is you can't spend too much time worrying about who you're real friends are. You just have to take everybody at face value. After all, if you start worrying, is this one going to be a real friend or behave badly, well it's a shame to have to think that way. At the same time, it's basically, difficult to trust anybody past a certain point. If you ask them to be faithful and non-demanding and be there to help you, to stick by you and never want anything in return, that's maybe asking a little too much from people. But you can't expect too much or you risk being disappointed. It was lonely at times while we were growing up. I think it's getting easier as I get older. Actually lots of things get easier as you get older. A lot of the nonsense fades away.'

One of the reasons is because she can see her parents reflected in herself as she raises her own children.

'Andrea is so funny. He was asking about his Italian grandma. I said that she's daddy's mommy and that his Italian grandpa is daddy's father and then I explained how they looked after daddy when he was a little boy. Then he asked about pappy and I said he is my daddy and he looked after me when I was a little girl. Then he asked about my mommy. I said she isn't here any more, she's up in heaven. I pointed to the sky and said, you know, in space, because outer space is a big thing with Andrea. Anything about going to the moon in rockets, that he understands. If you say something is magic, he also understands. He'll take magic as a pretty good answer. So I said my mommy is in space and she's magic because she can see us and hear us and she looks after us and protects us and if you concentrate very hard you might be able to see her too. I thought that should work. But then he asked me, "You mean she died?" My mouth fell open. Then he looked at me and said, "But you won't die will you? Because you're my only mother."'

In 1983 Caroline married Stefano Casiraghi, a tall, blond, quiet Italian from outside Milan who is some three and a half years her junior.

She joked at the time that he was the perfect husband for her because he had an interest in an Italian shoe company and there were few things in the world she liked better than shoes. He, in turn, had special labels made to put in her shoes saying they'd been created exclusively for her.

At about the same time she turned up in a sweatshirt that proudly boasted, 'I married an Italian'.

The son of a wealthy industrialist, Stefano settled in Monaco where he's expanded his own business interests to include real estate and boat building.

Their son, Andrea, was born in 1984, followed by daughter Charlotte in 1986 and their second son Pierre in 1987.

The five of them live mostly in Caroline's house on Le Rocher, dividing the rest of their time between Roc Agel, Paris and trips to Italy. Caroline and Stefano speak Italian at home together although she speaks French to the children.

With three children and a husband who seems to care very much for her, Caroline is obviously happy and content.

And that's a far cry from the woman she was when she married the first time.

As Madame Philippe Junot she learned some of life's more difficult lessons.

'It was very paradoxical. It all had to do with the way were brought up. Mommy said, "Of course he's the wrong man and you shouldn't marry him but now you've been compromised. You've been dating him for too long, so now either get engaged officially or stop seeing him and go off to the States and finish university there." She wanted me to go to Princeton. So, of course I said, "Okay, let's get engaged." I was 20 or 21 and didn't really want to get married. If I'd lived with him for six months, or even just three months, I'd have found out right away what he was like. But

I wasn't allowed to go off on vacations with him or even spend weekends with him, except at his parent's house, which was all very proper. I really didn't know him very well. Getting married was simply the correct way out.'

Caroline says that when she announced to her mother that she wanted to marry Junot, she added the proviso, 'But if you're really against it, I won't.'

'I told her, "I'm not going to run away and get married against your will. Maybe I'll be miserable if I can't see him any more but don't worry, I won't do it." She said, "Go ahead and get married. After all, what are people going to think after you've been dating this guy for two years?" How times have changed since then. It's amazing. I married Philippe because I was in love with him. That's a good enough reason for marrying anybody. But then one day you wake up and wonder what you've done. I guess I started to wake up and wonder what I'd done while we were still on our honeymoon. He'd arranged with a photographer friend of his to meet us there to have the exclusive rights to our honeymoon pictures. That's when it all started to click. That was terrible. The end started right there. But it took me a year and a half to finish it. A long time.'

When she finally gave up on Junot and wanted to come home, her parents were very supportive.

'Mommy was very helpful. I didn't dare divorce or even mention divorce because Catholics don't divorce. You're supposed to just make the best of it. But mommy said, "You have to get divorced." I said, "How can you talk like that? We're a religious family." I told her I was trying to find a way to work something out. But mommy said, "Religion is there to help people, not to make your life miserable."'

While Caroline goes to church every Sunday – she can't take communion but she's not excluded from the church – her annulment inquiry makes its way at a snail's pace through the Vatican bureaucracy.

'It will probably happen, except that I might be a grandmother by then. It's just kind of unpleasant to think that in the eyes of the church I'm still married to Philippe.'

Caroline is a competent pianist and an avid reader with a wide range of interests – from the classics to 19th century opera critiques to contemporary fiction. And at one point, just after her first marriage ended, she even flirted with the idea of writing.

In 1981 Caroline was approached by the *International Herald Tribune* in Paris to pen an article for them about her life in Monaco.

She titled her professional debut as an author, *A Compulsive Need for Blue*.

'The temptation is to glamorise one's childhood,' she wrote. 'It probably is in all small towns with beautiful surroundings. The weather is lovely throughout the four seasons. You spend a lot of time outdoors. But as children we were never quite aware of the total beauty. We never thought we lived in a place others considered unique.'

She wrote that it wasn't until she was older and had travelled more that she came to understand how much she longed for the Mediterranean and its cloudless sky. Then she gave an insider's view of the relationship shared by the locals and the invading armies of visitors.

'The rules are simple. If you're part of the jet-set you don't just go somewhere, you make an entrance. Your conversation centres on other people's private affairs. You have your dinner on the terrace of the Hôtel de Paris and fiddle with the caviar on your plate. The buses drive by endlessly. The people in them stare and point at the women, the champagne, at you. So on the one hand there are groups who stagger out of hot, smelly buses. On the other there are people trying to be beautiful and desperately cool, swelling with pride at the mere thought of showing off. Where and how do the Monégasques fit into this social jigsaw puzzle? Quite frankly, I don't think we do. We've had to learn to keep the visitor content, although it's not been without some grunting and groaning. Now we superbly ignore the anonymous masses as well as the insolent elite. Over the centuries, starting long before people travelled for pleasure, our unique concern has been to preserve a sense of national identity and to cling to it rather fiercely.'

Unfortunately, the newspaper printed no more than excerpts of the piece, putting it next to an insipid photo of her aged eight or nine. It was a personal disappointment to Caroline, who'd worked hard to make the article right, and also to her mother who'd read it and felt Caroline might one day take her writing further.

Undaunted by having her work mishandled like that, she started writing for French magazines and among her journalism credits is a very competent interview with the Italian opera star Ruggero Raimondi.

These days she still occasionally puts pen to paper. She and a few friends in Paris bring out an annual satirical magazine. But her writing has had to take a back seat to her family and her official duties in Monaco because when Grace died the burden of being Monaco's first lady fell on Caroline.

Albert became president of the Red Cross but he also had his own responsibilities.

Stephanie was most of the time in Paris and then in California.

So Caroline took over the Monaco branch of the Princess Grace Foundation and the Princess Grace Dance Academy, which is designed to help young dancers. She also assumed the president's chair at the Monaco Arts Festival.

'When mommy was president of the festival it was a sort of curious formula, spread out throughout the year, where various performances came under the auspices of the festival. I know she was thinking of grouping everything into a two or three week period but never had a chance to do that. One of the things I did was make it a proper festival, taking up three weeks in Easter.'

And Caroline has put her own stamp on it now.

'I get to choose what I like. It's quite eclectic. We've been concentrating over these past few years on reviving sort of forgotten 17th and 18th century operas. It's specialised because there are so many festivals in Europe with huge theatres. We've only got a small theatre here so we decided to cater to a more knowledgeable public. In September we do a Baroque Music Festival. We also run films on opera and music. There are sculpture exhibits and painting exhibits and photography exhibits. There's also some experimental theatre.'

In keeping with Monaco's tradition for ballet, Caroline completed her mother's work of creating a professional ballet company for the Monte Carlo opera.

'That was a lot of work. Setting it up, getting bookings and organising tours, setting up the repertoire and getting the right choreographers. We try to keep a careful balance between Diaghilev and Ballet Russe repertoire and the big classics like *Swan Lake* and *The Nutcracker*. We also do some modern, experimental suff.'

At the same time she established a project of her own, called *Jeune j'écoute*. It's a phone line to help young people in trouble with drugs, or the police, or their parents, or who are just unemployed and need some guidance. There's always someone to speak to and now there's also a place where they can go for refuge to find help.

'I guess I can't say that I have an average day. I try to spend as much time as I can with my children, the way my parents always did with us. I try to have at least one meal a day with my children, if not more. Usually the mornings are with them. I stay until they go off for their walk, then I go to the office and plough through the mail. I always have lots of files and dossiers to look at and then meetings. Either I'll go to my office in the Palace or my secretary will come to the house. Then there are all sorts of functions to attend. When it's calm, like in February, we go off to the mountains. Otherwise it's a full-time job doing the charity work that I do. Besides also being president of the World Friends of Childhood Association, I've taken over from my mother a charity that helps old people. Then there's the Garden Club, the Girl Guides and the Irish Library.'

Caroline accepts the fact that much of the void left by Grace has to be filled by her.

'It's because I'm here. I have a family and I'm here. Sometimes there's so much going on I don't even have time to think about it. The hardest thing is when you get these desperate letters from people who need help, whose lives are in a real mess. The hardest thing is to find a way to help them. Every day we get requests for help. I feel most of the time I'm really just a social worker trying to help people.'

In the meantime, she's asked, how about all those stories about wanting to take over the throne?

Her eyes light up.

'You mean the ones that say that I'm manoeuvring in dark corridors in the Palace? All that intrigue and counter-intrigue. Richelieu and Mazarin look like kids compared to what I'm apparently doing. The truth is that whenever I have any free time, instead of plotting, I spend it with the children. Frankly I can't wait for Albert to get married because then I can pass along a lot of my duties to his wife. Of course he keeps telling me he has to find the right girl. Well, at this stage I have so little time for myself and my children that sometimes, albeit only in my weaker moments, mind you, I think even I'd settle for Joan Collins.'

* * * *

13

Living in a Fishbowl

'*THERE'S* no way I can win,' she used to say. 'Whenever I put on a couple of pounds, everybody thinks I'm having a baby. Whenever I manage to lose a few pounds, everybody thinks I'm finally planning to make another movie. If I go three days in a row to visit a friend in the hospital, right away the newspapers write that I'm suffering from some incurable disease. If I stay in Paris for a few weeks so that I can be with my daughter while she's at school, it gets around that my marriage is collapsing, that we're going to separate. As adults we end up taking all that with a shrug. But the often malicious interest shown in my children is very difficult to accept.'

The Grimaldis have always ranked high on the list of the most written about, most photographed people in the world.

Yet with her hair wrapped in a scarf and sunglasses hiding her eyes, Grace was not always recognised.

Walking with a friend one day across the large, open square in front of the Palace, she was approached by a couple of American tourists carrying a camera.

The tourists said, 'Hi.'

Grace and the woman with her said, 'Hi.'

The tourists said, 'Where are you from?'

Grace and the woman with her said, 'America.'

The tourists said, 'Us too,' then thrust their camera towards Grace. 'Would you please take our picture?'

Grace said, 'Sure.'

The tourists found just the right spot so that the Palace was framed in the background. Grace took their picture. The tourists said, 'Thanks,' reclaimed their camera, waved, 'Have a nice day' and walked away.

They never knew.

Dressed much the same way, Grace once got into a taxi in New York only to notice the cabbie staring at her through the rear view mirror.

She smiled politely.

'You know what,' the driver called back to her through the meshed grill that separated his seat from hers. 'You look like Grace Kelly.'

She said, 'I do?'

'Yeah,' he said, 'you do. Except I think she's a little prettier than you are.'

Compared to the rest of the family, Rainier is probably the least approachable in public.

However, his face is just as well known and when he's outside Monaco there are often occasions when someone will come up to him, point a finger and ask, 'Don't I know you . . . aren't you . . . yes, of course, I've got it, you're Prince Rainier!'

Sometimes, especially if it's a very pretty woman asking the question, he admits he is. But most of the time he doesn't.

'I tell people, "It's funny you should say that because I'm often mistaken for him." I say, "In fact, you're the third person today who's asked me if I'm him." That's when they take another long look at me and decide, "Well, no, I guess you're not him. But you sure do look like him." After that they leave me alone. It almost always works.'

* * * *

When Prince Honoré V, travelling one day from Cannes to Monaco, chanced across Napoleon on his return from Elba, the two spoke for some time around a campfire.

By his own account, Honoré merely warned Napoleon that reconquering France would be a risky venture.

Years later none other than Alexandre Dumas reported on that meeting and got it so wrong that the Prince felt compelled to set the record straight.

He wrote to Dumas, 'The conversation you give as having taken place between the Emperor and myself is a travesty of the truth. He did not keep saying to me, "Good morning, Monaco", he never asked me to follow him and I did not reply that I awaited his orders. You must admit that your imagination is too fertile. I have certainly had nothing to complain about when reading your novels but history requires the truth.'

For the sake of the written record, history definitely requires the truth and in serious periodicals that requirement is usually met.

But tabloid newspapers and large-circulation down-market weeklies put their faith in shocking stories and sweeping head-lines because fantasy always outsells the truth, especially when it pretends to be the truth.

That's a battle the Grimaldis have been fighting since the days of Honoré V.

Rainier had to put up with a certain amount of it throughout his bachelor days. Every woman he was seen with became a potential bride.

Grace was more fortunate.

She managed to avoid most of the Hollywood scandal press while she was working there. Not only, perhaps, because she spent as little time as possible in California, which must have helped, but also because she was very discreet about her private life.

She did not however escape unscathed.

When she made *The Country Girl*, gossip columnists linked her to her leading man and the photo that proved it showed Grace with Bing Crosby sharing a very romantic dinner. But it was tête-à-tête only as far as the picture editor was concerned. He'd cropped the photo tightly enough to eliminate any sight of Grace's sister Peggy, who was sitting on the other side of Crosby.

Not long after that one of the Hollywood gossip sheets staked-out Grace's flat and wrote that William Holden's car was fre-quently parked outside at night. What they failed to say was that Holden had loaned the car to one of Grace's friends.

The person who gave Grace the roughest time of all during her Hollywood days was columnist Hedda Hopper.

For whatever reason, just before Grace started work on *A Country Girl*, the vitriolic Hopper phoned Crosby to warn him that his co-star was 'a man-eater'.

And when Rainier and Grace announced their engagement Hopper wrote, 'Half their friends are betting they never make it to the altar.'

Since Grace's death a great deal has been written about love affairs – real and imagined. All too often the sources quoted are dead and the stories, salaciously embroidered, are accepted as the truth merely because they are now in print and frequently repeated.

That she might have been in love with Ray Milland or Oleg Cassini or Jean Pierre Aumont or anyone else, for that matter, doesn't change the woman she became. Remember that when she got engaged to Rainier she told a reporter, 'I've been in love before but never in love like this.'

The point that a healthy, grown-up, single, working woman in her mid-20s had normal human feelings and desires 35 or 40 years ago, hardly seems like much of a revelation today.

It's no wonder that many people who find themselves in the public eye sometimes have turbulent relationships with the press.

'Even if you've lived with it all your life,' Rainier insists, 'you never get used to the pressures of living in a fishbowl. There's no denying that we've had our difficulties with the press but you have to understand that as soon as something gets printed it's too late. No matter what you do afterwards it's still always there in black and white. People believe what they read the first time. Retractions, when you can get one, are usually too little and much too late.'

In spite of their earlier experiences in dealing with the press, it wasn't until Rainier and Grace announced their engagement that they were truly baptised by fire.

Neither of them was prepared for the attention showered upon them.

They found themselves sitting through endless press conferences, forever answering the same questions.

Rainier might have been all right in the beginning, during the first few, but his patience quickly wore thin. Before too long he simply couldn't hide his extreme discomfort. You see that quite clearly in newsreel footage from those days. It's almost as if he's trying to become invisible. Grace obviously understood and tried her best to protect him. But at one press conference, just as Rainier thought he was finished, a photographer begged a few more pictures and, after Grace agreed, Rainier was heard to mumble under his breath, 'They don't understand that I'm not under contract to MGM.'

Then there was their wedding, a media nightmare.

The principality was bursting at the seams with journalists and photographers. The bar at the Hôtel de Paris became the unofficial press headquarters and there was such an overflow of scribes that the management had to fill the lobby with tables and chairs all the way to the entrance.

Mayhem reigned.

Part of the problem lay in the fact that most weddings are basically the same.

There is a bride and there is a groom and there are people who cry with joy. Afterwards there are drinks and there is food, so that friends can get together, offer congratulations and wish the couple luck as they run away on their honeymoon. But that's really all there is.

Had they employed a professional press attaché in those days, a few hand-outs could have filled in reporters on who was there, on who wore what, on how many eggs were used for the cake and how the smiling couple danced till dawn.

In the absence of any real stories, reporters wrote that Grace's hat was too big and hid her face from the cameras.

When a photographer tried to snap Randolph Churchill's picture on the steps of the Hôtel de Paris and Churchill punched the photographer, they wrote about that, forgetting to add that the general confusion had worn everyone's nerves to a frazzle.

They also wrote that Rainier's mother, Princess Charlotte, had been driven to Monaco by her chauffeur, formerly one of France's most wanted criminals – she was trying to rehabilitate him – and that since his arrival there'd been two burglaries at the Hôtel de Paris.

But there was nothing else to write about.

By the time the couple returned from their honeymoon, Rainier and Grace were in perfect agreement that they needed help.

Grace asked Rupert Allan if he could recommend someone. Allan told Grace about a young American woman in Paris named Nadia Lacoste who had experience in movie and show business public relations.

So Lacoste was asked to come and speak with the Prince.

'I met him in Paris in July. We talked for about an hour. Then he said he wanted to speak with the Princess and asked me to come to see both of them the next day. We made a verbal deal for a three-month job, to be renewed if they wanted to do that. I said okay and started right in because they were leaving for a visit to the States in September and we realised there would be a great deal of press interest in their first trip to America since the wedding.'

In a very real way, Lacoste got to know Rainier and Grace at a time while they were still getting to know each other.

'She was a warm, likeable person. But there was a big difference in those days in the way she behaved when we were alone or with the Prince and the way she was when she saw the press. It was odd because she had a lot of experience with reporters. I expected her to be relaxed but she wasn't. On the other hand, I expected him to be shy, which he was. But I discovered that he has a wonderful sense of humour. I remember going with them to fashion shows. The Princess would be on his right and I'd be on his left. As the afternoon wore on he'd start to get bored so he'd make remarks out of the corner of his mouth, without moving a muscle. He'd comment on everybody and everything. The dresses. The hats. The people in the room. He was so funny that I'd be in stitches.'

Rainier and Grace's first professionally arranged press conference was in September 1956 before sailing to New York on the SS *United States*.

Meeting at the Monaco Legation in Paris, Lacoste put journalists in one room and photographers in another. It was an old trick to give everyone a chance and keep the two groups out of each other's way.

And it obviously worked because Rainier and Grace were as comfortable as they'd ever been in front of the press.

From there, Lacoste, with selected members from the Legation and a few photographers, took the train with Rainier and Grace to Le Havre. Because they were relaxed, the photo story that followed was a good one. The group then gathered in their cabin for champagne and caviar before the ship sailed although Lacoste recalls that Grace would not eat the caviar.

'Someone had informed her that pregnant women should not have any kind of seafood. It was what pregnant women believed in those days.'

Once Rainier and Grace got to America, Rupert Allan took over and handled the press for them there.

'Grace was okay with the press,' he says. 'But Rainier was still usually pretty ill-at-ease. I'd arranged a few interviews for them and tried to make the ordeal as easy as possible, especially for Rainier. But when he was uncomfortable he tended to scowl. He'd see the photos published the next day, see himself scowling, and that merely served to re-enforce his discomfort when the next photographer appeared. I finally said to him, "Listen, every time you meet the press, just think of them all standing there in front of you in their shorts. Just react the way you would if they had nothing on but their underwear." And that old trick worked. The next time Rainier and Grace did a photo session, there was Rainier grinning.'

While they were in the States much of their publicity surrounded her new life.

'The biggest difference in my life isn't the title, it's changing from being a single career girl to a wife.'

And there was talk of the expected baby.

'I've already gained 26 pounds. When I became pregnant I was pretty sick for the first three months. They'd told me about morning sickness – but they didn't tell me you could be sick all day, every day. Once I got over that I started eating. The doctor says I shouldn't eat too much but I'm ravenous. I had this terrible craving for noodles and spaghetti all summer. I wake up hungry at night. The Prince is excellent at scrambled eggs but I had to teach him how to make sandwiches. Now he invents ones for me.'

With that Rainier chimed in, 'I'm the gendarme on her diet. I keep reminding her not to eat but it isn't easy. I really don't mind because she was so thin when we married.'

Grace said she wanted a boy, 'Because Rainier would like a boy a lot', then went on to explain that, although he'd helped choose the layette, he wasn't taking any special lessons on how to handle a baby.

There Rainier announced, 'When I show the baby to people, I promise I won't drop him. Though I may drop myself.'

Knowing that this kind of happy, friendly patter was a way of winning friends for them and for Monaco – which was the purpose of the exercise – Rupert Allan skilfully manipulated the interviews to highlight Rainier and Grace as real people with real concerns and all the more attractive for their sense of humour.

He got Grace to say, 'I suppose royal babies should be born in a Palace, but I'll feel better, more secure, in a hospital.'

And, 'No matter where the child is born, my husband won't be welcome in the delivery room because that's no place for husbands.'

She said she liked the name Henry but the Prince didn't, 'So it won't be Henry.'

She said she believed in spanking children, 'And royal children probably need more spanking than others.'

She said she'd eventually like to have at least three children, 'Not more'.

Then she pre-empted the next question by volunteering, 'So there's your answer as to whether or not I'll be making any more movies. I'll be too busy raising a family.'

By the time they returned to Monaco, Nadia Lacoste was beginning to understand that the key to Rainier's and Grace's public appeal was a combination of their natural charm and the 'handsome prince marries beautiful actress' fairy-tale.

Her three-month trial as their press attaché turned into a 33-year career.

'The difference between him and her, at least in the beginning, was that he had nothing to prove. He was born a prince. He knew who he was. But she believed she had to prove that the person being interviewed was not Grace Kelly the actress but Princess Grace of Monaco. She knew they were watching her carefully and she desperately wanted to do the right thing. She didn't want to make any mistakes. She didn't want to do anything that would embarrass her husband or reflect poorly on Monaco. It wasn't a part she could play like an actress. If it was, she could have gotten away with simply playing the role of a princess. That would have been easy for her and she would have played it beautifully. She would have been very comfortable playing a role. The problem was, being Princess of Monaco was real life. Finding her way was not very easy.'

Lacoste explains that once she got to know the Prince well enough she'd screen newspaper men so that no one ever got in to see him if she didn't feel the two would get along. She discovered that because the Prince takes an interest in the world and what's happening, he has a tendency to start asking the journalist questions. On more than one occasion journalists came out of an interview and reported to Lacoste, 'I told him more than he told me.'

But it took a long time before she could make it work that way with Grace.

'I can still see her during her very first in-depth interview with a French journalist in Monaco, literally sitting on the edge of her chair with her hands clenched together. She was grinning too hard and swallowing too hard and her answers were almost too practised. It must have been excruciating for her. I decided then and there not to ask her to do any other interviews for at least six months, at least until she could find her place in the Palace and get settled into her whole new life.'

Even many years later, once Grace had mastered French, she was never totally at ease speaking it for any length of time on radio or television.

'One afternoon, it might have been as much as 15 years later, I was trying to explain to her that the best way to let the public know about some of the things she was doing in Monaco like the Flower Show and the Princess Grace Foundation, was for her to talk about them. I argued that for me to tell the world about them was of no interest to anyone. She finally agreed to talk about the Ballet Festival.'

Lacoste offered the interview to a radio journalist she liked, one she'd always found to be knowledgeable about the arts.

But within 15 minutes Grace was in such a state, so unnerved by the whole thing, that Lacoste had to stop it and ask the journalist to please be kind enough to wait outside.

'Once he left she started to cry. Tears were running down her face. She said she felt totally frustrated being interviewed in French. Of course she'd made comments on French radio before, but when it came to expressing herself in a long, important interview, she said she simply felt too limited by a language which was not her own. She kept telling me, "This is terrible," I promised her, "Okay, never again in French." And I kept my promise. That was the first and the last in-depth broadcast interview in French she ever did.'

As Lacoste helped to sculpt a public image for Rainier and Grace, it was almost as if each story about them created bigger and bigger crowds wherever they went.

At the same time, those crowds generated more stories in the press.

Their arrivals and departures were announced.

Private visits, official visits, it was all the same as far as the media were concerned.

Once, while Rainier and Grace were stopping at the Connaught, a British paper reported, 'Big premiums were being offered last night to house and flat owners near the Connaught Hotel where the couple are staying. These Peeping Toms, for that is what they are, were eager to get a bird's eye view of Grace and Rainier, and blatantly said they wanted to use field glasses and binoculars. "I was astounded," said a Mount Street householder. "An estate agent telephoned me saying he would pay a premium if I let my flat, or one room in it, overlooking the hotel." Not since high premiums were offered to view the bed in which Mrs Simpson slept has there been such a rash of peepers.'

A few years later, on a visit to Dublin, a crowd along O'Connell Street – estimated by one paper to be 5,000 people and by another to be 20,000 – rushed to get a closer look inside the car bringing Rainier and Grace to their hotel.

Panic erupted and 50 people were hurt.

The papers reported, 'Princess Grace was escorted into the hotel, weeping and upset, and her appearance at the ball was delayed for more than half an hour. She later made an appearance on the hotel balcony to acknowledge cries of, "We want Grace".'

A couple of days after that, thousands of people lined the streets when Rainier and Grace travelled to County Mayo to see the home where her grandfather was born.

One journalist pointed out, 'Every bar and restaurant with Kelly in the name – and there are plenty, as I counted eight Kelly's Bars in Dublin alone – are laying on celebrations tonight.'

Another wrote, 'Among their 800 pounds of luggage was one marked "fragile". It contained presents for everyone including, I'm told, all the Kellys in County Mayo.' To that he added, 'Since Princess Grace has been expected, everyone around here has discovered their name is Kelly.'

While a third journalist disclosed, 'At a conference among close relations which went on until the early hours today, a compromise was reached. Originally only second cousins of Princess Grace were to be officially received by her. But it was finally decided that one third cousin would also be allowed in.'

When Rainier and Grace returned to Ireland on their next trip, this time with Albert and Caroline in tow, they got even bigger headlines.

'A prince and princess were "at home" yesterday to representatives of the press,' commented Mary Lodge in the *Irish Press*.

'There just is no other way to describe the disarming informality of the press conference given by Prince Rainier and Princess Grace of Monaco. The quote of the day came from Albert who announced in the middle of his parents' conversation with the press, "I want to milk a cow."

At least until the children grew up, the Grimaldi family was, unlike any other royal family in Europe, written about in the press as just that, a real family.

What no one realised at the time was how the media's interest in them as a family would turn into a nightmare.

'We got request for interviews with the family every day of the year from all over the world,' says Lacoste. 'I think the only country I've never spoken to is Russia. Even the Chinese have asked for interviews. I'd say that between interviews, appearances and photographs we got at least 20 requests a week. That's over 1,000 a year. For obvious reasons we accepted very few. I don't think I ever set up more than five or six interviews a year for Princess Grace. In later years it was even less, maybe two. For the Prince there were usually a bit more but they tended to be on specialised subjects. Let's say, the architectural press requested an interview to discuss something about the development of Monte Carlo or a financial journalist wanted to talk about the Monégasque economy. Maybe he did as many as eight or ten interviews a year.'

As long as Lacoste could control who got to see Rainier and Grace or any of the children, everything worked out reasonably well, most of the time.

The main problem was the paparazzi.

Says Rainier, 'You can imagine the kinds of photos they're looking for because they all walk around with huge telephoto lenses and hide behind bushes. What no one ever seems to understand is how distressing it is for us to live our lives knowing that they could be anywhere, spying on us. It was especially terrible for the children when they were younger. It wasn't fair to them. They were paralysed by it, never knowing how to play or what to play because they were always afraid that someone might be photographing them.'

Rainier explains that the whole system is based on making someone look ridiculous. The more ridiculous the photo, the higher the price.

'I remember dear David Niven, who always hated interviews,

telling me how some journalist did an interview with him in London and at the end of it asked if he could take a few pictures. David said yes, okay, thinking he was going to shoot one or two. Well, this chap went through several rolls of film, standing on chairs, bending over and lying on his back. David just sat there politely while this fellow shot away. But when the story ran, David said that the only picture they used was one where he scratched his nose.'

Especially embarrassing – and all the more infuriating – was the photo of Grace at a Monaco carnival shooting gallery. She'd gone there with her children on a Friday morning to open the carnival and walked around with them to play at various booths. She stopped at the shooting gallery, took aim with a rifle and fired at some clay pipes. No one recalls whether or not she won a Kewpie doll because it was Friday, 22 November 1963.

And the photo of Grace with the rifle ran in newspapers around the world the following day. And the caption under it berated her for being so insensitive as to have played with a rifle when John Kennedy had just been murdered.

But Monaco is seven hours ahead of Dallas.

The photo of Grace with the rifle was taken a full nine hours before Kennedy was killed.

Rainier's profound suspicion of photographers has, she says, proved over the years, to be well placed. But the day the paparazzi discovered there was a market in photos of his children, their lives took a turn for the worse.

The paparazzi paid people at airports to ring them when Caroline arrived. They came to Monaco disguised as tourists with cameras strung around their neck to blend into the background. They sprinkled roads with tacks so that Albert would have to stop his car or risk a flat.

They even rented ultralight gliders to sail over the family property at Marchais hoping to get a glimpse of Stephanie.

One photographer, after checking the family flat in Paris to see if anyone was home, discovered there was an empty apartment next door. He somehow got inside and waited there for several nights. The picture he got for all his trouble was of someone – it turned out to be Caroline – closing the curtains. She was dressed and you couldn't see her face but that didn't matter. The photo ran.

'It became unbearable for all of us,' Rainier shakes his head. 'Once, on a skiing holiday in Switzerland, Grace found Stephanie hiding in her room in tears, afraid to go outside because the paparazzi frightened her. It was obvious they didn't want pictures of the kids skiing well, they were waiting for someone to take a fall. I wonder how those photographers would have reacted if their own children had been subjected to those same pressures.'

Grace found it just as aggravating to watch the press abuse her children. She was able to accept certain things in the papers about herself but when they wrote about her children she looked at it differently.

There were times when she'd be so incensed at the treatment her children were receiving that she'd write to editors to ask them please to leave the family alone, or she'd write to correct them when they published something about her children that struck her as being particularly stupid.

When that failed – which it usually did with the German press in particular – she showed her frustration by lashing out against the nation in general.

'Germany is a horrible country and the Teutonic press is disgusting. I read some of the things written about my family in German magazines and newspapers and there are times when they say such despicable things that I can't bear it any longer.'

However the thing that truly panicked Rainier and Grace was when the French or Italian papers publicised the family's address in Paris.

They looked on that as a direct threat to their children's security.

'I went after them for that,' Rainier says. 'Happily, the law in France protects people from that sort of thing. Once they printed pictures that showed where Caroline lived in Paris. You could very clearly see the number of the house and all the nuts in the world starting ringing her doorbell. I wouldn't stand for it. We went to court to stop that.'

Over the years, Rainier and Grace have taken photographers and magazine editors to court on several occasions.

Back in the 1970s an Italian magazine superimposed Caroline's face on the nude photo of another girl. Magistrates sent the editor to jail.

In other instances there's been very little Rainier and Grace could do.

The paparazzi have photographed Caroline in low-cut dresses bending over in a nightclub and sunbathing topless on a boat. The pictures were published. They used their long lenses to get Albert and a girlfriend nude together on a boat. Those pictures were published too. They once even got Rainier in his underwear through a second-floor window.

Certain big-circulation magazines and downmarket tabloids in the United States, France, Italy and Germany refuse to put a price limit on embarrassing photos of the Grimaldis. It's well known in the trade that anyone with the right photo can name his own price and probably get it.

Certain smaller picture agencies in France, Italy and Germany still consider photos of the Grimaldis to be their bread and butter.

Faced with that kind of market pressure, and not necessarily helped in every country by privacy laws, Rainier concedes 'In the end you can't really do much. You have to let a lot of things go. You just have to write some of it off as part of the apprenticeship of life.'

Most of the time the dual burden of structuring the family's public relations and at the same time defending them against the press fell on Nadia Lacoste.

'Right after the Prince and Princess were married, whenever they were in Paris, there were always four or five photographers stationed outside their apartment snapping pictures of them coming in or going out. Okay. But as the years went by, the photographers became less and less reserved. They'd follow them on motorcycles through the streets of Paris. Or, during the summer in Monaco, they'd hide in the small stretch of public beach just around the corner from the Old Beach Hotel because from there, with their long lenses, they could photograph Grace in her bathing suit. In the winter, when the family went skiing, the photographers would follow them to the slopes and hide in the bushes so they could get pictures of them, hopefully falling in the snow.'

The solution Lacoste proposed was to arrange a family photo-call.

Wherever they went, especially if it was on a private holiday, Lacoste would make a deal with the photographers. She'd get Rainier and Grace and the children to pose for 15 or 20 minutes. Once they got their pictures the photographers had to go away and leave the family alone.

It was a good idea on paper and it even worked the first few times.

Then one photographer stuck around for a few more days to get the picture that everyone else missed and before long all the other photographers were doing it too.

Eventually it got so bad that instead of four or five on guard in front of the apartment in Paris there were 20.

In 1980, word went around that there was big money in any photos anyone could get of Stephanie at school.

To protect her from daily harassment and allow her to get on with her life, the question became how to keep the press from finding out which school she was attending.

It wasn't easy because the family always tried to get together at weekends, either in Monaco or Paris. The paparazzi therefore knew that Stephanie would be going back to school on Monday mornings. Their game plan became to find out where they were spending the weekend, then wait them out until Monday.

So Rainier and Grace, with the help of Nadia Lacoste, had to devise new ways every week to get Stephanie back to school without being followed.

Life for Stephanie quickly deteriorated into one, big, unhappy race between the family's chauffeur and the photographers.

'Dad always told me,' she says, '"If you and your sister weren't beautiful, no one would care, so take it as a compliment." I guess he's right. If we were ugly dogs and never did anything exciting except sit home desperately seeking a husband, the magazines wouldn't have bothered with us. I guess they're interested in us because we're well brought up and not too bad looking and we do things with our lives. It's hard sometimes, but I always try to find the good side of things.'

Stephanie notes that Grace was often philosophical about the situation, telling her children there was nothing anybody could do but accept the fact that the photographers would be hanging around.

'She urged us not to let it get to us or to depress us or to make us go completely nuts. She was a great help because she'd gone through this sort of thing when she was in films. She didn't over-dramatise things or allow it to have more importance than it should have. When we were children she tried to get us used to it and warn us that we were going to be hassled and chased around by a lot of photographers. So in a way, when I got older, I was expecting it. I don't think it was so much Caroline's experience that taught me anything because there really isn't anything to learn. Even if I wanted to use the same tricks she did to avoid the photographers, they already knew them. I had to find my own.'

Being as strong-willed as she is, Stephanie was the one who always seemed to react in the most candid ways when she was hassled by the press.

There were times when she'd even stick her tongue out at them and tell them to go to hell.

'Yeah, I did. When they were rude to me I never saw why I should have been anything else to them. Now, mainly because of my career, I work with those people and if they're polite with me, I'm polite with them. If they ask for a picture, I let them take one on the understanding that once they've got what they want they leave me alone. But if they're rude to me, yelling obscene names to me, I'm going to be just as rude back to them. That's the way I am.'

Still, there were times when even her best sword-rattling bravado in the face of Nikons let her down.

Late one winter afternoon, Grace rang Lacoste to announce that the paparazzi had been massed in front of the house all day and that because of them Stephanie was now in tears. Grace said she refused to leave the house and would not go back to school as long as they were there.

'Can you blame me?' Stephanie asks these days. 'Do you realise how embarrassing it is to be that age and to arrive at school with a horde of photographers behind you? The other kids made fun of me or stayed away from me because of the photographers. It didn't bother me as much when I was with my family but at school it was horrible. I felt as though it scared them off and I didn't want that. What kid would?'

So it was up to Lacoste to plot Stephanie's escape.

As it was easy for her to second guess the photographers' behaviour – obviously they were going to follow Stephanie to school – Lacoste phoned Prince Rainier's chauffeur and told him to drive away slowly from the residence. She told him to make absolutely certain the paparazzi saw that Stephanie was not in the car. He was then to wait nearby but out of sight.

Lacoste arrived at the apartment a few minutes later in the ambassador's car.

She stayed in the flat until it began to get dark.

Then, with a scarf wrapped around her head, she climbed into the back seat of the ambassador's car, bent down, and told the chauffeur to drive in a hurry down the Champs-Elysées.

As soon as they pulled out of the garage, the photographers swarmed the car.

Lacoste and the ambassador's driver sped away.

Convinced Stephanie was in the back seat, the paparazzi raced after them.

It wasn't until they converged at a red light along the Champs-Elysées that the photographers realised they'd been duped.

By that time, the Prince's chauffeur had been called on the car phone to say that the coast was clear, had returned to the apartment and had fetched Stephanie.

'Those were the sorts of silly games we were forced to play,' Lacoste says. 'It became a constant battle of wits between us and the photographers. Maybe a grown-up can understand that sort of thing but it's awfully difficult to make a child understand. It got so bad in the last two years before Princess Grace died that once she stopped her car in the middle of Paris, got out and berated the photographers to please leave them alone. She said, "You've been following me around all day. I can take it. But please don't do it to my children. Please stop doing to them what you've been doing to me for years."'

Her case fell on deaf ears.

The photographers merely took pictures of her pleading with the other photographers.

Lacoste goes on. 'They became so aggressive that they'd follow her into shops and restaurants. And no one would stop them. Although one day when she was in a store and couldn't find anyone to help carry her packages, she turned to a photographer who'd followed her inside and said, "The least you can do is make yourself useful." She loaded him up with packages and led him back to her car.'

Of the three Grimaldi children, Albert has fared best with the press.

'I was lucky. When the press started getting interested in Caroline and then Stephanie – I'm talking about the European social press – I was at Amherst. I wasn't hiding but I was far removed from that whole Paris disco scene. Also, as a guy, I was more capable of defending myself. Yet I think the real reason they pretty much left me alone is because pictures of Caroline or Stephanie or my mother sell more magazines than pictures of me. Sure, we were all bothered at official functions and on holidays, like when the whole family went skiing in Switzerland. I've had to deal with the press from an early age. But, thankfully, I've never been harassed like my sisters were.'

He says the only time the press bothered him during his four years in the States was the first week of college and at graduation. The rest of the time he was free to roam around and do his thing.

'I guess you might say I was semi-incognito. It was great. And that's why I have such fond memories of those years. I can still be that way when I go to the States. Not too many people there know me and if I don't tell them they don't necessarily know where I come from. After the 1988 Winter Olympics I took a road trip with some friends. We drove from Texas to Los Angeles and stopped at some pretty cheap motels in Arizona and New Mexico. It was great fun. No one knew who I was. And no one cared. I enjoyed that.'

But these days, living in Monaco as heir to the throne, life is not as easy for him as it used to be.

'I don't like to see my face spread all over the scandal sheets, so I try not to give them a lot of opportunities to do that. I have to be careful where I go and who I go with. But I try not to let it get in the way of my social life. It's hard to do and as time goes on it will be increasingly difficult. Though I'm sure there's always a way to be relatively anonymous.'

It's never very easy for him to be seen in public with a girl, because the photographers are always hoping to get the first pictures of Monaco's next Princess.

They've even been known to hound him when he goes somewhere in Paris with one of his sisters.

More than once he's had to enlist the aid of a friend to drive a second car behind his just to keep the photographers from catching up. One night a friend swung his car sideways to block the street, allowing Albert and Stephanie time to get away. Just as he did, the car with the pursuing photographers slammed into him.

The friend complained that they'd ruined his car.

The photographer who'd been driving replied, 'It doesn't matter. With the money we make selling pictures of them we can buy you three cars.'

*   *   *   *

For the Grimaldis, the media event of the 1970s was Caroline's two-day wedding to Philippe Junot on 28 and 29 June, 1978.

It was a star-studded affair, highlighted by the fact that the press was openly predicting that her marriage with playboy Junot would never last.

There was even a betting line started a week before the event that it wouldn't happen at all.

Caroline, however, seemed determined to marry Junot.

And so they got married.

The bride wore white. The groom was nervous. Frank Sinatra was there. Cary Grant was there. Ava Gardner was there. But the press corps of nearly 200 reporters and photographers were not. They were kept as far away from the ceremony as the police could keep them, which in this case was outside the security-tight Palace. They were left to jostle for hand-out photographs and what few morsels 'spokespersons' would fling at them, like volunteers in a Bowery soup kitchen.

That Princess Caroline became Mrs Junot could not have been a surprise to anyone who'd spent the first half of 1978 on the planet Earth.

Their engagement and every step of the way that would take them to the altar were hyped in newspapers and magazines to such an extent that, at least for a short time, they rivalled Burton and Taylor, the Windsors, Rainier and Grace and maybe even Romeo and Juliet in history's 'most-hyped-love-affair' category.

Unlike White House weddings with live television coverage or Buckingham Palace weddings with souvenir tee-shirts on sale across the street, this one was held in the strictest family privacy with an official guest list of a mere 600.

Because the Palace throne room is far too small for that number, only the immediate family – about 50 people – attended the Wednesday morning civil ceremony. Thursday morning's religious service, planned for the Palace chapel, was finally held outside, a last-minute change, because Rainier and Grace decided to include all their guests.

They succeeded in avoiding the kind of chaos that overshadowed their own nuptials, but they didn't quite manage the calm that comes with simple family affairs. How could they – with 200 reporters and photographers encamped in Monaco, each of them trying to outscoop the other, and none of them having anything more to report on than printed hand-outs.

The first of those hand-outs, a press kit free for the asking to any reporter or photographer in English or French, noted that the press would be permitted to operate in total freedom, without special permission, in spite of the fact that they would not be admitted into any official ceremony or any of the several parties planned to fête the bride and groom. The rest of the press kit contained potted histories of the throne room, the chapel, Princess Caroline and what everyone was wearing. A late entry, complete with photograph, was everything anyone ever wanted to know about the wedding cake – 500 eggs, 145 pounds of sugar, 45 pounds of almond paste, lots of smiling chefs, etc.

Then came the news that Mr and Mrs Junot could be photographed while they walked from the Palace to City Hall. As for photos taken during the official ceremonies, Grace had asked an old Hollywood chum, Howell Conant, to take pictures. His films were rushed off to be developed so that six photos could be chosen as official press photos. In other words, every reporter got the same six photos. It meant that anyone who could have managed to get past the Palace walls with a tie-clasp Pentax would have cleaned up.

As a matter of fact, a few tried.

One of the paparazzi even dressed up like a priest.

But they were all caught and no one managed to come up with anything more than those hand-outs.

So the press did what they usually do when there's no one to talk to, they talked to themselves.

They formed four main groups: Germans, Italians, British, and others, with the few American reporters on hand forming the mainstay of that fourth category.

As for the French, they got lost somewhere around the first hand-out.

Under normal circumstances, Italy's *Oggi* magazine reporters have no love for Italy's *Gente* magazine reporters and Germany's *Bunte* reporters don't usually tell their secrets to Germany's *Wochenende* reporters. However, there is a certain kind of brotherhood in journalism – much like there is among streetwalkers – so the usually opposing forces joined hands and went off in search of a story.

The Italians bribed taxi drivers, bar-tenders, croupiers, shopkeepers, barbers, manicurists, hotel concierges, and anyone else who might be able to tell them anything at all about the wedding.

Admittedly they didn't get very much because none of the people they bribed were on the guest list.

The Germans put out the word that they were prepared to pay up to DM 30,000 – then about $15,000 or £7,000 – for any unofficial pictures taken during the ceremonies, parties, balls, anything at all. The money went unspent.

The British traipsed off to David Niven's house on Cap Ferrat and they might indeed have come up with the only scoop of the week – Gregory Peck's car backed into Cary Grant's car. There was no damage, no one was hurt and everyone involved remained friends. Still, cables were rushed off to Fleet Street.

Yet the best stories were the ones they didn't get. For instance, the night before the wedding, Grace was up until 4 a.m. trying to figure out how to seat everybody at the celebration luncheon. There were royals and there were heads of state and protocol was a nightmare. Tables were set up under the trees on the square in front of the palace. The whole area had, of course, been roped off from the general public. It was, as Rupert Allan described it, 'The luncheon of the century in that part of the world.'

After the ceremony, before going to the lunch, Allan was standing under the Palace portico next to the Sinatras and the Pecks while Sinatra's bodyguard was dispatched to case the area to make certain that the coast was clear of photographers. When he came back to report that all was not good, Frank and Barbara Sinatra decided they would not stay for lunch. So Gregory Peck and his wife decided they wouldn't stay either.

Rupert Allan was incensed. 'Sinatra's bodyguard gave him the wrong advice. That doesn't excuse anything but it explains why he didn't stay. But how could Gregory Peck and his wife leave also? I can't understand anyone doing that to someone like Grace. How dare they do that to Grace?'

Then there were the two great British gentlemen stars, Brian Aherne and David Niven.

Allan explains, 'Brian has always been the best-dressed man in the movies, and that includes Cary Grant. He was looking fantastic that day in a wonderful Panama hat. But this wasn't one of his luckier days. He was standing with his wife and the Nivens when a seagull took his revenge on the world and got both Brian and David. I mean he really got them both.'

Not that all official channels of information were turned off, they were just mostly useless.

Question: 'Where is the couple going on their honeymoon?'

Official answer: 'Only Philippe knows and he hasn't told anyone, not even Caroline.'

To get the scoop of the week, the Italian team headed down to the harbour to check out the yachts, found the Niarchos boat there and tried every trick they could think of to squeeze information out of the crew. When the officers and boatswains alike refused to say anything, the Italians convinced themselves that Niarchos was in on the honeymoon plans and accordingly wired Rome and Milan.

Not to be outdone, the German contingent suddenly pinpointed the honeymoon spot to one of the Greek islands. They wired Frankfurt and Munich, swore the Italians were off course in betting on the Niarchos yacht and took back the lead by naming another, equally fancy boat.

It turned out the Junots flew Air France to Tahiti.

The Fleet Street bunch was still reliving the Peck/Grant car crash so they didn't bother trying to come up with any honeymoon stories at all, which therefore put the heavy betting on the German version.

One learns very quickly that German reporters come up with better rumours than Italian reporters, even if both fall short of the more thorough, direct-from-behind-the-scenes reporting of British rumours. That's not, by the way, a comment on the state of journalism in Germany, Italy or Great Britain. It's merely an observation about rumours.

As the first day melded into the second, there were more handouts.

Some of them were intriguing enough to include 'the night was balmy, the moon was full', in spite of the fact that they'd been written the week before, that the night was decidedly not balmy and that the moon was anything but full.

Then there were phone calls from 'official unofficial sources' intent on setting the record straight.

'Deep Background' wanted it known that Mr Junot was not staying in the Palace with Princess Caroline before the wedding.

Whether anyone had actually dared to pose such a delicate question was a moot point.

The 'official unofficial source' simply wanted it known that everybody was playing by the rules, even at the Palace.

And so they got married.

The bride wore white. The groom was nervous. Everybody got their free press kit and their six official photographs.

But then, just down the beach in Nice, at almost the very same time, Maurice Brocart wed Marie-France Gaillard. The bride wore white. The groom was nervous. And anyone who showed up was welcome to take all the photos they wanted.

*   *   *   *

Caroline shudders when she looks back on that.

'Not one of my better days,' she says. 'Mother once told me she hated the whole fiasco of her wedding too. Of course I wasn't there, so I don't know all of the details, but I remember mommy saying that it was just a circus. Not only didn't they look at their wedding pictures for years after that, on their honeymoon they didn't talk about it. It was madness. She didn't want that for mine.'

It's hard to see how Caroline could have avoided it.

Her face sells magazines.

She even made it to the cover of *Time* at the age of 16.

'That wasn't my idea at all. They were writing a piece on Monaco and it turned out to be on me. When they said they wanted to ask a few questions, I was frightfully rude. I didn't want to talk to anybody because I was about to go on to university where I'd decided I wanted to be anonymous. I wanted to be forgotten about. But I was told they were going to take a picture. I'd just come back from school, walked into the apartment and the photographer was there. So we went out onto the balcony. As I remember it was a pretty lousy picture.'

She is still pursued by the paparazzi, although not so much now that she's married with a family as when she was single.

And she agrees with her father that you never got used to it.

'When I was living in Paris I went everywhere with my German shepherd dog. As long as I was with my dog they tended to keep their distance. Or at least they only used their long lenses. Even today when I go out I worry that somebody is following me or hiding behind bushes. You never think you're completely alone or completely free to move around. It's a terrible feeling. The pressure of being spied upon is awful. Lots of people can't understand why I've tried to stop it whenever I can because they think I love it, they think we love the publicity.'

Just in case anybody is wondering, she insists that she does not collect her own press cuttings. They do arrive regularly in her mail, usually from people who think she might want to have them. But she says she very rarely reads them.

'Yet when I do read something, it's like reading about somebody else's life. I look through some of the articles and for the first ten minutes I giggle because it's so absurd. They write such complete nonsense. Then, all of a sudden I say to myself, but they're writing about me and they're lying. That's when I get furious. When they have nothing else to write about they invent things.'

As for his own press these days, Rainier feels, 'I don't interest them so much any more because I don't do enough that would interest them.'

Although that's not quite the way the papers see it.

Hounded by a photographer in New York, Rainier made headlines when he took a page out of Frank Sinatra's book and threw a punch at a photographer. Depending on which account you read, he might even have thrown two punches at two photographers.

Not quite five months after Princess Grace's death, Rainier had gone to see *Cats* with the wife of an American friend. Photographers swarmed him coming out of the theatre, insinuating that the 'unidentified' lady on his arm might become the next Princess of Monaco.

First he shouted at one of them.

Then he let his Mediterranean temper get the better of him and he hit the guy.

More photographers showed up the next day at his hotel and he was alleged to have taken a swing at another photographer. However, reports of the two incidents named three different photographers.

Another version of the story had it that Rainier, in a fury, jumped into a limousine thinking it was his, ordered the driver to pull away fast and was told he'd mistakenly climbed into the wrong car. The punchline of that story is that the car actually belonged to Oleg Cassini.

The best any of the serious press could hint at was, 'Prince Rainier's behaviour in New York recently has suggested that his nerves are not perhaps as settled as they might be.'

But those stories paled when word leaked to the press that Rainier was about to marry Princess Ira von Furstenberg. Her title came from the first of what are now three well-publicised marriages, this one in 1955 at the age of 15 to an Austrian prince.

In a less than tasteful way, the Rainier–Ira marriage stories ran on the third anniversary of Grace's death.

With great authority, one scandal sheet noted, 'His 28-year-old daughter, Princess Caroline's second marriage to wealthy former Italian playboy Stefano Casiraghi is shaky. And his other daughter Stephanie, 20, is constantly in man trouble. Rainier hoped that strong-willed Ira, a close friend of the Grimaldis for many years, could help him overcome these problems.'

Describing her as 'Racy Ira', the London-based *Daily Mail* explained that she is the niece of Fiat magnate Gianni Agnelli, her mother being Agnelli's sister. After an early divorce from husband number one she was married briefly to Brazilian playboy, 'Baby' Pignatari.

They then went on to point out, 'Ira has never been one to let the ageing process catch up with her. She is proud that she has undergone extensive cosmetic surgery and once even had her bottom lifted. Rumours that if you press her tummy button her ears flap are probably exaggerated.'

While all of this was going on, both Rainier and Ira were denying that anything was going on.

Before long, her son Christoph announced it was a sure bet that his mother would marry Rainier.

And, just as the ink dried on that story, she did get married – however, it was to somebody else.

The way the story got started was innocent enough.

Von Furstenberg came to Monaco on business in 1985. She'd taken a stand to exhibit antiques at Monaco's bi-annual show. Because she happens to be a distant cousin of Rainier's and as he'd been to school with her first husband, they were in a sense old friends. It was only to be expected that when Rainier toured the exhibit he stopped at her stand to say hello. They were photographed together there.

A few days later Gianni Agnelli arrived in Monaco on his yacht for the Red Cross Ball. He hosted a luncheon on his boat and quite naturally invited both his niece and Rainier. As it happened, they arrived together.

Next, Rainier invited von Furstenberg to join him at his table for the Red Cross Ball. She sat on one side of him, his sister Antoinette sat on the other.

The photographers now had them together all over Monaco, which quickly led them to the obvious conclusion that their engagement would be announced at any moment.

Her son's quote, 'They'll be married by the end of the year', was enough to keep the rumours alive and on the front pages for over a year.

Yet Rainier says there was never any talk of an engagement.

There were never any plans to marry.

They were only friends.

And even if there was a brief flirtation or a minor romance, it stopped well short of the altar.

'Her father was friendly with my grandfather,' he says, 'so they used to come to Monaco when she was growing up. We've known each other a long time. She's good company and she's amusing, but that's all. There's never been any question of marriage. But I guess each time I go to say hello to a woman the press immediately invents a romance because it makes for a better story than the truth.'

Nadia Lacoste points out that very same photo of Rainier and von Furstenberg walking onto Agnelli's boat was later run by newspapers and magazines around the world as Rainier and his fiancée in the Caribbean, Rainier and the future Princess of Monaco in the South Pacific, Rainier and the new Princess of Monaco on their secret honeymoon.

Wearily, Rainier shrugs, 'What can I say? It sells magazines.'

*   *   *   *

14

The Accident

ONE AFTERNOON in Monaco, late in the 1970s.
She was driving alone in her converted London Taxi.

It was an amusing car, easy to handle in the narrow streets. And with its big back seat there was always plenty of room for other people and piles of packages.

She was a slow, deliberate driver. So slow in fact that whenever her children came along they'd tease her, 'We could walk there faster.'

Now she pulled the old cab out of the Rue Grimaldi and into the Place d'Armes.

She had her glasses on – she always wore them when she drove – but she must have come into the intersection without looking because an Italian, with the obvious right of way, shot across the square directly in front of her.

She rammed him broadside.

Startled but unhurt, she got out of her car to apologise. She was clearly in the wrong and she was willing to admit it.

But the Italian was too furious for polite conversation. He jumped out of his car, pointed to the damage and screamed at her.

She tried to calm him down, saying, you're absolutely right and please don't worry because my insurance will cover all the damage.

The Italian didn't want to know. He yelled at her and insulted her.

Within seconds, the policeman guarding the road that goes up to Le Rocher rushed over, saluted her and asked the irate Italian to calm down. He told the man, 'Madame says she's sorry and will take care of all your expenses.'

But the Italian was too far gone. 'This bitch ran into me.'

The policeman strongly advised the man to keep quiet.

With arms flying about, the Italian shouted at her again, his vocabulary descending into the gutter.

Now the cop took control. He warned the Italian in no uncertain terms, 'If you open your mouth one more time you're going to jail. If you insult the Princess of Monaco one more time, I'll arrest you.'

That stopped the Italian.

He spun around to take a close look at the woman who'd smashed into his car and now realised who she was.

She reassured him, 'It was my fault and everything will be taken care of.'

A car soon arrived from the Palace to fetch her. The damages to the Italian's car were made good by her insurance company. And she began telling friends, 'I'll never drive again.'

It was a promise she failed to keep.

*   *   *   *

September 1982.

On Friday morning the 10th, Stephanie returned to Monaco from Antigua where she'd been spending the last few weeks of her summer holidays. While she was in the West Indies she'd suffered a water skiing accident and split open her head so badly she needed stitches. A chauffeur brought her from Nice airport to Roc Agel where she spent the next few jet-lagged days trying to reassure her parents that she was all right.

On Saturday morning the 11th, Nadia Lacoste rang Grace at Roc Agel. Stephanie and Grace were booked to catch the train from Monaco to Paris on Monday night, arriving early Tuesday morning so that Stephanie could start school on Wednesday. Lacoste was concerned with how Grace planned to keep the paparazzi away from Stephanie on her first day back. She suggested Grace and Stephanie should not spend Tuesday night at the family apartment in Paris. She told Grace, 'The photographers will undoubtedly be hanging around the apartment on Wednesday morning, so why not spend Tuesday night at someplace like the Hotel Maurice? It's close to the school and no one will find you there.' Grace thought it was a reasonable idea. Although she did have to concede, 'No matter what we do, they're bound to find out.'

On Sunday the 12th, Grace's former secretary, Phyllis Blum, now Phyllis Earl, rang from London to talk about Grace's trip to England in 10 days' time and the poetry readings that were planned for the third tour of America. At one point in their conversation, driving was mentioned and Earl told Grace, 'Don't forget to wear your seat belts.'

That same afternoon, Caroline flew to London. A friend met her at Heathrow airport and drove her into town. They spent a few hours together before she took the train from Waterloo Station to Forest Mere, a health farm in the Hampshire countryside. The friend told her, 'If the place is great, I'll visit you there later in the week. If it's not, I'll still visit you there later in the week but I'll also smuggle in a lot of food.'

On Monday the 13th, at around 9 a.m., Grace woke Stephanie. Then she went into Albert's room to say good morning. He'd been to Italy over the weekend to see a soccer match with some friends and had got back to Roc Agel late the night before.

'Mom came to wake me up and we talked a bit. Then she said, "See you later." I had to come down to the Palace for something that morning so I said, "Sure, see you later."'

While Grace was getting ready to leave for the Palace, her chauffeur brought the 11-year-old, metallic green Rover 3500 out of the garage and parked it in front of the house.

Normally Stephanie would have done that.

All three Grimaldi children had been allowed to drive the car from the garage to the house at Roc Agel before they had a licence. All three had scooted around in Rainier's golf cart or played with his jeep there. All three practised driving at Roc Agel. But Rainier and Grace laid down very strict rules that, as long as they were under age, they could only drive on the family's private property. Until they had their licence, none of their children could take a car beyond Roc Agel's gates.

When Grace came out of the house, her arms were full of dresses which she spread flat across the rear seat of the car.

A maid followed with other dresses and large hat boxes and together they filled the rear seat.

Then she called for Stephanie who was still trying to wake up.

Grace's chauffeur was standing by the car ready to drive the two of them down to the Palace.

Grace didn't much like driving and didn't do a lot of it, although she liked the Rover. There wasn't a lot of mileage on it because she didn't use it much. Still, she always insisted it be well maintained. It hardly, if ever, went any further away from the Palace garage than Roc Agel. And even then it was usually driven by a chauffeur.

Now, however, with the back seat covered, there wasn't room enough for Grace and Stephanie and a chauffeur.

Grace told her chauffeur that it would be easier if she drove.

He said, there's no need to do that. If you leave the dresses here I'll drive you down now and then come back for them.

She said, no, please don't bother, I'll drive.

He said, it's better if I drive. Why don't I call the Palace and ask someone to come up for the dresses straight away?

She said, no believe me, it's all right like this.

He kept trying to convince her. I really don't mind coming back for them.

But she kept saying, it's just easier if I drive.

So Grace got behind the wheel and Stephanie climbed into the passenger seat.

At about 10 a.m. they pulled away from Roc Agel.

The chauffeur watched them leave.

The road from the farm winds down the hill and eventually into La Turbie. There you must skirt the large Roman monument in the centre of town to arrive at a narrow point in the two-lane road where you turn left, across oncoming traffic and in front of an old woman who sells wicker baskets from a stall at the edge of the village car park.

The road from there down to the Moyenne Corniche, which takes you into Monaco, is called the D37.

It's two lanes, but in most places the road is so narrow and winding that you can hardly ever overtake another car.

It's straight for a while, running between old, yellow stucco two-storey houses with green shutters and geraniums in window boxes, and sometimes you see laundry hanging out of a top-floor window to dry.

There's a slight bend to the right where you find yourself going fairly steeply downhill. A few hundred yards more and there's a bend where you pick up speed again as the road down gets steeper still.

To your right, an angular valley cuts through the mountains, leading to the sea with houses teetering on the edge, just waiting to tip over and tumble down.

For a moment, the road straightens out, but it is never straight for very long – bending right, bending left, then snaking back again – always getting steeper as it brings you down the hill.

A sign says, 'Beware of falling rocks.'

Far below, the stubby thumb of St Jean-Cap-Ferrat juts out from where the water comes to meet the valley and forms a small beach.

Now the whole expanse of sea is there in front of you, a huge greenish-blue semi-circle.

And now there are several very sharp turns.

Approximately two miles from the monument at La Turbie, there is an especially steep bend where you have to brake very hard and fight with your steering wheel to follow the road 150 degrees to the right.

Grace missed that turn.

The Rover slammed into the small retaining wall.

And went through it.

The car somersaulted as it crashed 120 feet through branches of trees, careening off the side of the slope, tossing Grace and Stephanie around inside.

*   *   *   *

Rainier was called at Roc Agel.

He rushed into his car and immediately drove to the hospital in Monaco.

Louis de Polignac was already there.

Albert came down from Roc Agel in his own car and met them at the hospital.

Members of the government started to arrive.

Everyone stood around waiting for the doctors' reports.

It took a long time before the news came that Stephanie was badly hurt but that she was going to be all right.

Grace was hurt too.

And at this point the doctors felt she would be all right as well.

As late as three hours after the accident, all Caroline had been told was that Grace had broken her collar bone, fractured her hip and had lacerations. She was assured that Grace's injuries were not serious enough to warrant her return home that night. So she made reservations on the first flight from London to Nice on Tuesday morning.

Over the next few hours, with the entire hospital staff mobilised and specialists called in, three medical bulletins were released by the hospital. None of them suggested the true extent of Grace's injuries.

Stephanie, only semi-conscious and in terrible pain, was diagnosed as having cracked her vertebra. No other serious injuries and no internal bleeding were found. They secured her neck in a brace and eventually announced that with proper care she could be home in about two weeks.

But Grace, now in a coma, was not responding to treatment.

Doctors began to suspect a brain haemorrhage.

They needed to do a CAT scan but the hospital, ironically named for Princess Grace, didn't yet have one.

The doctors debated their options.

A helicopter to a Swiss clinic was ruled out because they feared she'd never make it.

Even taking her to nearby Nice was considered too dangerous.

In the end, Grace was secretly moved about 400 yards in an ambulance to the office of a private physician where the CAT scan was performed.

While the accident had caused some light, external brain damage, the scan showed that Grace had suffered two severe brain lesions.

The first, before the accident, caused her to black out.

The second, brought about by the accident, was so extensive that the French neurosurgeon who'd been rushed from Nice to Monaco determined that no surgical intervention was possible.

After examining the CAT scan results, Dr Jean Duplay told his colleagues that the second stroke was so massive, Grace would have needed treatment within 15 minutes to have had any chance of survival.

And even then, as Professor Charles Chatelin, the doctor in

charge, told Rainier later, had she somehow managed to survive, at least half her body would have been paralysed.

Grace was brought back to the hospital and placed on a life support system.

On Tuesday night, 14 September, Rainier, Caroline and Albert assembled outside Grace's room to speak with Dr Chatelin.

He wanted them to know the truth.

Rainier and Caroline and Albert listened as he gently explained that Grace's condition had deteriorated and that she was now far beyond anyone's help.

'We had a long talk with him,' Rainier says. 'He was an extremely nice man and very understanding with us. He explained the uselessness of continuing with the life support machine. He showed us the pictures and helped us to understand in a very clear way that the machine should be turned off.'

Rainier and Caroline and Albert made the decision together.

Now the Prince's voice gets very soft. 'It was a difficult decision sentimentally.' He pauses. 'But from a rational, human standpoint it was an obvious decision. There was no reason to keep her on the machine.'

Rainier and Caroline and Albert went into Grace's room to say goodbye for the final time.

When that was done they left her to Dr Chatelin.

And the life support system was turned off.

*   *   *   *

First came the rumour.

There's been an accident.

Next came disbelief.

It's not true. The Princess is in Roc Agel and Stephanie is with her and so is the Prince and so is Albert.

Then word spread throughout the principality that the rumour was true.

Disbelief turned to shock.

Next came confusion.

People believed only what they wanted to believe. The Princess is all right. Stephanie is all right. The car was badly damaged but they've both escaped.

People wandered through the streets of Monaco reassuring each other, they're all right, there's nothing to worry about, they're going to be fine.

Then the press swarmed in on Monaco, like a plague of locusts, and now the rumours exploded. She's dead. They're both alive. She's in a coma. Stephanie has escaped unhurt but Grace is critical.

Shops closed. Offices closed. People went to church to pray. Photos of Grace began appearing in windows, draped in black. People went to stand in front of the Palace, waiting for news.

The announcement came late on Tuesday night.

Her Serene Highness, Princess Grace of Monaco, died this evening at 10:15 p.m.

Total silence blanketed Monaco.

Like a thick, eerie fog hanging heavily, it made its way through the streets and into the corners of every home.

At the Palace there was shock and disbelief and confusion.

A state funeral had to be arranged.

But no one seemed to want to take the initiative.

It was almost as if everyone knew that once they began making arrangements, that would mean it had really happened.

For the longest time no one could summon up the strength to begin.

The one person who might have been able to organise such an event was Grace.

The burden fell on Rainier, Albert and Caroline.

And although the government and the cabinet carried some of the weight, it was the Prince who, despite his enormous grief, somehow found the courage to carry on.

Albert and Caroline did their part.

But it was Rainier himself who took charge.

'Daddy was wonderful,' Caroline says. 'He was so brave and strong. He was amazing. It was such a lesson to watch him handle that. I can see now, all these years later, that my mother's death brought the family closer together. Not that we were far apart before she died. But after she died we learned to work more together, to be more careful about each other, to pay more attention to each other's lives.'

Over the next several weeks, thousands of telegrams and tens of thousands of letters poured into the Palace from all over the world.

Someone counted 450 baskets of flowers, many of them from complete strangers.

Grace lay in state for three days in the tiny private chapel at the Palace, constantly surrounded by a guard of honour and flowers – white roses, white and purple orchids, white lilies.

Her hands held the green stones of her rosary beads.

Her wedding ring was clearly visible on the fourth finger of her left hand.

And thousands of people filed past her.

At precisely 10:30 a.m. on Saturday, 18 September, she was taken from the chapel and brought to the Cathedral in a procession – marked by the mournful beat of a single drum – led by her husband, her son and her eldest daughter.

Stephanie, in traction, lay on her back in her hospital room looking up at a television mounted high on pillows so she could watch the funeral. Paul Belmondo was with her. But as soon as it began she broke down and after a few minutes she was so distressed that she passed out. Belmondo turned the TV off.

For the rest of the morning he just held her hand and they wept together.

Once the high mass was said, Grace lay in state for the remainder of the day.

A private burial had been planned for later that afternoon. But at the very last minute Rainier decided Grace would not be buried in the crypt that night.

He said he wanted it made larger.

So she was buried the next day, once workmen had prepared a place next to her where one day he too will rest.

*   *   *   *

The Monégasques had lost their Princess.

The dignity that characterised their mourning was only surpassed by the elegance of the woman herself.

There were, however, a few incidents that posed a minor risk to the solemnity of the event.

When Nancy Reagan's limousine came within sight of the Cathedral, the Secret Service spotted someone on the roof. They whisked her round to the rear door while agents cornered the man who turned out to be a specially assigned film photographer with authorisation to be there.

Even most of the paparazzi showed their respect.

Although a few of the principality's foreign residents had an oddly warped view of the future.

Some of them had grown smug in their belief that, as long as Grace and Rainier were on the throne, all was well with the non-taxable world. Now, with Grace gone, the main things that concerned them were: Will all of this change? Will Rainier abdicate? Will Monaco collapse? The death of an ideal is sad, the death of one's financial security and one's quality of life is something serious.

Other people, especially those who lived their lives vicariously through hers, pretended that they were, as always, very much on the inside.

For example, while Grace was lying in state at the Palace, with thousands of people lining up to walk past her coffin, one particular foreigner with a vague association to the family showed up in the courtyard every day, literally to hold court. He'd stand off to the side, under the arched walkway, and console friends, or reassure them that everything was under control. There was a lot of whispering in ears, and arms around shoulders and hugs with promises about getting them better seats inside the Cathedral for the funeral.

Then there were those who had once found themselves on the fringes of friendship with the family, the ones who never hesitated to drop Grace's name. They suddenly found themselves unprotected. Those are the ones who are still forever suggesting that Rainier and the children are lost without Grace.

They are also the ones who still today claim, 'Even if Stephanie was not driving . . . and by the way, I'm not totally convinced she wasn't . . . there's been a cover-up and we'll never know the truth about the accident, although I know what happened but I can't say for fear of reprisals.'

Nonsense.

There was no cover-up.

Stephanie was not driving.

Caroline is the only member of the family to have spoken to Stephanie about what happened in the car that morning. She moved into Stephanie's hospital room, to live there with her until she was fit enough to go home. And the two girls talked about the accident a few days after it happened.

'Stephanie told me, "Mommy kept saying, I can't stop. The brakes don't work. I can't stop." She said that mommy was in a complete panic. Stephanie grabbed the handbrake. She told me right after the accident, "I pulled on the handbrake but it wouldn't stop. I tried but I just couldn't stop the car."

Stephanie has never discussed the accident with her father or brother. There are even some people close to the family who sincerely believe that Stephanie has since blocked the accident out of her mind, that she remembers nothing of what happened that morning.

This is not the case.

'I remember every minute of it,' she says, trying to control her emotions. 'It's only in the last few years that I've been starting to cope with it. I had some professional help and especially in the last eight months I've been learning to deal with it. I still can't go down that road, even if someone else is driving. I always ask them to take the other road. But at least I can talk about it without crying. Although it's hard for me to get it out in front of my dad. As far as I'm concerned, I can live with it. But I still can't talk to my dad about it because I know it hurts him and I don't want to do that because I love him.'

To set the record straight, once and for all, this is what happened.

Grace had gone through a very busy summer.

She was always exhausted at the end of the season, but this one had been even more hectic than usual.

The cruise on the *Mermoz* had helped. But she was still tired, irritable, suffering from high blood pressure and going through a very difficult menopause.

Caroline confirms, 'She wasn't feeling too well. She was incredibly tired. The summer had been very busy. She hadn't stopped going places and doing things all summer long. She'd done too much. She never mentioned it or complained about it though. But she wasn't in great form.'

On that fateful morning, Grace and Stephanie drove past the French policeman directing traffic near the monument at La Turbie. He later reported that he'd recognised Princess Grace at the steering wheel and had saluted.

A French lorry followed the Rover down the D37.

The driver later testified that Grace was driving.

Somewhere along the road Grace complained of a headache.

It continued to bother her as they headed down the hill.

Then suddenly a pain shot up through her skull.

For a fraction of a second she blacked out.

The car started to swerve.

When she opened her eyes she was disorientated. In a panic, she jammed her foot on the brake.

At least she thought it was the brake.

It appears now that she probably missed the brake and hit the accelerator instead. The French lorry driver reported that he was 50 yards behind the Rover, nearing that very steep, sharp curve, when he saw the Rover swerve violently from side to side, zig-zagging across both lanes. Then the car straightened out and shot ahead very fast. He knew the road and knew that the bend was coming up and, in those two or three seconds when he didn't see any brake lights on, he realised what was going to happen.

At that instant, Grace screamed to Stephanie, 'I can't stop. The brakes don't work.'

Stephanie lunged across her seat to grab the handbrake.

She also somehow managed to put the car into park.

But the car kept going.

Stephanie says she'll never know for sure if her mother got the accelerator and the brake pedal mixed up or just didn't have the use of her legs. But when the police investigated the accident and checked the road, there were no skid marks.

Neither Grace nor Stephanie were wearing their seat belts.

The gardener who heard the car crash onto the property where he was working knew the sound from past experience. He later reported that in 30 years it had happened at least 15 times. He also later claimed to have pulled Stephanie out of the driver's window, giving the impression that Stephanie had been driving. Seeing the interest he created with those remarks, he continued embellishing his own role in the tragedy through so-called 'exclusive interviews' which he sold to any magazine or newspaper that paid him.

The fact is, he wasn't the first person on the scene.

And he did not pull Stephanie out of the car.

She got out herself from the passenger side.

'I found myself huddled under the space below the glove compartment. I lost consciousness as we fell down. I remember hitting the tree and the next thing I remember is waking up and seeing smoke coming out of the car. I thought the car was going to blow up. I knew I had to get out of there and get my mom out of there and so I bashed down the door with my legs. It wasn't hard because the door was half gone anyway. I ran out and saw a lady standing there and started yelling, "Please get help, call the Palace, I'm Princess Stephanie, call my father and get help."'

The woman, who lived at the house, sat her down.

Stephanie was in shock. The stitches in her scalp from her water skiing accident had opened and she was bleeding badly. She'd also cut her tongue and lost a tooth.

And now pain began shooting up through her back.

She was screaming, 'My mother's in the car, call my father.'

The woman and her husband kept asking who her father was.

She told them, 'He's the Prince. I'm Princess Stephanie and he's the Prince of Monaco.'

It was several minutes before anyone understood her and several minutes more before they believed her.

'I kept pleading with the woman, "Call my father at the Palace. Please get help. My mother is in there." Everything else is blurred in my mind until the police came.'

Grace had been tossed into the rear of the car, shoved into the back seat and pinned there by the steering column which opened a severe gash in her head.

She appeared to be conscious but was covered in blood.

Stephanie says, 'The firemen got mom out of the car and put her in an ambulance. I waited there for another ambulance.'

The car was severely damaged and someone who examined it closely later that afternoon asserts that the only area not twisted beyond recognition was the space under the glove compartment in front of the passenger seat. Only someone hunched down in front of that seat could have survived.

When something like this occurs, there are always lingering, unanswerable questions.

For instance, why didn't Grace let the chauffeur drive?

For example, why was she fated to black out at exactly the wrong spot on that road. If she'd blacked out 100 yards further up the road, Stephanie might have been able to swing the car into the hill and stop it. It it had happened 100 yards further down the hill, they would have passed that dangerous hairpin turn.

Another thing, the CAT scan revealed that the first haemorrhage, a mild one, caused the accident. But the massive stroke that killed her was brought on by the accident.

Ironically, a few years later, Grace's brother John, Jr, would die while jogging of an identical cerebral haemorrhage.

As the accident had occurred in France, Rainier was approached by the French Government who'd immediately ordered an official investigation and asked if, under the circumstances, he'd like that investigation accelerated.

He said no.

He said that everything should be done step by step, by the book.

'I wanted them to do whatever they had to do without any interference. All right, the car was taken away from the spot right away. We were criticised for that in the press. But we had to do that otherwise we would have had tourists chipping off bits of it as souvenirs. It was the French gendarmerie who told us to take it to a police garage in Monaco. The local French judge who was in charge of the investigation told his colleagues in Monaco to seal off the garage so that no one could tamper with the car. They did that right away. No one in Monaco had anything to do with the final report or could influence it in any way.'

Rover engineers were also flown in from Britain and they went over the car to check for mechanical failure. They also investigated the possibility of sabotage. But no mechanical failure was found. The brakes, they wrote in their final report, had been in perfect working order.

The French investigation concluded that the accident occurred when Grace blacked out and lost control of the car.

But even now, even all these years later, doubts remain.

Not, Rainier says, in his mind. It's the press who won't let the story alone.

'When I got the phone call at Roc Agel that morning, I drove down to the hospital immediately. The doctors didn't want to say anything in the beginning because they wanted to do a thorough examination. But the press was diagnosing faster than the doctors. Based on the information supplied by that wretched gardener who says he found the car, and supplemented by the gendarmes, rumours spread very quickly. But it took a long time before the doctors knew what the situation was. They'd come out and tell me they'd found a fracture here and a fracture there, then go back inside and look for more. As they went on finding things they'd tell me. I waited a long time before I knew how serious her condition was and I knew before the press did.'

That didn't much matter to the press, especially to the downmarket tabloids who rushed teams of journalists to Monaco. One American rag sent no less than 17 reporters.

Armed with cash, they were happy to pay anyone who'd speak to them. The result was a continual stream of speculation about how the accident happened, who was driving and how the medical teams at the hospital were too slow in their treatment of Grace.

'They did their best to keep the story running and didn't show much human compassion for the pain that we were suffering. It was dreadful. There was all sorts of speculation about what we should have done to save Grace. I just can't understand why. Practically everybody at the hospital was mobilised for her. And I don't know how many times we've had to say that Grace would never have allowed Stephanie drive her down to Monaco, especially on that road as dangerous as it is. Yes, Stephanie did drive the car from the house to the garage at Roc Agel but she never drove that car off the property.'

He stops for a moment to shake his head, then confesses, 'When the press makes up a story about the Mafia wanting to kill Grace, though I can't for a moment see why the Mafia would want to kill her, if there was some interpretation that seemed even only minutely possible, I'd say, all right. But when they keep rehashing the story that Stephanie was driving and they know it's not true, when they know it's been proven that she wasn't driving, it hurts all of us. It's done a lot of damage and that isn't fair. Maybe if there had been some sort of mechanical error, I don't know, but if there had been, Stephanie might have been able to master it better than her mother. But that's not the point. The point is people don't know to what extent Stephanie has suffered.'

Psychiatrists say there is a fairly common reaction when someone survives an accident in which someone else is killed.

It's known as the 'why me?' syndrome.

The survivor keeps replaying the accident over and over again, asking, why did I survive and the other person die? In Stephanie's case the unanswered question is made even more perplexing by those well-meaning people who, since the accident, have reminded her what a wonderful woman her mother was and then added, 'Too bad she had to die.' It's a way of subtly suggesting, 'Those of us who admired your mother would have found it easier to accept your death instead of hers.'

Two other things make the problem especially complex.

The press, by constantly playing up the possibility that Stephanie was driving, have subjected her to enormous stress. She's tried to fight back by saying, 'How can they think I killed my mother?' But because her voice isn't as loud as theirs, no matter how much she continues to protest, the stress does not easily subside.

Even then, the tabloid press might not matter so much if there wasn't also the guilt that lingers every time she thinks about grabbing the handbrake, every time she tells herself she tried to save her mother and every time she remembers that she could not stop the car.

How many times have we all thought, if only I could turn back the clock?

It's clear that if this was anyone else besides a Grimaldi, a Windsor or maybe a Kennedy, what happened that day in September 1982 might be accepted as an understandable explanation for the way she's behaved since.

But lurid stories linked to Stephanie Grimaldi – true or false – sell newspapers and magazines.

In the end, from her point of view and from her father's, the way Stephanie has been treated in the press since the accident is in some ways almost as tragic as the accident itself.

*   *   *   *

Nearly 100 million people around the world watched Grace's funeral on television.

But at the time, neither Rainier nor Caroline nor Albert in the church, nor Stephanie in the hospital, knew just how widely the world was sharing their loss.

Any solace that might have come from the outside escaped them that day.

And like that scene so long ago when a three-year-old boy stood on the steps of the Capitol as the caisson rolled by bearing the casket of his father, and that little boy saluted – the scene so indelibly etched in the memory of that morning in Monaco is of Rainier, in his uniform, shattered with grief and of his oldest daughter, ashen and veiled in black, reaching out to touch him.

*   *   *

15

Dusk

THE WATERS turn dark.

The sun falls behind the hills.

Those buildings at the port are no longer salmon pink. They're now more of a fading strawberry red.

The post office sells the last stamps of the day.

The souvenir shop facing the port sells the last picture postcards of the day.

The pastry shop around the corner and down a narrow alley from City Hall on Le Rocher sells the last loaf of bread on the shelf.

And now there is a pause.

A small fishing boat chugs slowly back into the harbour.

Traffic comes to a halt on the roads leading out of town.

Cabana boys at the Beach Club pick up mattresses and fold umbrellas. A sign says that you swim at your own risk after 7 p.m., and someone does. Later the police will patrol the beaches, just in case there are any campers who think it would be sexy to sleep on the beach at Monte Carlo. It's done elsewhere along the coast but other beaches aren't this one.

A croupier arrives late for work because he couldn't find a space in the private lot behind the casino for his bright yellow Mazeratti.

Four cocktail parties are about to begin, all within 500 yards of each other. They serve the same champagne and the same canapés. Two are sponsored by jewellers. One is sponsored by an art gallery. One is sponsored by a chap who sells luxury cars privately. Everyone who shows up at the first party will inevitably meet everyone else again at the other three.

Shops close.

Girls in white smocks struggle to pull heavy metal grills down across the store-front windows which are covered in a rose film or a yellow film so that the sun will not spoil the bottles of perfume on display.

Men meet their mistresses.

Women meet their lovers.

The first train of the evening leaves for Paris.

A commuter trains pulls in from Nice on its way to Ventimiglia.

A stockbroker sits in front of a computer screen checking Wall Street because when it's 6 o'clock in Monte Carlo it's only noon in New York.

Chefs all over town ready their kitchens.

Sommeliers all over town consider their stock of wine.

The maitre d' at the Cafe de Paris is counting reservations when an American couple come in to ask if gentlemen are required to wear ties because if gentlemen are required to wear ties they won't be able to dine there, as the gentleman is tie-less. He assures the couple that they will be welcome.

The daily card game finishes at the café near the high school.

One last round of pastis is served.

A used-to-be-famous old English actor is paged at the bar in the Hôtel de Paris, the way he is paged every evening at the same time, because that's what he's tipped the barman to do.

*   *   *   *

16

Rainier Reminisces

*R*AINIER and Grace had been invited to a small dinner party by some friends, who'd also planned to ask Phyllis Blum, Grace's secretary, to come along. But at the last minute the hostess realised there were too many ladies at the table.

The hostess excused herself, saying she hoped Phyllis wouldn't mind.

Phyllis said she understood. So, encouraged by Maureen King and with her hostess's complicity, she went to the dinner party as a man.

Dressed in a wig and a borrowed suit, and made up with a beard and dark glasses, Phyllis was introduced to everyone as a famous Polish pianist, in the west for the first time.

When presented to Princess Grace, Phyllis bowed gallantly.

Grace said that she was very pleased to meet him.

When the famous Polish pianist didn't respond, Grace was informed that he didn't speak English.

At one point before dinner Rainier quietly remarked to someone that the famous Polish pianist seemed to him to be, 'A bit on the feminine side'.

He was told, 'Oh well, you know how those musical types are.'

Over dinner, Grace found herself sitting next to the famous Polish pianist and, being polite, tried to determine what languages he spoke.

The hostess informed her, only Polish and German.

So Grace now asked the famous Polish pianist in German if he
liked the soup.

When the famous Polish pianist didn't answer, Grace supposedly mumbled, 'Perhaps he doesn't like the soup.'

Not one to give up, Grace continued trying to make small talk
with him in German.

But Phyllis was unmovable.

Exasperated, Grace finally turned to her hostess and whispered,
'Who is this person?'

That's when the hostess confessed everything.

And it was Rainier and Grace who laughed the loudest.

*   *   *   *

Rainier has spent the day at his desk.

His office, in the tower of the Palace, is a good-sized room, filled
with 40 years worth of stuff.

There is a table to the right of the door, covered in folders
and silver picture frames – Caroline and her children, Albert
and Stephanie – and near that there is a large, very old safe
that is locked shut, protecting, one imagines, large, very old
valuables.

His desk is set back in the far corner of the room, facing
the door, with a couch and a chair and a coffee table in front
of that.

On the tables next to his desk there are more silver picture
frames.

Of course, there are pictures of Grace.

In the corner of the room there is a private lift, a sort of decorated triangular cage that takes him up one flight to a second office
he uses as a conference room.

The same size as the main office, there's a round, green felt
table off to one side and a small desk against the opposite wall.
There are more family photos on the tables but here there are also
several glass cabinets filled with mementos, such as a collection
of life-sized sterling silver crustaceans and fish.

There's a large bronze telescope aimed out of the east window
and a huge architect's mock-up of the museum Rainier is building
to house his automobile collection.

There are several paintings on the walls, including a particularly striking one called 'Storm', which depicts a small boat being hurled about by waves far out to sea.

The sky in that painting exactly matches the steel-grey blue of those office walls.

Back in his main office, dressed in a blue blazer with grey slacks and a white shirt with a blue wool tie, he reaches for a cigarette, then sits down in the chair next to the couch.

There are no lights on in the room.

And as the sun fades, as the room grows dark, he talks quietly about the last 40 years.

'Mistakes? Yes. Who doesn't make mistakes? One would be terribly boring if one didn't. But I'd like to think there have not been any major mistakes which have handicapped the principality in its development. I suppose, though, there have been minor ones. In fact I'm sure there have been. Maybe sometimes our timing was bad in some decisions that were made.'

Such as?

'Such as certain construction in the country. Maybe we shouldn't have built as many skyscrapers as we did, or at least controlled the building better. But as I've said, it all happened very fast. Of course we learn from our past. When you look down from here you see La Condamine, the port area, where there are a lot of old buildings that will one day have to come down. Some of them date from 60 or 70 years ago and haven't the proper sanitary installations. So we're remodelling that quarter. But we're not building high.'

Building might well be a key word when it comes to his reign, and some people even feel that his legacy will be that of 'Le constructeur' – the builder.

He ponders that.

'The builder or the constructor is a nice image and I like it. But I must explain that it hasn't been building just to please the speculators. Far from it. Fontvieille is a project that's brought a great deal to Monaco but that was a major gamble because it meant reclaiming so much land from the sea. Then again, I'm not sure if the builder or the constructor is the way I would describe my legacy. Perhaps I'd rather it read that I did good for the country. That my reign was successful. That I was right.'

And that, when the time came to make unpopular decisions, he had the courage to make them.

'It's not easy to take an unpopular decision but there are times when you don't have a choice. I'm open to advice. I've never wanted yes-men around me. I always tried to insist that everyone give me their point of view before I make a decision. It's generally easy to spot the yes-men because they're the ones who wait for me to say what I think. So I find that at meetings I generally don't begin by telling anyone what I think. I ask everyone in the room for their opinions before I express my views. Naturally there are times when some people are sitting there merely trying to second guess my opinion but they can't be right all the time. I've learned this through experience. Believe me, it works. Albert is now in on these cabinet meetings so he's seeing my style and hopefully learning something from it.'

When Albert eventually does take over, he will – as he knows only too well have a tough act to follow because no one could argue that Rainier hasn't done well for the Monégasques.

Compare Monaco with any city in the world whose population is only 30,000.

Not many have an acclaimed symphony orchestra, a recognised ballet company, a world-renowned opera company, quality public gardens, a beach, a port, high-class restaurants, high-class hotels and the same kind of international sophistication.

All of this in a place that only 40 years ago was pretty dreary.

The Monégasques are prosperous and healthy and educated and safe.

In fact, they might be the safest people in Europe.

Monaco's police force is only 450 strong.

It doesn't sound like a lot, but when you consider they only serve 30,000 people, London's Metropolitan Police force of 28,000 would need a total of 108,000 officers to achieve the same police to population ratio.

'I'm a great believer in the idea that a strong police presence is an obvious answer to crime. That and modern equipment so that the police can do their job. There is no real crime here. Nor is there a serious drug problem here. Of course there are some petty crimes and there are young people I guess who sniff glue but there are no serious crimes here and drugs are not sold here. The only time there's been any shooting is at a get-away car when some bank robber has tried to escape. The great thing is that there are only four roads leading in or out of the principality and the police can very quickly and very efficiently shut them off. We have a system of rakes with points that can be pulled out and blow the tyres of any car trying to get away. We are fortunate enough to have an easy border to defend.'

Street crime in Monaco is almost unheard of.

There are occasional murders of passion and burglars have been known to break into wall safes or steal valuable paintings. But muggings are rare, prostitution is illegal – at least the street-corner variety – X-rated films are not shown and you can't even walk barefoot in the streets without risking a police warning to put on your shoes.

Monaco is always billed as one of the last places on earth where a woman can wear her jewels.

That's very much by design.

Rainier is proud of that and intends to keep it that way.

'We have video cameras in key locations around the principality, on street corners, in passageways and in public lifts. It's proven very dissuasive so we're extending the system. Let's face it, if a fellow sees a camera on a corner he's not going to do much because he knows that the police are watching.'

But cameras on corners and cameras in lifts have brought on cries of 'Big Brother'.

'I think that's very unfair. This isn't a police state. I've heard that comment but I don't agree with it at all. Come on, what is a police state? It's a place where the police interfere with your life, with who you see, with what you say, with what you think. That's not the case here. There are no restrictions on any of your liberties. The strength of our police force is for protective reasons, not restrictive ones. The major part of the force is in plain clothes. But let's face it, this is a small community and everybody knows everybody else. How long do you think you could be a plain clothes policeman in this place before everybody knew who you were? You know, there's a great imbalance in the world. Some people seem ashamed to show authority and discipline. Well, I don't agree that authority and discipline are a threat to liberty. Without authority and discipline there is only anarch. And that is a threat to liberty.'

He says, for example, that the state religion is Catholicism but there are all sorts of places of worship in Monaco.

All the major sects and religions are accounted for, as are many small ones.

'We didn't invent ecumenicalism, but I think we thought of it long before the Pope did.'

Obviously the state religion is Catholicism because the Grimaldis are Catholics. Yet Rainier admits to having had many questions over the years about his faith.

He credits Fr. Tucker with keeping him in the Church.

'I rebelled the way many people do. I had a lot of questions and no one could give me satisfactory answers. But Fr. Tucker understood my rebellion from the Church and didn't over-dramatise it. That's the way he got me coming back towards the Church. He explained things. He didn't force anything on me the way some other priests probably would have. Let's be honest, most of them, I suspect, would have tried to convince me that by questioning my personal relationship with the Church I'd committed a great sin. He had an important influence on my life.'

Among other things, he helped Rainier see what the Church should be.

'What is the Church? It's charity, tolerance and understanding, isn't it? That's also what Fr. Tucker was all about. You know, I've always been appalled by those schools conducted by nuns for little kids where they have a triangle on the wall with an eye in the middle representing God and they tell the kids, that's God watching you. I don't think that's the right image of God at all. I see God with a smile. Or maybe more with the heart than with the eye.'

As a Catholic royal, Rainier enjoys a special relationship with the Vatican. They sent a representative to his marriage and together with Grace he's called on all the popes since Pius XII.

'He was an extraordinary man, absolutely saintly. I always had the impression with him that he was the closest one could ever get to God. He didn't receive us around the coffee table with chummy talk. I don't want that from a pope. He received us in a little throne room. Grace and I sat on each side of him. He was affectionate and nice but deeply committed to his faith and deeply inspiring.'

Their visit with John XXIII was slightly less formal not only because he, as a pope, was less formal than Pius XII, but because Rainier had known him when he was nuncio in Paris and he'd stayed at the Palace.

'He was then Monsignor Roncali and came here for some official ceremony, although I can't remember which. He was a jolly, more down-to-earth man. Pius was a cerebral pope, a deeper thinker, a more reflective pope. John was probably the right pope for that time. He was social, more outgoing, and wanted much less ceremony. The style changed again with Paul VI. I always thought of him as a pope for transition. A man of ample goodwill who didn't make waves.'

There wasn't much time to get to know John Paul I, but John Paul II is a man about whom Rainier has strong opinions.

'He's very conscious of the media. He's very conscious of his image in the press. I think I'd like to see him spend more time tending to the flock.'

Grace's deep commitment to her faith inspired a Monaco–born, Rome-based priest to suggest within a few months of her death that she be put forward for beatification.

Father Piero Pintus announced on the first anniversary of Grace's death, at a mass he held for her on that occasion at his church in Rome, 'I propose to make Grace Kelly a saint. As an actress, I preferred Ingrid Bergman. But Grace of Monaco was a faithful wife and an impeccable mother. She lived in a world where it was more difficult to preserve one's faith. She was rich in temperament and rare in potential. She had the gift of grace and not only in her name.'

The idea of having her mother canonised struck Caroline as a lovely thought but she wasn't sure it was possible. So she started to look into it and discover that, in fact, it is highly unlikely.

'To become a saint', she says, 'you need to have performed some miracles when you were alive and those miracles had to have been recorded in the church. Now, there is something in the church called "Blessed," which is one of the steps towards beatification. Maybe mommy could become that.'

Father Pintus claims there are people in Europe and the United States collecting miracles attributed to Grace. There are stories about mothers with sick children praying to Grace, seeing a vision and watching as the child is cured.

But until some of these claims are fully substantiated, Saint Grace seems a long way off.

Even Rainier suggests, 'The priest involved with that movement made a lot of noise but I don't think it's very serious.'

Caroline agrees with her father. 'I'm afraid we're a little short on documented miracles.'

The Grimaldis are not, on the other hand, short on friends.

And Rainier proudly counts the Reagans among his.

Politically, Grace might have leaned more towards a John
Kennedy style of Democratic party politics but if Rainier had
been American he'd almost certainly be a Reagan Republican.

'That's been a very warm friendship,' he says, 'We got to know
them very well and got to see their life in the White House up
close.'

Rainier, Caroline, Albert and Stephanie visited the Reagans
there on a couple of occasions. Rainier stayed in the Lincoln
Room – which Lincoln himself never had the honour of sleeping
in – while the others had rooms upstairs.

On the night table next to the bed in everyone's room – just
like those fancy hotels where they leave a piece of 'sleep well'
chocolate on your pillow – there was a little gift bottle of jelly
beans with the presidential seal.

'The President took Albert and myself to see the Oval Office
and told us that the only time he got any exercise or any fresh
air was when he went downstairs from the private apartments
to the office. I thought to myself, what a change. Eisenhower
had a putting green on the lawn there and he could move about
pretty freely. Now the White House is like a fortress. When you
look out of any window all you see are fellows in uniforms with
guns patrolling the grounds with dogs. At the entrance you have
a huge reinforced concrete triangle so you can't just crash through
the gates and drive straight in.'

Visiting the Reagan White House for the first time just after the
President was shot, Rainier found security so tight that it was like
a prison.

'We had very nice accommodation but every time you went
into the corridor some security man would pop out from behind
the curtains to see what was going on. You couldn't possibly
switch rooms there.'

Nancy mentioned to Rainier one evening how she loved the
theatre but complained that the only theatre she and Ron could
go to was the Kennedy Center because it was modern and had been
planned with presidential security in mind.

'Kind of sad, no? She said the only movies they ever saw were
ones they showed in the White House. I thought to myself, who'd
want a job where you had to live like this. It might be the worst
in the world. But then Gorbachev's job can't be too nice, with
all those old cronies watching over his shoulder, with all the
conniving that must go on. He may not be as physically restricted

as the President but I'd think he's severely politically restricted. Although I suspect he's got files on everybody. He must know where a lot of skeletons are buried. He'd have to in order to survive in that job. I hope so anyway, for his sake.'

The Reagan–Grimaldi friendship was such that Nancy Reagan was one of the first people to arrive in Monaco when Grace's death was announced. A gesture, Rainier says, that was very much appreciated.

'Nancy was very sweet to come to Grace's funeral. We put her up in the Palace. Although the Secret Service started being a bit rude when they decided there wasn't enough security in the Palace with all the guards. We finally told them that if she stayed here she was our responsibility and they had to accept that. Frankly, I think the Secret Service just likes to show off. And maybe they could use a little dusting off because you can spot them immediately. They have wires coming out of their ears and they speak to their watches. You don't find many other folks like that.'

It's interesting that, when you speak to the people who knew Rainier and Grace as a couple for a very long time, they all tell you that their friends were very devoted to them. Possibly it's because people who weren't devoted to them didn't stay around too long. But friendship for Rainier and Grace was never a one-way street, as Khalil el Khoury can testify.

'When the Lebanon fell apart, we didn't have to flee our home but there was nothing more I could do for my country, unfortunately, as the odds were too great and the players were too big. So my family and I left. We didn't have any place to go until Rainier gave shelter to me and my wife and our children. He offered us passports. He gave us new roots, Mediterranean roots which are our natural roots, and the feeling of security to have this place and this nationality. It was a gesture of love and friendship.'

Over the years it's a gesture often repeated for the same reasons.

King Farouk used to spend a lot of time in Monte Carlo. He'd take the entire second floor of the Hôtel de Paris, about 20 rooms, and even as ex-king he travelled with an entourage of about 40 people. Whenever he wanted to go somewhere he needed several dozen cars.

Rainier and Grace got to know him and they both liked him.

'He was an interesting man,' Rainier says. 'I always shock people by saying I liked him. I'm not saying that I agreed with everything he did politically in his own country or how he behaved or certain decisions he made. But the times I saw him I found him to be a very nice man, although he was also a very lonely man. He was concerned about his country, about his family, about his son. He once told me, "We have a saying that a man who has a son never dies." I think he believed greatly in this. When he asked me to be his son's protector, of course I accepted.'

Rainier admits another reason he liked Farouk – much the same reason he liked Onassis – was the man's flamboyance.

'I like it for others but not for myself. It wouldn't fit in with my way of living.'

While he was king, Farouk used to come to Monaco because he enjoyed gambling.

And most of the time he'd arrive on his yacht.

'The first time I went on board I was taken back by how very obvious it was that he didn't trust anyone around him. He couldn't trust anyone, from his personal barber right down to the sailors.'

When Farouk returned to Monaco after he was exiled, Rainier still received him the same way as when he was king.

'That pleased him. I think it also astonished him. Don't forget how young he was when he became king and what he had to go through. I'm talking about the intrigues and the assassination plots, with the British trying to kill him I don't know how many times, and the isolation in which he found himself. Members of his own family encouraged him to perform every vice possible. He was a sad character and he had no place else to go. Of course I gave him asylum. It was the right thing to do. He didn't live here but he came here once or twice a year and carried a Monégasque passport. I'm still in touch with his son. He was married in Monaco. He's developed into a very nice man who has great respect for his father. It turned out to be quite a good family. They stayed together. They live very quietly and simply in Switzerland.'

Monégasque citizenship is a rarity.

Basically, you must be born anywhere in the world of a Monégasque father, or in Monaco of a Monégasque mother and an unknown father.

If you're simply born in the principality, that doesn't count. Unless you happen to be born there of unknown parents. In that case you can claim citizenship.

The other route is through naturalisation. But getting a Monégasque passport that way is not easy either. It helps if you have family there, grew up there and have lived there all your life. Still, there are relatively few naturalisations each year.

When cellist Mstislav Rostropovich needed a passport, Rainier made him and his wife Monégasques. Neither of them spend much time in the principality but that's not the point. As Russian exiles a Monégasque passport allows them to travel.

Rainier's gift of a passport was also extended to the Shah of Iran when he went into exile.

'I thought it was only right. I was revolted with the way the rest of the world treated him when he was down and out. Everybody at Persepolis was licking his boots, shining up to him. Remember how every country in the world tried to get money out of him? Persepolis was just the grand finale. He was the policeman of the Gulf and the best friend of the west as long as the west needed him. But as soon he went into exile everybody slammed their door on him, especially the countries that had once gotten the most use out of him.'

High on that list, he says, were the United States and France.

'Tell me what they ever got from Khomeini? When I saw everyone close their to doors to him, I went to my Minister of State and said, "Why can't we invite him here?" The Shah was pretty much alone at that point. There was just his immediate family because most of his entourage had deserted him. France not only refused to take him in but, after having given asylum to Mr Khomeini, they allowed Khomeini to return to Iran. And the Americans were worse. They could have offered him so many possibilities. All right, don't move him to Los Angeles because there's a big Iranian population there. But how many of those Iranians now living in America went to school there thanks to the Shah's generosity? The United States is a big enough country. They could have found somewhere he'd be safe. Sure, there was a security problem but we were assured that he was willing to handle most of that himself. So we offered him asylum here. The Empress and the children still have Monégasque passports. Maybe the way the world treated him brought out of the boy scout in me.'

*   *   *   *

There are Monégasque embassies and consulates representing the principality in 51 countries.

While most of the nearly 170 Consuls-General are honorary, there are full-time ambassadors in certain countries, notably France, Switzerland, Germany, the Benelux countries and Italy. Embassies are maintained, Rainer says, not because they're necessarily ever going to accomplish anything of earth-shattering proportions, but because it's important to establish Monaco's right to independence.

Keen to do that whenever possible, Rainier recently ratified a treaty with France defining Monaco's air and sea rights.

It's only a narrow strip of water that goes to the 12-mile limit and a tiny corridor of air space but these are the kinds of things that re-enforce Monaco's status as an independent country.

Accomplishing it took some time, however. Rainier opened negotiations with President Valéry Giscard d'Estaing in the mid-1970s but couldn't get a formal treaty signed until well into François Mitterand's presidency nearly 10 years later.

The comment is made, 'It sounds as if international diplomacy is a pretty tricky business.'

He mugs a startled expression. 'Do you believe in international diplomacy?'

'Don't you?'

'Not at all. Come on, how well do you suppose your thoughts and your wishes are translated when you have to go through other people who will always allow their own interests to get in the way? Nine times out of ten somebody in the middle will think, maybe I should wait on this until I have my own candidate in a position to do it. It happens all the time. Tell me, for instance, what's the use of ambassadors? What do they do? They go to parties. They're not given wide enough powers to really negotiate a solution to a problem so there's little else they can do. I mean, what serious peace initiatives have ambassadors ever come up with in the Lebanon or anywhere in the Middle East, for that matter? Or, if you really want to get me started, let's talk about the United Nations.'

'Okay. What about the United Nations?'

'Maybe I'm over-simplifying things, but I can't see why we make the same mistake with the United Nations that we made with the League of Nations. The United States gets one vote and the Fiji Islands gets one vote and the result is nothing but oratory.

It doesn't make sense. For example, they're in a position to do something about world hunger and yet 75 per cent of the world population is underfed. It's the same thing with the Common Market. Food stocks in Europe are bursting at the seams and people are dying of starvation. It's disgusting that when too much milk is produced it's thrown away. I don't care if they throw away wine but I do care that they throw away fruit and grain and do nothing more than talk about helping to feed people who are starving. Look at UNICEF. They compile statistics and announce that only 14 million children have died of starvation and disease, not 19 million like last year. Only 14 million? It's disgraceful. What are these baboons talking about?'

Monaco does not have a seat on the United Nations. It is officially present as an 'observer'. Any thoughts they might wish to raise must, by treaty, come through the French spokesman.

'At one point I did look into establishing a UN seat for Monaco. I went to Charles de Gaulle and expressed my wish to be represented. The government of the day studied the matter and finally said all right, Monaco could gain admittance as a full-fledged member of the United Nations, with the blessing of France, as long as we agreed amongst ourselves that no matter what, Monaco would always vote with France. I said no thanks and the question has never come up again.'

Acting independently, Rainier has nevertheless seen to it that Monaco does what it can.

For example, when the south-east Asian boat people were looking for homes around the world, Monaco officially and without fanfare accepted eight families.

Proportionally, it was the second highest patriation after Canada.

More recently, Monaco bought and shipped to Africa two brand-new trucks which were filled with rice and condensed milk.

'It's obvious that only a small quantity of food shipped to the starving Third World ever gets to the people who need it, that most of it winds up in the wrong places. We sent those trucks to Africa but as soon as you go through diplomatic channels you can never be sure that it gets where you hope it's going. I honestly don't have any idea where those trucks are today or whatever happened to the food we sent. We can only hope it got to the people who needed it.'

*   *   *   *

'Did you know', he asks, 'that the Russians sometimes come here?'

'The Russians come to Monte Carlo?'

'That's right. Soviet hydrographic ships come here because there is an International Hydrographic Bureau here. It's interesting because they always let people visit the ship. School children, or anyone else who might be interested. We also get Russian trawlers stopping here. But they don't let anyone visit those ships. I've often wondered what they can fish because they've got so many antennas sticking out of them. I'm always amused when they pull in here because the Russian sailors are allowed to walk around and see this capitalistic inferno. Funny, but I think most of them rather like it.'

'What's not to like?'

'There are some things I don't like.'

'For instance?'

'For instance, some of the sailors who come here on shore leave. When the Americans call here, they generally behave very well. I'd have to say that the Americans are the best. The American shore patrol works well with the local police and they're fine. But I can't say I always like it when the ships of other countries call here. We've had a lot of warships stop here over the years and I'm sorry to say that the worst are the English. They get drunk and raise hell. They wreck cars, break windows, and generally behave very badly.'

'Any other for instances?'

'Gossip.'

'You mean, gossip as in – have you heard the latest?'

'Like I've already told you, gossip was invented in Monaco. Except that I couldn't care less about it. If somebody is going to bed with somebody else and they enjoy it, good for them.'

'What about gambling?'

'It doesn't interest me. No member of the sovereign family is supposed to go into the casino here anyway. No nationals are supposed to play. It was clever of Prince Charles to do that. He didn't want Monégasques to lose their money and become a burden to the state.'

Rainier does, though, occasionally enjoy horse racing.

'That's fun. You go down to see if the horse has blue eyes or if the jockey is dressed in the right colours and bet on him. My father-in-law, Jack Kelly, used to invite friends and business associates, all men, to go to the Kentucky Derby every year I went two or three times. He'd rent an entire train to take us from Philadelpia to Kentucky. It was really one gigantic booze-up. We'd arrive on Friday and stay on the train for the races on Saturday. The mint juleps never stopped. It was great.'

Fondly remembered as the greatest of all was the trip when Rainier proved he could pick horses.

'You have to understand that I don't know anything about horses except the front from the back. But one Friday, I think it was the last race, there was a horse called Caine Run and the odds were so high they couldn't even post it. I decided to bet $25 on it. Jack Kelly Jr and a few other guys tried to talk me out of it. They thought it was out of the question that the horse could win. Well, I felt this was such a poor horse that someone ought to put something on it. I finally talked them into forming a little syndicate and we each put $5 down. Guess what? The horse came in. I was worshipped from there on out.'

Frank enough to admit he's never quite been able to match that performance again, he says that he still likes to go to the races in Paris every now and then.

'I like it because you can see what's happening. I could never get fascinated with a little ball spinning around a wheel. Although I will say that black jack can be fun. For a while. I used to play a little gin rummy but I get bored with card games if they last too long. Poker is too slow. And as for board games, like Monopoly, I've never had much fun doing that. It goes on forever.'

His grandfather never played any card games but his mother adored bridge.

'They'd play bridge all the time at Marchais and all I ever heard were arguments. "Why didn't you bid spades?" Or, "Why did you play a heart instead of a club?" It would go on for days like that. People would get so annoyed with each other that I've made it my business to stay away from it.'

With Grace's death, Rainier's sister Antoinette has come back into the mainstream of the principality's life.

More and more over the past few years, she's appeared with Rainier at certain functions, among them the Red Cross Ball.

Her son wrote a book about the Grimaldis not long ago that was anything but flattering. For the most part it was dismissed as sour grapes, the nasty musings of a spoiled young man who renounced his responsibilities, defied his uncle, subsequently saw his inheritance cut off and now weeps for the free ride he'd long taken for granted.

While Caroline and Albert have taken over most of Grace's duties, and even Stephanie is managing a few long-distance from California, Antoinette has assumed the role of elder stateswoman, when that's been needed.

Taking into account the way their lives have gone, Rainier seems more than willing to put their past behind them.

'I went away to school when I was 11 and she stayed home, living either with my mother, my father or with my grandfather. So from that time on there wasn't very close contact between us. We grew up, each on our own side. You say she attempted to take the throne but I wouldn't go that far. She may have criticised me. And maybe she even went further than criticism. But I've always been on fairly good terms with her. The incident at the time was grossly over-exaggerated. She's conducted her life and I've conducted mine but the bridges have never been taken down, the conversation has never been cut off. All right, I might have been annoyed with her and she might have been annoyed with me. We've had our differences. But we've remained on speaking terms and, anyway, I don't know of any brother and sister who have never had their differences.'

Antoinette's attempt to take the throne might not have been a fully fledged pretence but there have been others.

George Grimaldi, who ran a pub and then a garage in the south of England, used to claim to be the 13th Marquis and the rightful prince but it never got him very far. However, a lawyer outside Turin, Italy, insists he does have a genuine, documentable claim to Rainier's throne.

Augustus Maria Olivero Grimaldi says he's a direct descendant of a Grimaldi who, in the 16th century, had the throne illegally taken away from him by his own brother.

When Honoré I died in 1581, Charles II assumed power.

He died without an heir and sovereignty then passed to Hercule I.

Rainier comes from that branch.

Augustus Maria Olivero Grimaldi is related to a brother he insists would have become prince had Hercule not jumped the queue.

His problem is, however, the old adage that possession is nine-tenths of the law. In this case, as long as Rainier possesses the throne, it's probably eleven-tenths of the law.

There was also a time when someone in the German branch of the family tried their hand at pretending. But that claim to succession is so obscure Rainier isn't entirely sure how they're related.

'These people pop up every now and then,' he says. 'Grimaldi is a common name in Genoa and so there are always a few people there who pretend to be the rightful Prince. Recently there was one in Corsica. There are lots of Grimaldis there too. This chap announced that he was really the rightful heir to the throne but that he didn't particularly want to rule. He said he'd do me a favour and let me stay.'

Interestingly enough, the 85-man Carabinier – Monaco's equivalent of an army – is made up entirely of Frenchmen. Monégasques are not to serve in the Carabinier, one of the 19th century Princes ruled, so that there could never be a *coup d'etat*.

His throne therefore safe, Rainier's title as Prince of Monaco is actually only one of 142 that he happens to have.

There is a whole series of Dukes, Marquises and Counts that make up the list. As a matter of fact, he is said to be the most titled man in the world.

Many of his titles bring with them some sort of medal. Add various awards and honours that have been bestowed on him over the years and it turns out that being highly decorated can be a real problem when you have to wear your finery at official functions.

'I must be frank and say that medals don't particularly interest me. They're given by people who are perhaps expressing a kind thought or recognise something I've done. I appreciate that and accept the medal in that spirit. But I don't attach any importance to medals and have never been anxious to get them. Nor am I especially anxious to wear them. However because they're given in a certain spirit it's difficult to wear one and not others. So I usually wind up having to wear them all. But contrary to whatever gossip you sometimes hear around Monaco – and you already know what I think about that – I do not spend my days looking at my medals, admiring them and polishing them.'

He suddenly can't keep a straight face.

'Nor do I wear my medals on my pyjamas.'

*   *   *   *

Grace was, he says, as much of a matchmaker as most women are, always amused at the possibility of trying to bring couples together.

One story had it that she wanted to reunite Onassis and Tina, but, Rainier claims, he can't recall her having tried too seriously.

Another story has Grace trying to come up with a mate for Elsa Maxwell.

Here Rainier has to laugh. 'Grace, you see, was an optimist.'

She did not, however, play matchmaker where her own children were concerned.

'Grace and I always encouraged our children to make their own choices because in the end it's their own life.'

But then, he adds, it's not always easy to let a child go ahead and do that, especially when you can see that it's the wrong choice.

'Caroline's first marriage wasn't a happy one. Both Grace and I knew it but we hadn't got much choice. When you have a child come up to you determined to share her life with somebody, what do you say? I think it was better to go along with it than to fight it. I think the most important thing when a parent has a crisis or conflict with a child is to keep the door open all the time so they know they can always come home to find shelter and refuge.'

There was hardly any doubt that when Caroline announced her engagement to Philippe Junot her parents disapproved.

'He had a very bad reputation and not much of a personality. I didn't like his background. He didn't have much of a job. I didn't know what he did besides being part of a Paris clique who had some money and spent their nights out at clubs.'

On one occasion before the marriage when someone asked Rainier, 'What does Junot do?' the answer shot back, 'Anything or nothing.'

By the time word got out that the marriage was on the rocks, a story was circulating that Rainier and Grace had, literally up to Caroline's first step down the aisle, constantly reassured her that if she wanted to change her mind, if she wanted to back out of the wedding, she could and they would stand by her.

No, Rainier says, it wasn't quite like that.

'I think you have to play the game as sincerely as you can. That's really the issue. You have this child who is in love. All right, we did try to stop her up to a reasonable point, at least to talk her out of it. But she was intent on doing it, so what else could we do except go along with it? Now she's married to a very nice boy. He's a good father and they seem happy. But you can't forget that growing up has been difficult for our children. They've had very public lives. It hasn't been easy.'

Because of the accident it has been especially difficult for Stephanie.

When she went off to do her own thing, Rainier says, he wasn't always pleased.

It sometimes hurt.

But deep down, he likes to think he understands that she was merely doing what she felt she had to do.

'Parenthood is never easy. You have to swallow a lot and let things go. But the main thing is to keep talking. To keep the door open. The child should know where home is and how to get back there, to know that no one is going to wave a wooden finger and say, I told you so.'

Some time ago Stephanie remarked to a woman's magazine, 'My father is the only man who never betrayed me.'

In one way it's a sad comment for any 23 year old to make. In another, it shows she's aware that he's there for her.

'I was very pleased about that. I hope that's a result of the fact that we've never closed the door. You know, you can say, please don't do something, and give a child all the reasons in the world but if the child wants to go on doing something, there's nothing left to do but say, all right, be careful. What else can you do? I have very different relationships with my children. Albert is my son, and fathers and sons are special. With Caroline, she's a parent now too and she's very daughterly towards me. As for Stephanie, she has a mind of her own. I know that. I also know that she's got a tremendously strong character, maybe even the strongest of the three.'

Rainier is now in the latter half of his 60s.

He doesn't know how much longer he'll reign.

He says he'd like to step aside and will as soon as he and Albert decide that Albert is ready.

After all, with Grace gone, it isn't like it used to be.

'When this kind of ending occurs, there are always regrets. You regret not having spoken enough together, not having spent enough time together, not having gotten away enough together. Not having dedicated enough time to each other. When you look back over 26 years you find moments when you think to yourself, why didn't we go on that vacation the way we always said we would. And why didn't we do this or talk about that? I regret we didn't have more time together. I just hope she's remembered the way she would have wanted to be remembered, as a caring person. She was. She really did care about other people. She was extremely demanding of herself.'

In the meantime, he soldiers on.

Enough time has passed but if there are any ladies in his life now he won't talk about them.

'I live in a fishbowl. It complicates life and puts you off doing a lot of things. I have to be extremely discreet.'

Yet taking a lady to dinner is one thing.

A second marriage is something else.

He shakes his head.

'I don't see the necessity for marrying again. I find it very difficult to even imagine. I enjoy the company of women, sure. But at this point in my life there are no thoughts of marriage. Anyway, second marriages are things I don't necessarily understand. If a marriage ends because you can't stand your wife or she can't stand you, so you split up, you separate and go your own way. Then perhaps if you meet someone who can make you happy you might want to try again. But as it happens for me . . .'

He pauses for a moment.

'I have a wonderful family and I had a wonderful marriage. And everywhere I go is so filled with memories of Grace. We lived here together for 26 years. She's still everywhere. I couldn't have another woman here. I see Grace wherever I go. Anyway, I couldn't do it because it would be very difficult for my children. It wouldn't be fair to them.'

He pauses again and then says softly, 'So I won't.'

*   *   *   *

17

A Personal Note

W E EACH have our own favourite memories.

Mine is of that Saturday afternoon before her last Christmas on earth.

She'd spent the morning baking butter cookies cut into stars and Christmas trees and Santas carrying sacks of toys.

Once they were ready, she walked alone from the Palace to Caroline's house, about 500 yards along a winding, narrow street, between three-storey fading yellow clay houses with green shutters across the windows and freshly washed laundry hanging out of some of them.

Dressed in dark slacks with a cream cashmere sweater and a simple string of pearls around her neck, flat shoes, her hair wrapped in a scarf and large sunglasses, no one recognised her except the Palace guards in their winter uniforms who saluted smartly as she nodded to them and smiled, 'Bonjour'.

She let herself in and came up the front steps into the hallway. Finding no one there, she peeked into the kitchen. 'What's for lunch?'

I answered, 'How would you like scrapple and eggs?'

She gave me a suspicious look. 'Where can you get Philadelphia scrapple in Monaco?'

'Alas,' I shrugged. 'Will you settle for a western omelette?'

'Sounds great,' she said, placing the bag of cookies on the counter near the sink and reaching for an apron. 'I'll supervise.'

The years had been kind to her. She'd put on some weight

but her eyes were as magic as they'd ever been and her voice was exactly the same as it was in *Mogambo* and *High Noon* and *Rear Window*. Her face was a bit rounder now. But it was softer, more gentle than in her Hollywood days. The ice-goddess image had melted away and that once-so-beautiful movie star of 22 was now a still-so-beautiful woman of 52.

'I thought you were from New York.' She started to scrub the green peppers. 'How do you know about scrapple?'

'I went to school in Philadelphia. I went to Temple.'

'So did I,' she said. 'I went to Temple.' She paused, 'Although I think it must have been a few years before you.'

'Well,' I politely suggested, 'only a few,' then pointed to the paper bag. 'Is that for the tree?'

'I baked cookies. What did you do?'

Caroline had phoned to ask, 'Want to make lunch on Saturday for my mother and me?' She'd explained it was the day she was going to decorate her Christmas tree. 'This year everything on the tree has to be edible. You know, cookies, candy, dried fruit, whatever you want to bring.' But I had my own idea of edible decorations.

'It's not quite the same as if I'd baked.' I reached for my shopping bag. 'Nevertheless,' I assured her, 'everything is edible.'

She said, 'Let's see.'

I pulled out Santa-encrusted tins of tuna fish and several packages of Christmas-ribbon-wrapped pasta.

When she laughed her whole face lit up.

'Your hair is a little long, isn't it?' she said once we'd started cooking the omelettes together. 'Tell you what, after lunch get me a pair of scissors and I'll give you a haircut.'

I turned to her. 'It's a deal. But you must understand that if you cut my hair, my mother will tell everybody in Florida that Grace Kelly is my barber.'

She chuckled, 'You're on.'

That's when Caroline came into the kitchen. 'Hi. What's for lunch?'

Right away her mother said, 'Scrapple, dear.'

Caroline made a face.

Her mom and I just laughed.

When lunch was over we went into the winter garden where the tree was waiting. We hung cookies and striped candy canes and the ribbon-wrapped pasta.

As the afternoon wore on, as we only barely managed to keep Caroline's dogs from eating the decorations, all sorts of people stopped by. There was a constant stream of friends, some carrying presents to put under the tree, almost everyone bringing more food to hang on its branches. No one else brought decorated tuna fish.

Before long Caroline's mom and I drifted off into a corner of the room, the two of us sitting Indian style on the floor. We talked of many things – of shoes and ships and sealing wax, of cabbages and Hollywood.

'It was very different in those days,' she said. 'Not like it is today. It was a much gentler place then.'

'With gentler people?' I wondered. 'Hitchcock never struck me as being particularly gentle?'

'Hitch was wonderful. He was very secretive and mysterious. He was naturally shy so he was always playing hide and seek with everybody.'

'But he was known to be very demanding.'

'He had to be. Movies were an expensive business, even if they didn't cost anywhere near what they do today.'

'He was at Paramount, wasn't he?'

'Well, *Rear Window* was at Paramount and so was *To Catch a Thief*. But *Dial M For Murder*, which was the first film we did together, was at Warner Brothers. Moving around like that always presented problems because I was on a salary at Metro. Whenever Hitch wanted me for a film he had to get me from them. MGM kept renting me out to other studios. And they made a lot of money doing it. Unfortunately I didn't. I think I actually made more money modelling in New York than I did acting in Hollywood.'

'Do you miss Hollywood?'

'I miss some of the people, yes, because I was lucky enough to work with some fabulous people, like Hitch. But I never much cared for California and never really lived out there. Everything in Hollywood seems to be affected by the exaggerated importance of money. I worked out there but I always came back to New York when I wasn't working.'

'Except that you worked out there a lot.'

She shook her head. 'I only made eleven films and don't forget I made six of the eleven in a little over a year between 1953 and 1954. And then, only one of those six was for MGM.'

'Did you have the right to turn stuff down?'

'Not really.' She began to giggle. 'In fact I once even got suspended for it. You could only say no when they let you say no. A director once wanted to cast me as Elizabeth Barrett Browning in a production of *The Barretts of Wimpole Street*. I was about 25 at the time and in the movie she would have been in her early 40s. He thought I'd be marvellous in the role. I told him I was much too young. And he said, "No problem. We'll make her younger." I couldn't believe it. I tried to explain to him that the whole beauty of her story lies in the fact that she was 40 when she had this great romance. Luckily the project was dropped. In the mean time my reputation as a difficult young actress was greatly enhanced.'

'Were you difficult?'

'Who me?' She grinned broadly. 'Well, MGM thought so.'

'Do you still get fan mail?'

'Yes. And I'll have you know that every letter gets an answer.'

'Are the letters ever still addressed to Grace Kelly or is everything Princess Grace?'

'Of course most of my mail is addressed to Princess Grace but yes I still get letters from people who say they've just seen one of my movies on television. Or they say that their mother and father were fans and ask if they could have my autograph for them. Or they ask for photos or recipes. So we send them a photo of the family or some of my favourite recipes, you know, local dishes that are cooked in Monaco. Or they ask for advice.'

'What kind of advice?'

'All sorts of advice. I get questions on just about everything, from raising children to how to get into the movies. Although I stopped giving advice about how to get into the movies in about 1949 or 1950.'

'Why?'

'Elia Kazan called me one afternoon to ask if I'd like to help a young actor rehearse for an audition. I said sure. I remember that the guy came up to our apartment on a Sunday afternoon. He explained that he lived somewhere outside New York, in the suburbs, and couldn't rehearse with me during the week because he was married and had a young family and had to work for his father. But he said he really wanted to be an actor. Well, the girls I lived with were home that afternoon and they had dates over and the record player was going, so the only place we could rehearse was the kitchen. Of course, it was one of those really tiny New York City kitchens so we were very cramped. He read okay. But he wasn't great. And when he asked me what I thought I tried to find a kind way of letting him know that he wasn't going to make it. I explained how difficult it was to get work and reminded him that most actors in New York were hungry most of the time. I advised him to keep his job so that he could support his wife and child and maybe act as a hobby in amateur productions. I tried to convince him as nicely as possible to forget acting as a career.'

She stopped right there and stared at me.

'Okay,' I asked, 'Who was it?'

And she answered, 'Paul Newman.'

JR/Monto Carlo
1989

* * * *

Index

A

Adventures of Quentin Durward, The 56
Aga Khan 119
Agnelli, Gianni 146, 256
Aherne, Brian 252
Albert, King of Belgium 198
Albert, Crown Prince of Monaco 12, 13, 219–25, 119, 220
  and the accident 262, 264
  career 222
  childhood 129
  education 126–7, 144, 222
  eligible bachelor 221
  and his mother 223–4
  and his sisters 224–5, 219
  official duties 230, 292
  and press 243, 248–9
  schedule 221
  sports 130, 222
  and succession 280, 295, 223
Albert I, Prince of Monaco 23–4, 98–100
Alden, John 164
Alexander 54
Alice, Princess of Monaco 98–100
Allan, Rupert 59–60, 61, 67, 69, 71, 89, 236, 238, 252
Americans, drawn to Riviera 170
  sailors 290
  soldiers 33
  tourists 100–1, 141, 145
  warships 43
Anka, Paul 182
Antoinette, Princess of Monaco 26, 27, 291–2
Arabs, tourists 124, 126
Ascari, Alberto 176
Atlantic City 148
Atwood, Bill 66
Aubrey 171
Aumont, Jean Pierre 235
Austin, Russell and Edith 69, 70
Automobile Club of Monaco 174

B

Bacharach, Burt 184
Bad Homburg 93, 95
Baden-Baden 93
Baker, Josephine 184–5
ballet 230, 99
Bandini, Lorenzo 176
Basehart, Richard 53
Beaverbrook, Lord 122
Bel Geddes, Barbara 53
Belle Simone (yacht) 145
Belmondo, Paul 210, 266
Bennett, James Gordon 170
Bernhardt, Sarah 172–3
Bertie, Prince of Wales (Edward VII) 169
bidets 150
Blanc Camille 97, 100, 101
Blanc, Louise 97
Blanc, François 95–7, 115, 167
Bloom, Ron 217, 218
Blum, Phyllis 133, 134, 260, 277–8
Bohan, Marc 210
Bonaparte, Prince Charles 95
border closure 42
Brando, Marlon 199
breaking the bank 95, 96, 168
bridge 291
Bridge at Toko-Ri, The 55
Brocart, Maurice 254
Browning, Elizabeth Barrett 300
Brynner, Yul 198
bull fighting 120
bureaucracies 16–18

C

Callas, Maria 108, 110, 119, 120
Callingham, Clement 154
Cannes 126
Cannes Film Festival 60
Carabinier 293
Caroline, Princess of Monaco (mother of Charles III) 93
Caroline, Princess, 41, 118, 130, 225, 228

and the accident 260, 263, 264,
    267–8
at Connaught Hotel 207–8
childhood 128–9
education 126, 208
and her children 135, 226–7
and her mother 225, 226
marriages 136, 227–8, 294
official duties 230, 292
and press 243, 250–1, 254
sawn in half 136–7
wedding 250–1
work 231, 230, 292
writing 229–30
Carroll, John 200, 202, 203, 204, 205
casino 22, 93–4, 102, 148, 165–6
Casiraghi, Andrea 226
Casiraghi, Charlotte 227
Casiraghi, Pierre 227
Casiraghi, Stefano 227
Cassini, Oleg 61, 235, 255
Charles II 292
Charles III 22, 98, 93
Charlotte, Princess of Monaco
    (mother of Rainier) 25–6, 28–9, 75,
    118–19, 236
Château de Marchais 9
Chatelin, Professor Charles 264
Chevalier, Maurice 103
Children of Theatre, The 202
Chirac, Jacques 145
Christina (yacht) 105, 110, 111, 119
Churchill, Winston 86, 106, 122–3
Circus Festival 123, 173, 219
Ciro 170
Civil List 104
Clark, Petula 205
Clemenceau, Georges 101
Coki 8
Collins, Joan 231
Collins, Sir William 155
Conant, Howell 251
Connaught Hotel, London 207, 241
Connery, Sean 196
Constitution (ship) 83–4
Cooper, Gary 54
Cosby, Bill 45, 184
Country Girl, The 55, 234
Court of Revision 36
Cousteau, Jacques 15, 38

crêpes Suzettes 169–70
Crosby, Bing 55, 234
croupiers 157
'Curse of the Grimaldis' 80

D

da Silva, Howard 53
Daly, Derek 176
Davis, Sammy, Jr 184
de Gaulle, Charles 39–44, 197, 289
de Havilland, Olivia 62
de Lara, Isidore 100
de Laurentis, Dino 145
de Polignac, Louis, Prince of Monaco
    26, 79, 125, 126, 136, 262
de Segonzac, Gladys 62
de Taglia, Alex 122
Debré, Michel 40
Delon, Anthony 210
Deo Juvante II (yacht) 84, 85, 119
Designing Woman 196
Diaghilev, Sergei 99, 119–20
Dial M for Murder 55, 299
Dickinson, Angie 198
Dior, Christian 210
Docker, Lady Norah 154–6
Docker, Sir Bernard 155–6
dog's birthday party 133
Domingo, Placido 205
Dommanget, Ghislaine Marie
    (Princess Ghislaine) 35
Donat, Dr Robert 66, 70–1, 74, 77
Douglas, Paul 53
Dreyfus affair 99–100
Dumas, Alexandre 234
Duplay, Dr Jean 263

E

Earl, Phyllis Blum 260
Eisenhower, General Dwight 34
el Khoury, Khalil 58, 120, 285
Elizabeth, Queen of England 86–7, 114
Elizabeth, Queen Mother 203
Escoffier, Auguste 169
Europe Number One 39

F

Fahd, Crown Prince of Saudi Arabia
    125
Fairbanks, Douglas 102

family values 127–8, 130, 217
Farouk, ex-King of Egypt 285–6
Father, The 52
Faure, Felix 99
Field, Sally 199
Fitzgerald, Ella 180
Florestan, Prince of Monaco 11, 21–2, 141
Fonda, Jane 199
Fontvieille 149, 279
Ford, John 54
Fourteen Hours 53
France, relation with Monaco 160, 161
Franco-Monegasque Pact 24, 40, 101, 288
François 'Le Malizia' 6
Franz Josef, Emperor of Austria 171
Frederick, Major General Robert Tryon 33
From Here to Eternity 55

G
Gable Clark 54, 60
Gabriel, Peter 216
Gaillard, Marie-France 254
Gaither, Gant 53–4, 116, 198
Galante, Pierre 62
galas 103, 116, 121, 180–5
Gallico, Paul 193
gambling 95–6, 125–6, 141, 290–1
    systems 167, 168–9
Garden Club of Monaco 204
Garden of Flowers, A 204
Gardner, Ava 55, 59–60, 89
Garland, Judy 183
Ghislaine, Princess 36–7
Gibert, Caroline 22
Giscard d'Estaing 41
Grace, Princess 188–91, 232–3
    acting career 51–6, 195, 299
      after marriage 195–204
    change in career 117, 187, 238
    childhood 48–50
    and clothes 81, 192
    driving 258
    education 49–50
    engagement 79–82
    fan mail 300
    fatal accident 259–64, 268–71
    flower arranging 204

funeral 265–6, 273–4
health 268
and her children 127–8, 132, 239, 244
hobbies 193
and Hollywood 54–6, 299
humour 132
and interviews 240
and Lady Docker 155–6
and languages 131, 193, 203, 240
letter writing 192
matchmaker 294
meets Rainier 62–6
modelling 51–2, 299
and Monégasques 187
moves to Monaco 82–5
and music 10
Oscar as Best Actress 55
in Paris 136, 199
and poetry programmes 200–4
pregnancies 118, 119, 127, 131, 187–8, 237, 238
and press 234, 237–9
private side 190–1
reading 194
and Red Cross Ball 180–3
and religion 205
sailing 119
self-improvement 116
teamwork with Rainier 44, 115–37
and television 53, 199, 205
ties with America 194
work schedule 190
Grand Prix 174–80
Grande Corniche 94
Granger, Stewart 55
Grant, Cary 87, 94, 123, 252
Green, Julian 36
Green Fire 55, 196
Grimaldi, Augustus Maria Olivero 292
Grimaldi, George 292
Grimaldis 6–7, 24
    chart of dynasty 20
    curse of 80
Guinness, Alec 66, 132
Gunsbourg, Raoul 99
Gustav V, King of Sweden 103

H

Hamilton, Lady Mary Victoria
  Douglas 25, 86
Harlow, Jean 55
Hathway, Henry 53
Hawkins, Jack 198
Hayworth, Rita 198
Hedren, Tippi 198
Hine, Alice (Princess Alice) 98
Heiress, The 52
Hemingway, Ernest 33
Henley Regatta 46
Hercule I, Prince of Monaco 292
Hermitage 32, 35
High Noon 54
High Society 80, 203
Hill, Graham 178
Hitchcock, Alfred 55, 196, 299
Hoffman, Dustin 199
Holden, William 55, 234
Honoré I, Prince of Monaco 292
Honoré V, Prince of Monaco 21, 233
Honoré-Charles (Charles III), Prince of
  Monaco 22, 93
Hopper, Helda 234
Horowitz, Vladimir 120
Hôtel de Paris 32, 35, 96, 102, 106,
  138, 147, 167, 171
Howard, Trevor 198
Hunter, Jeffrey 53

I

Ilona 171
Institute of Human Palaeontology 23
International Herald Tribune 170,
  229
International Institute of Peace 23
Iran, Shah of 112, 287
Ireland 241
Ittleson, Henry 145

J

Jaggers, William 168
Jews 32, 33
John, Elton 184
jokes 132–5, 136–7, 277–8
Jourdan, Louis 66
Junot, Philippe 227–8, 294
Jutard, Mario Olivier 214

K

Kazan, Elia 300
Kelly, George 51, 52, 53
Kelly, Grace (aunt) 50
Kelly, John Brendon (Jack) 45–7, 70–1,
  76, 80, 291
Kelly, John (Kell) 47, 48, 271
Kelly, Lizanne 47, 48
Kelly, Margaret Majers 47, 48, 49, 70,
  76
Kelly, Peggy 47, 48
Kelly, Walter 50–1
Kennedy, John 243
Keppell, Alice 170
Khashoggi, Adnan 124–5
Kiley, Richard 200
King, Maureen 133–5
Kramer, Stanley 54

L

La Condamine 279
La Turbie (D37 road) 94, 261
Lacoste, Nadia 116, 197, 245, 246,
  247–8, 259
  becomes press attaché 236–7,
  239–42
Las Vegas 148, 218
Lawrence of Arabia 123
Le Broq 165
Le Mermoz 136
Le Rocher 142
Le Rosey 31
Lehman, John 43, 115
letter writing 58, 72, 224
Levasseur, Andre 181, 183
Levitt, Bill 145
Levy-Soussan, Louisette 189
Livanos, Tina (Mrs Onassis) 105
Lodge, Mary 242
Loews Hotel 148
Louis II, Prince of Monaco 14, 25, 27,
  34, 102
Louvet, Marie Juliette 25

M

Mangilo, Silvana 145
Manxmouse 194
March, Frederick 55
Margaret, Princess 202
Marnie 196–7

Massey, Raymond 52
Mata Hari 172
Maxwell, Elsa 102–3, 116, 119, 120,
  294
Mediterranean, pollution 15, 16–17
Merzagora, Cesare 41
MGM 55–6, 66, 81, 195, 299
mice, pottery 193–5
Michael, George 213
Milland, Ray 55, 235
Minelli, Liza 184
Mississippi bonds 163–4
Mitchum, Robert 60
Mitterand, François 288
Mogambo 54, 59, 225
Monaco 5–7, 14, 21–44, 138–40, 146,
  149, 275–6
  banks 162
  budget 141
  building 279
  claims to throne 28–9, 365, 102,
    292–3
  coins 153
  constitution 144
  economy 14, 135, 150–1, 159
  embassies and consulates 288
  and Europe 222
  farming 18
  festivals 173
  foreign aid 289
  foreign investment 158
  aid France 160
  government 24, 156–7
  independence 288
  light industry 149–50
  museums 173
  police force 280
  postage stamps 152–3
  religions 281
  street crime 281
  taxes 159, 161
  tourism 104, 145
Monaco Arts Festival 230
Monaco Banking and Precious Metals
  Society 37
Monaco Red Cross 116
Monaco Zoo 9, 65
Monégasque Assembly 28
Monégasques 5, 23, 93, 144, 187, 197,
  229, 280

  citizenship 286
  employment 158
  gambling 290
Monoecus 6
Monroe, Marilyn 57
Monte Carlo 1–3, 22, 23, 138–40,
  275–6, 146
  urban development 151
Monte Carlo Beach Club 138
Monte Carlo Opera 99
Monte Carlo Orchestra 116
Monte Carlo Tennis Club 103
Moore, Grace 103
Moorehead, Agnes 53
Morgan, J P 170–1
Morocco, King of 9
Moss, Stirling 177

N
Napoleon 233
National Council 37, 38, 156–7
  wedding gift 87–8
national identity cards 17–18
National Museum 173
nationalisation 109
Nazi occupation 32–3
Neal, Mr 170
Neiman Marcus 81
New York Times 52
New Yorker 194
Newman, Paul 301
Niarchos, Stavros 106
Nicholson, Jack 199
Nijinsky 120
Niven, David 243, 252
Nuvolari, Tazio 176

O
O'Brien, Jack 78
Oceanographic Institute 23, 25, 38
Oceanographic Museum 15
Old Beach Hotel 103
Olympic Maritime 92, 106
Onassis, Aristotle 57, 92, 104–11, 121,
  171, 182, 286, 294
Onassis, Jackie Kennedy 97, 135
Onassis, Tina 105, 294
Otero, Caroline 172

P

Paget, Debra 53
Palace 10, 117–18, 142
paparazzi 242–9, 253–4, 267
parties 167–8, 133
Pascal, Gisèle 8, 56–7
Pasco, Richard 200, 202
Pears, Sir Peter 201
Peck, Gregory 252
peepers 241
Pelletier, Emile 40
physiognomists 96, 165
pickpockets 177
pieds noirs 39
Pierre, Prince, Count of Polignac 26, 28, 102
pigeons 115, 168
Pintus, Father Piero 283
poetry readings 200–4, 206
pollution 15, 16–17
Pope John Paul II 283
Pope John XXIII 197, 282
Pope Paul VI 283
Pope Pius XII 282
Powell, Jane 181
press 82, 84–5, 234, 242–9, 267, 271–2
    at Caroline's wedding 251–4
    taken to court 244
press conferences 237–8
Prince Pierre Prize 36
Princess Grace Dance Academy 230
Princess Grace Foundation 182, 191
Princess Grace Irish Library 136
publicity 232–57

R

Rabagas 11
Radio Monte Carlo 32–3, 39
Radziwill, Prince Constantine 97
railway 37, 94, 96
Raimondi, Ruggero 229
Rainier, Prince, of Monaco 7, 10, 26, 29, 120, 293
    25th anniversary in office 135
    and the accident 262, 264
    and automobiles 9–10
    as bull fighter 120
    as businessman 143
    childhood 27
    and de Gaulle 41

    education 29–31
    as eligible bachelor 56
    engagement 75–7, 79–80
    in French army 34–5
    and his children 214, 217–18, 220, 295
    interests 19, 290–1
    as 'le constructeur' 279
    leaves Monaco 35
    medals 293
    and Monégasques 144
    music 10
    and oceans 15
    office in Palace 278
    personality 12, 58, 132, 214, 237
    and press 234, 235, 238, 239, 255
    pro-American 43
    regrets 296
    and religion 282
    retirement 18
    sails to Africa 8, 57
    show-down with Societe des Bains de Mer 104
    visits United States 66–7, 70–1, 74–5, 217–18
RAMOGE 16
Ratoff, Gregory 52
Ravenhill Academy 49
Reagan, Nancy 284
Reagan, Ronald 198, 284
Rear Window 55, 299
Rearranged 204
Red Cross Ball 116, 180–5
Reed, Donna 55
Revson Charles 145
Rey, Jean Charles 37
Ritz, Cesar 169
Robbins, Gwen 204
Roc Agel 7–8, 10, 117, 119
Roosevelt, Franklin 47
Roquebrune and Menton 22, 94
Rose, Helen 81
Rostropovich, Mstislav 203, 287
royalty 113–14, 126
Russians, in Monaco 290

S

St Jean-Cap-Ferrat 36, 56
St Mary's College, Ascot 208
Saint-Mleux, André 116

salles privées 166
Schary, Dory 196
Schwab, Charles 171
Schweitzer, Albert 121
secret tunnel 171
Shaw, Irwin 33
Siam, King of 9
Sinatra, Frank 55, 89, 121, 123, 180, 182, 183–4, 252
Smith, Constance 52
Société des Bains de Mer 23, 27, 35, 87, 92–111, 135, 156
    renamed 96
    take-over 147
Spencer, Diana (Princess Diana) 204–5
Spiegel, Sam 145
Sporting Club 35, 92, 105, 106
Starlight Room 181
Stephanie, Princess 127, 131, 260
    and the accident 214, 259–61, 266, 267, 268–70, 272–3
    and actress mother 196
    in California 214
    childhood 129–30
    education 208–10
    and friendship 212
    growing up 295
    and her father 214–15
    kidnap attempt 213
    modelling 211
    music and acting 212, 215–16, 218
    official duties 218–19, 292
    and paparazzi 243–4, 246–7
    swimsuit designer 211–12
Stewart, Jackie 178
Stewart, Jimmy 55
    Stewart, Rod 216
    Stowe 30
Streisand, Barbara 199
suicides of gamblers 172–3
Summer Fields School 29
Summer Sporting 107, 181
Suvorov, Princess 167–8
Swan, The 66, 132

T
taxation 39, 43, 161
Taxi 52
Taylor, Dahart 56
Tele-Monte Carle 39

Tito, Marshall 113, 114
To Catch a Thief 61, 94, 299
tomahawk 132
Torch Bearers, The 50, 51, 52
tourists 148
Tucker, Father Francis 58–9, 66, 69–71, 74, 282
Turner, Norah (Lady Docker) 154–6

U
Ultima II (yacht) 145
United Nations 288–9

V
Varzi, Achille 176
Victoria, Queen of England 100
von Furstenberg, Princess Ira 256–7

W
wedding, Caroline 250–1
    Grace and Rainier 85–91, 236
Wells, Charles 168
Wells, Mary 189, 206
Westbrook, John 201–2
White House 284
Wild Peaches 201
Wilhelm II, Kaiser 99, 169
Windsor, Duke and Duchess of 102
Woollcott, Alexander 173
World War II 31–3

Z
Zaharoff, Basil 101–2
Zelle, Gertrud Margarete (Mata Hari) 172
Zimbalist, Sam 54
Zimmermann, Fred 54
Zola, Emile 99